Snake River Fly Fishing

Through the Eyes of an Angler

Boots Allen

Snake River Fly Fishing

Through the Eyes of an Angler

Boots Allen

Frank Amato Publications, Inc.

About The Author

Photo Courtesy of Jackson Hole News and Guide

Boots Allen is a third-generation fly-fishing guide from Jackson Hole, Wyoming who, since 1991, has guided 100-plus days each season on the Snake River, South Fork of the Snake River, the Green River, and the streams and lakes of Yellowstone National Park. In 2004, 2005, and 2008 he was the high-scoring guide in the prestigious One-Fly Contest. Boots has penned numerous articles for national publications such as *Fly Tyer*, *Flyfishing & Tying Journal*, *The Drake*, and *Sports Afield*, and has made several presentations and fly-tying demonstrations at expos and conclaves throughout the country. In 2006, he was awarded a Ph.D. in Sociology from the University of Texas at Austin, where his research focused on rural development in mountain communities. Shunning the world of policy making and academia, Boots has returned permanently to the Rocky Mountain West to continue to work in the fly-fishing industry and lend his expertise to local communities dealing with issues of growth and development. Boots is a board member of the Snake River Fund and, in the winter, he guides at Kau Tapen Lodge in Tierra del Fuego, Argentina. This is his second book.

For Mom and Jim. Thanks for tons of support over the years.

In 2009, the Snake River in Wyoming was granted status as a National Wild and Scenic River, with protection under the National Wild and Scenic Act.

All inquiries should be addressed to:
Frank Amato Publications, Inc. • P.O. Box 82112 • Portland, Oregon 97282
503-653-8108 • www.amatobooks.com

Book & Cover Design: Mariah Hinds
Photography by Author Unless Otherwise Noted
Illustrations by Loren Smith
Fly Photos by Jim Schollmeyer

LIMITED HARDBOUND EDITION
ISBN-13: 978-1-57188-459-6
UPC: 0-81127-00298-6

SOFTBOUND
ISBN-13: 978-1-57188-458-9
UPC: 0-81127-00297-9

Printed in Hong Kong

1 3 5 7 9 10 8 6 4 2

Contents

Jason Sutton

Acknowledgements

The research for this book began several years ago, well before I considered a career in the fly-fishing industry, much less becoming a writer. When I was five and six-years-old, my father and uncle took me on a number of fishing trips to the South Fork of the Snake River in Idaho. I was throwing a spinning rod at this age, and using bait and spinners, yet I was learning a lot about fly-fishing and fishing in general—where trout hold, how to work a lure through particular currents, how to play trout to the boat, and how to properly release trout and return them to the river.

A few years later, I had a fly rod in my hand. This time around, in addition to my river excursions with my father and uncle, my grandfather Boots Allen was accompanying me to Flat Creek and the Gros Ventre River. There were also daily sessions at the tying vise to learn how to construct Humpies, Royal Wulffs, and Hare's Ear Nymphs. This is when my true education in fly-fishing began. I began to learn more about trout food, how to properly present a fly to trout in various situations, and I started to gain a respect for the region's one and only native trout—the cutthroat.

Thus, my first-and-foremost thanks must go out to my grandfather, father, and uncle. These three individuals helped to pioneer the fly-fishing industry in the Snake River region. I knew at a very early age that they were highly respected individuals on the fly-fishing scene, but it was not until years later that I began to understand their true impact. It was also not until several years later that I began to understand how much they taught me. Much of what I have learned from them is included here. I hope that what I have written repays them for my education, at least in some small way.

As these acknowledgements suggest, research for this book comes in large part from conversations with, and observations from, those who fly-fish the Snake River and call it their home river. The number of people who deserve recognition for this is almost uncountable. I must thank my brother, Richard. Although four years my junior, he was always a more observant guide and fly-fisher than myself. I recall how one day, while fishing a spring creek we had no legal right to be on, he pointed to a caddis cocoon in the water that I initially had dismissed as a simple piece of debris. Then I realized what a special gift he has, how much there is to learn in this sport, and how much more I had to learn. I must also thank my cousin—Tressa. I still consider her to be among the best guides on the Snake River, who also happens to be one of the best casters. Whenever my head gets too big in regard to my own abilities, she quickly puts me in my place.

To fly-fish and tie in the Snake River region is to be a part of a fraternity that has a sincere concern for the ecosystem and readily shares information about the river, its tributaries, its trout, and its trout food. Growing up here, I have had the privilege to know and learn from some of the local industry greats. These include Jack Dennis, Scott Sanchez, Jimmy Gabettas, Jay and Kathy Buchner, Marcella Oswald, Howard Cole, Jimmy Jones, Joe Bressler, Dave Brackett, Joe Burke, Jeff Currier, John Simms, Will Dornan, Reynolds Palmeroy, and Tom Montgomery. Each one of these individuals has shared something with me that is a part of this book. They all deserve my gratitude and all of our thanks for their commitment to the protection of the Snake River and its trout.

For eight months every year, my life revolves around guiding, so it is not hard to conclude that I am in constant contact with guides, be it on the water, or at local restaurants, bars, and various fundraisers and functions. Guides are amongst the highest of fraternal orders on the river—disseminating information to each other readily and expecting nothing but the same in return. I have learned bits and pieces from more guides than I can count, but some stand out more than others. Key among these are: Ken Burkholder, Gary "The Wedge" Willmott, and Carter Andrews. These three are absolute legends on the Snake River. Willmott and Andrews inparticular have been most generous in sharing information with me. They have also taught me an incredible work ethic, which I have applied to my guiding, research, and writing.

Other guides who provided important information for the completion of this book include Jason Sutton, Brandon Murphy, Mike Bean, Jaason Pruett, Mike Janssen, and Mike Dawes, all whom I consider to be amongst the best guides on the Snake River today. Additionally, Melissa Thomasma, Jim Hickey, Josh Cohn, Brandon Payne, Beau Strathman, Cole Sutheimer, Curt Hamby, Lucas Donaldson, Dean Burton, Bill Happersett, Bart Taylor, Brenda Swinney, Kasey Collins, Carlos Ordonez, John Griber, Ooley Piram, Mark Fuller, Dave "Sammy" Samuels, Phil "Smiley" Steck, Keith Smith, Jason Wright, Klay Mangus, Elden Berrett, Rick Schreiber, Scott Smith, Ben Smith, Billy Pew, Mark Rollans, James Osmond, Don Wackerman, Bob Barlow, Pat Kelly, Guy Turck, Kim Keeley, Dan Oas, Larry Larson, Chris Jansen, Scott Hocking, Ben Brennan, Shannon McCormick, Brandon Payne, Rhett Bain, and Pat Kelly have shared valuable information with me.

Officials from the Wyoming Department of Game and Fish, the Idaho Department of Fish and Game, and several regional/local organizations provided a wealth of data for this book. I would like to thank John Kiefling and Ralph Huddleson from the Wyoming Department of Game and Fish who provided rich contextual data on the historical stocking of non-native trout in Wyoming and the historical progression of the State's fisheries management policy. Rob Gipson and Tracy Stephens provided data regarding trout abundance and redd counts on the upper Snake River in Wyoming. Jim Fredericks and Bill Schrader of the Idaho Department of Fish and Game, and Rob Van Kirk of Idaho State University, provided information on total trout abundance and stocking history on the South Fork of the Snake River. Matt Woodard, Trout Unlimited's watershed project manager for the South Fork of the Snake River, provided valuable information regarding the impact of the current rainbow trout reduction program.

Several individuals provided important historical information regarding early fly-fishing practices on the Snake River before the industry began to take off in the 1950s and 1960s. Tom Carmichael gave detailed information about his father's Moose Tackle Shop and his professional relationships with Don Martinez and Roy Donnelly. Despite being well into her 90s, Marcela Oswald provided time for interviews regarding her and her husband's influence on the South Fork of the Snake River in the early post-war period. Useful information also came from Wes Newman and Kevin Radford.

The writing of this book was spurred on by two individuals who also provided more information than I could have ever gathered on my own. Bruce Staples has been a semi-mentor for me ever since I started writing magazine articles in 2000. Staples is an accomplished writer, a Buzsek Award winner, and one of the primary historians on fly-fishing in the Yellowstone region. I have learned much from Bruce about the history of our sport, about researching its origins, and about writing. He is a terrific friend and, in many ways, a kindred spirit of mine because of our common interest in the angling heritage of the Snake River area.

Paul Bruun knew me well before I could even speak in complete sentences. Growing up, I was a consistent fan of his articles in *Fly Fisherman Magazine* and weekly outdoor articles in the *Jackson Hole News*. From these writings, I learned a lot about the Snake River and its tributaries. Bruun, along with Staples, reviewed my outlines for this book and provided constant criticism and encouragement. Once, when the publication of this book was in doubt (for market reasons) only weeks after the acceptance of the initial proposal, Paul said, "Just write the book anyway. This is going to be the first book ever regarding fly-fishing on the Snake River and you are one of the few who have the knowledge to do this." I kept those words with me throughout the entire writing process.

There are two individuals who have been inspirations for me during the writing process. Jessica Kany was the first person to encourage me to write about my experiences in fly-fishing, especially on the Snake River. She reviewed the first of several magazine articles I began to write in 2000 and, in many ways, taught me to write. I have not seen Jess in many years, but there were numerous times while writing this book that, upon reaching a rut where I could not put into words what I wanted to say, I would lean back and think to myself, "How would Jessica say this?" She is as much a contributor to the success of this project as those I have named previously.

Lastly, I must thank Lucy Flood, my forever friend, who shot into me a new source of inspiration and determination to complete this project. There are no words to truly explain the impact she has had on me, my writing, and my life. The only way I can thank her is to let her know that there is much more to come.

Foreword

In the fly-fishing world the Snake River in its upper reaches has been relatively unknown compared to such rivers as the Madison River, the Henry's Fork, and the Bighorn River. Reasons date back into the early twentieth century and come from the commercial world, from development of regional infrastructure and from a former perception of native salmonid sporting qualities. Now there are compelling reasons for bringing this most beautiful of rivers to the same degree of attention held by these other fine salmonid hosts. To begin, the Snake River courses through some of the most breathtakingly beautiful and nearly pristine parts of our country. Wildlife in uncountable numbers relies on it and its riparian zones for habitation. Most of all, as far as the angling world is concerned, it is a last stronghold for Yellowstone and Snake River fine-spotted cutthroat trout.

The Rocky Mountains hold the only waters where wild populations of inland cutthroat trout survive. But within this region, environmental changes continue to reduce cutthroat trout populations to a shadow of their former selves. This is ongoing in the upper Yellowstone River drainage. Now champions are emerging to raise the banners of preservation of this species that so much symbolizes Rocky Mountains waters. These champions come in the form of organizations and individuals, and the Snake River is in the focus of their efforts.

Joseph "Boots" Allen is one of the individuals emerging as a champion for preserving the Snake River and its salmonids in as natural a state as possible. Our friendship spans a decade. Kindred spirits, we are both avid fly-fishers, we frequent and love Snake River drainage waters, we hold passionate interests in preserving these waters, we love their salmonid bounty, and we herald the rich fly-fishing heritage nurtured by the quality of this drainage. We live on opposite sides of the Grand Teton Range, that crown jewel of the Rocky Mountains. Thus much of our friendship is communicated electronically, but it thrives on these mutual passions. When Boots asked me to compose this Foreword, I knew he did so out of appreciation for my interest and passion for retaining our Greater Yellowstone fly-fishing heritage and salmonid populations. Knowing his passion for such I could not decline.

Jackson Hole hosts many accomplished and generous contributors to fly-fishing, to the Snake River preservation efforts, and to the preservation of native cutthroat trout populations. But it is fitting that Boots Allen, a Jackson Hole native, offers this work. His grandfather, Leonard "Boots" Allen, came over Togwotee Pass from the east to Jackson Hole eighty years ago. Some sixty years ago, after obtaining extensive fly-fishing experience, he established one of the first fly-fishing retail shops in Jackson, Wyoming. Boots' father, Joe Allen, extended the business, was a famed guide on the Snake River, and a creative fly tier. To grandfather Boots and father Joe, the Snake River's cutthroat trout population was more than a source of income; it was a treasure to be preserved and loved.

Thus Boots came into a family that revered the river and its cutthroat trout population, so beginning in youth's formative years a passion for the river and its trout was planted. It spread roots in those early fishing trips with grandfather or father that we all remember with warmth and appreciation. It grew into the curiosity of teen-aged years to explore all facets of the river and its tributaries. It matured to a passion when as a young man he guided along the river, always hoping to instill in his clients appreciation for the river and its trout. More recently came literary skills, honed through obtaining a doctorate degree, to give ability in expressing his nearly matchless experience in fly-fishing and guiding on the upper river from eastern Idaho's "South Fork" reach to the spectacular run through Jackson Hole. So he offers this work, the first in such detail on the river and its salmonid treasure. In it the reader will observe more than successful strategies for seasonably taking trout in locations along the river, more than the personalities that developed the associated heritage, and more than recommended fly patterns. The reader will also feel the love Boots has for the river, its trout, and its surroundings. Thus a purpose of this work is to instill in the reader an appreciation for all these, and a resolution to help in the efforts to preserve these. So consider joining these efforts to preserve the river and its drainage, perhaps the remaining great bastion for inland cutthroat trout on the face of this earth.

—Bruce Staples

Introduction

The greater Yellowstone region is among the most storied freshwater ecosystems in the world. It boasts a diverse set of streams that read like a who's who registry of classic trout water. From the north flow the Yellowstone and Madison rivers, two streams that, along with their tributaries like the Lamar and Firehole rivers, are famous for their abundant trout populations. In the extreme south of the region, the Green and New Fork rivers drain the Wind River Range and contain healthy populations of large brown trout. From its east flows the Wind River that eventually becomes the famed Bighorn before leaving Wyoming. And from its west flows the legendary Henry's Fork, a renowned rainbow trout fishery, and home to some of the most influential names in all of American fly-fishing.

At the center of all this is another celebrated trout stream that in many ways acts as the crown jewel of the Yellowstone region. This stream is the Snake River. The Snake begins as a series of small creeks deep in the backcountry of the Yellowstone National Park and the Teton Wilderness. It ends 1,040 miles downstream as a massive waterway flowing into the Columbia River near Pasco, Washington. In between, it drains approximately 107,000 square miles of land, flows through three national parks, four states, more than a dozen reservoirs, two of America's most productive agricultural regions, and one of the world's deepest canyons. The Snake River is a massive stream. In fact, it is the tenth longest river in the United States. But in this book, I am concerned primarily with the first 200 miles of water, from its headwaters to its confluence with the Henry's Fork of the Snake River. The vast majority of this length is considered part of the Greater Yellowstone Ecosystem.

There are two distinct features that set the Snake River apart from other streams in the Greater Yellowstone Ecosystem. The first you will notice before you even remove your rod from its case. The river flows through what is arguably some of the most stunning and scenic landscapes in

The lower canyon reach of the South Fork of the Snake River.

the United States. The Grand Tetons, Jackson Hole, Snake River Canyon, Swan Valley, and the Canyon of the South Fork make the Snake River a lasting experience even on those few days when the fishing is subpar. It is truly one of the most beautiful places on Earth.

The second characteristic that sets the Snake River apart is undoubtedly much more important than the dramatic surroundings: it is one of the last remaining streams in the United States where native cutthroat trout are found in abundance. Cutthroat (*Oncorhynchus clarki*) are the only true native trout species in the upper reaches of the Snake River, and the vast majority of the Rocky Mountain West. Yet through more than a century of over-harvesting, habitat destruction, hybridization, and stream mismanagement, cutthroat have almost disappeared. Unfortunately, this applies to many of the rivers found in the greater Yellowstone ecosystem. For example, except for secluded high mountain lakes and streams, the Green River drainage of Wyoming is almost devoid of native Colorado cutthroat (*Oncorhynchus clarki pleuriticus*). The Madison River system, where once only westslope cutthroat (*Oncorhynchus clarki lewisi*) and Montana grayling lived, is almost exclusively a rainbow and brown fishery today. It is difficult to find anyone who can recall actually catching native Yellowstone cutthroat (*Oncorhynchus clarki bouvieri*) on the Henry's Fork. And on the upper Yellowstone River, native Yellowstone cutthroat populations are thought by many area anglers, guides and fisheries scientists, to be in decline due to increasing pressure from the introduction of mackinaw lake trout to Yellowstone Lake.

The Snake River remains one of those very few streams in the western U.S. where cutthroat trout, inparticular the Yellowstone cutthroat and the Snake River fine-spotted cutthroat (*Oncorhynchus clarki behnkei*), are the dominant trout species. This is by no means an indication that mankind has not attempted the same policies of mismanagement that have wrecked havoc on other western streams.

When I catch a cutthroat on the Snake River, cradling it in my hand after having brought it to the net, I am often amazed by its perseverance. The particular "cuttie" I may be holding is a direct descendent of ancestors that were victims of severe damming and leveeing. The fish in my hand may have just withstood yet another brutally dry summer and the disruption to the natural flow of the river to meet irrigation needs farther downstream. If I inspect this cutthroat's mouth as I remove the fly, I may find a number of scars created by other hooks over its lifetime, a sure sign of the increasing pressure these trout are under from sportsfishers. As I release the trout into the stream, I may look into its eyes for one last time and wonder about the dramatic changes it is experiencing from the introductions of exotic species. How many times did this cutthroat flee for its life from a predatory brown trout as a juvenile? If a female, were her eggs unexpectedly fertilized by non-native rainbows?

It is a sad tale that has been repeated on streams throughout the American West. Yet, as this cutthroat that I have just released returns to the swift currents of the stream, I cannot help but feel a sense of optimism for these trout. Despite all of the destruction wrecked upon their habitat, Yellowstone and Snake River fine-spotted cutthroat continue to thrive on much of the Snake River in Wyoming and eastern Idaho. It is a true testament to their toughness and adaptability. So while the mountains and canyons present a stunning venue, it is the abundance and strength of the cutthroat population that truly sets the Snake apart from other streams.

As a native fly-fishing guide from Wyoming, I have a very intimate link to this river system and its native cutthroat. While growing up, it was always special to travel just a short distance to the Green River, the Madison River, and the Henry's Fork and fish these streams with more diverse trout populations. I still enjoy fishing these waters and I always look forward to guiding a portion of my trips on them each year. But I will always return to the Snake River and its native cutthroat.

In this book I will deal separately with the two different segments of the Snake River, which happen to be conveniently divided by the Idaho-Wyoming border. Part I is concerned primarily with what I define as the Upper Snake River, a segment which flows from its headwaters in the Teton Wilderness to Palisades Reservoir, a distance of approximately 130 miles. This piece of the Snake River is exclusively on the Wyoming side of the border. In Part II, I examine Idaho's portion of the Snake River, what is popularly called the South Fork. This section runs 65 miles from Palisades Reservoir to Menan Buttes, just downstream from its confluence with the Henry's Fork. I will also examine various tributaries of the Snake River and important area lakes in each section too.

My decision to analyze these two segments separately is not arbitrary, nor is it based on the convenience of a state border and differing administrative bodies managing the water. While they are technically the same stream, the Upper Snake River and the South Fork of the Snake River differ in very subtle but important ways. Each has different characteristics that extend to their tributaries. Each has a different history of human encroachment and stream management, including the stocking of non-native species. Each has a different concentration and variety of trout and aquatic insect life. And each is fished with subtly different strategies, tactics, and flies. I will examine these differences separately in each section.

In Parts III and IV, I conclude by first, introducing the reader to the important patterns that I consider essential for a productive day of fishing and then, by paying homage to the legendary people that have made the Snake River the incredible fishery that it is today. This includes early pioneering outfitters and tiers such as Bob Carmichael, Marcella Oswald, Leonard "Boots" Allen, and those carrying on the tradition today, like Jack Dennis, Bruce Staples, Paul Bruun, and Ken Burkholder. These individuals have not only contributed to our understanding of the Snake River and how to fish it successfully, they have also been at the cutting edge of stream conservation and the protection of its trout. They have been instrumental to the creation of important conservation groups, organizations like Jackson Hole Trout Unlimited, The Snake River Cutthroats, the One-Fly Foundation, and the Snake River Fund. They have assisted with the preservation efforts of other, more regionally focused groups like the Greater Yellowstone Coalition, the Jackson Hole Conservation Alliance, and the Nature Conservancy. I consider it an honor to have known many of these individuals personally. As such, this section of the journal means the most to me and is the one I take the most pride in presenting to the reader.

Research forms the backbone of this book, but as with almost everything in fly-fishing, a considerable portion is based on personal experience and opinion. Not everyone who fishes the Snake River regularly may agree with all I present here. I believe this is common to all trout streams, but none more so than the Snake. If you were to ask a dozen different anglers their opinion regarding tactics, fly selection, even insect and trout abundance on the stream, you would probably get a dozen different answers. But this is what makes fishing the Snake River special. It has a reputation as a relatively easy stream to fish, yet at the same time, it can present challenges to even the most experienced angler. While the Snake is known as a classic dry-fly stream, there are days when subsurface flies are the only game in town. This is to say nothing of the variable runoff, variable flow regiment, and hatches that vary in their size and density from year-to-year and reach-to-reach. The Snake River is complex, but it is probably one of the most enjoyable streams an angler can fish. I hope what I present here will let you experience all that this wonderful river has to offer.

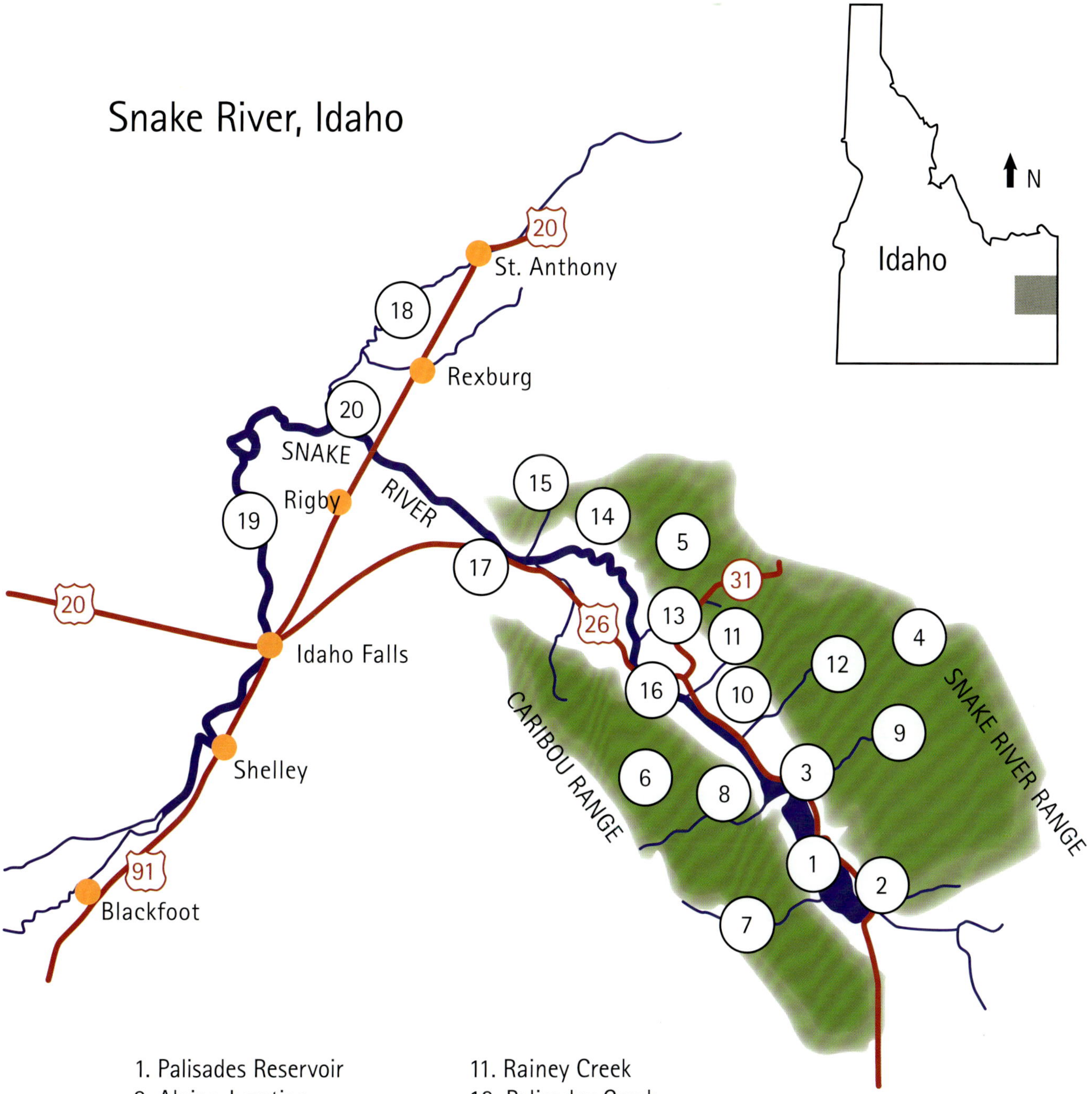

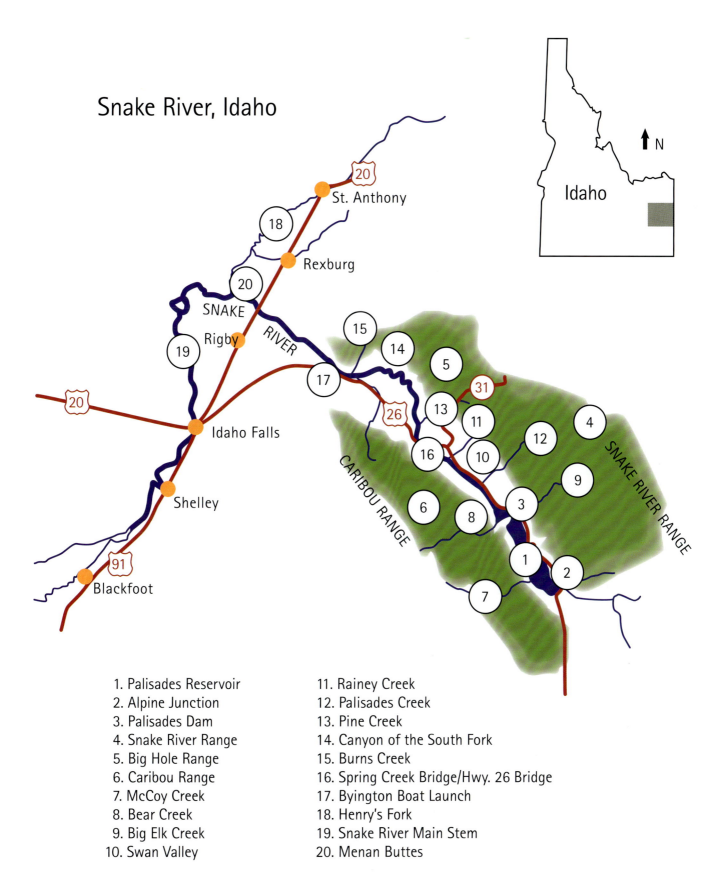

1. Palisades Reservoir
2. Alpine Junction
3. Palisades Dam
4. Snake River Range
5. Big Hole Range
6. Caribou Range
7. McCoy Creek
8. Bear Creek
9. Big Elk Creek
10. Swan Valley
11. Rainey Creek
12. Palisades Creek
13. Pine Creek
14. Canyon of the South Fork
15. Burns Creek
16. Spring Creek Bridge/Hwy. 26 Bridge
17. Byington Boat Launch
18. Henry's Fork
19. Snake River Main Stem
20. Menan Buttes

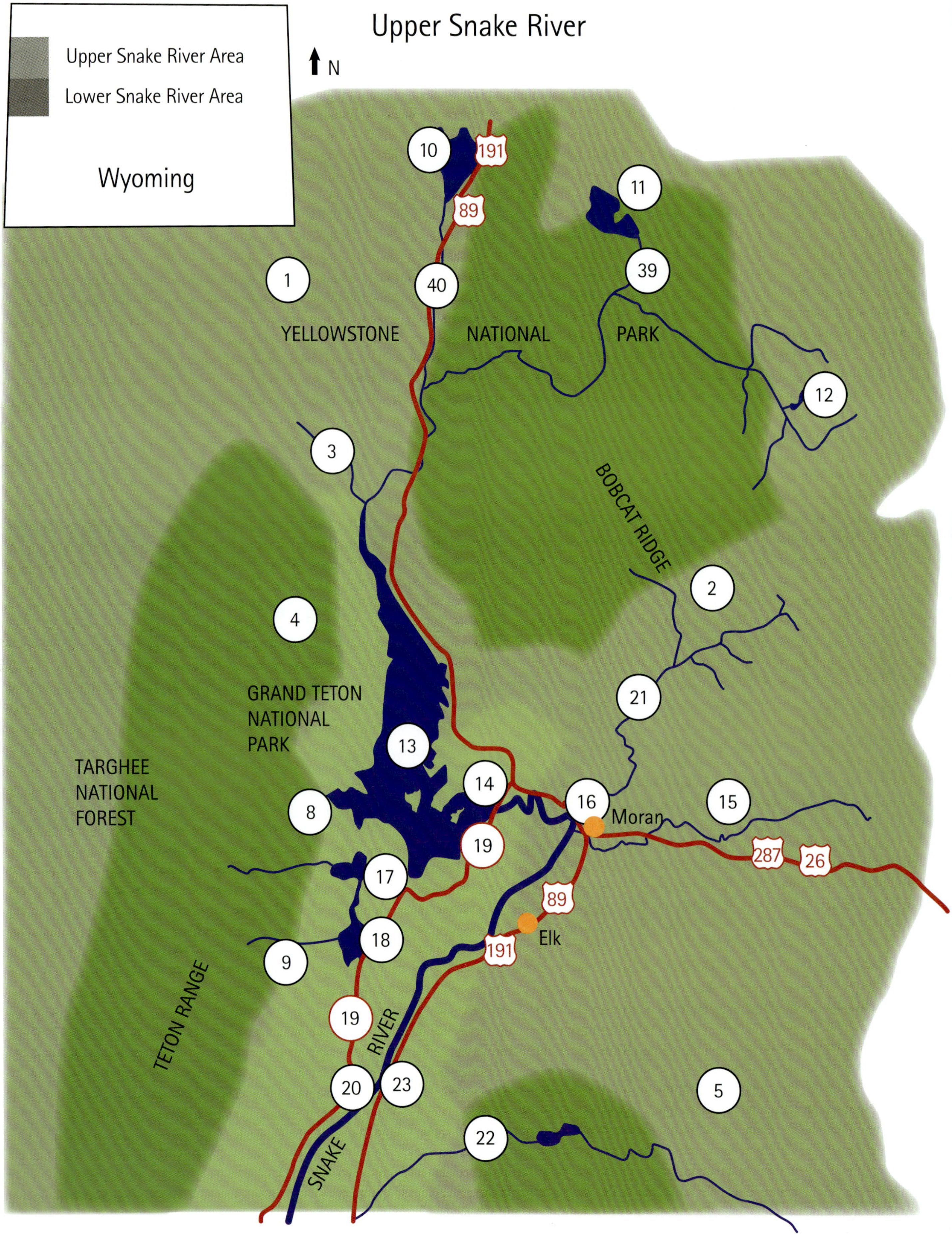
Upper Snake River
Upper Snake River Area
Lower Snake River Area
Wyoming
N
YELLOWSTONE
NATIONAL
PARK
BOBCAT RIDGE
GRAND TETON
NATIONAL
PARK
TARGHEE
NATIONAL
FOREST
TETON RANGE
SNAKE
RIVER
Moran
Elk
191
89
287
26
1
2
3
4
5
8
9
10
11
12
13
14
15
16
17
18
19
20
21
22
23
39
40

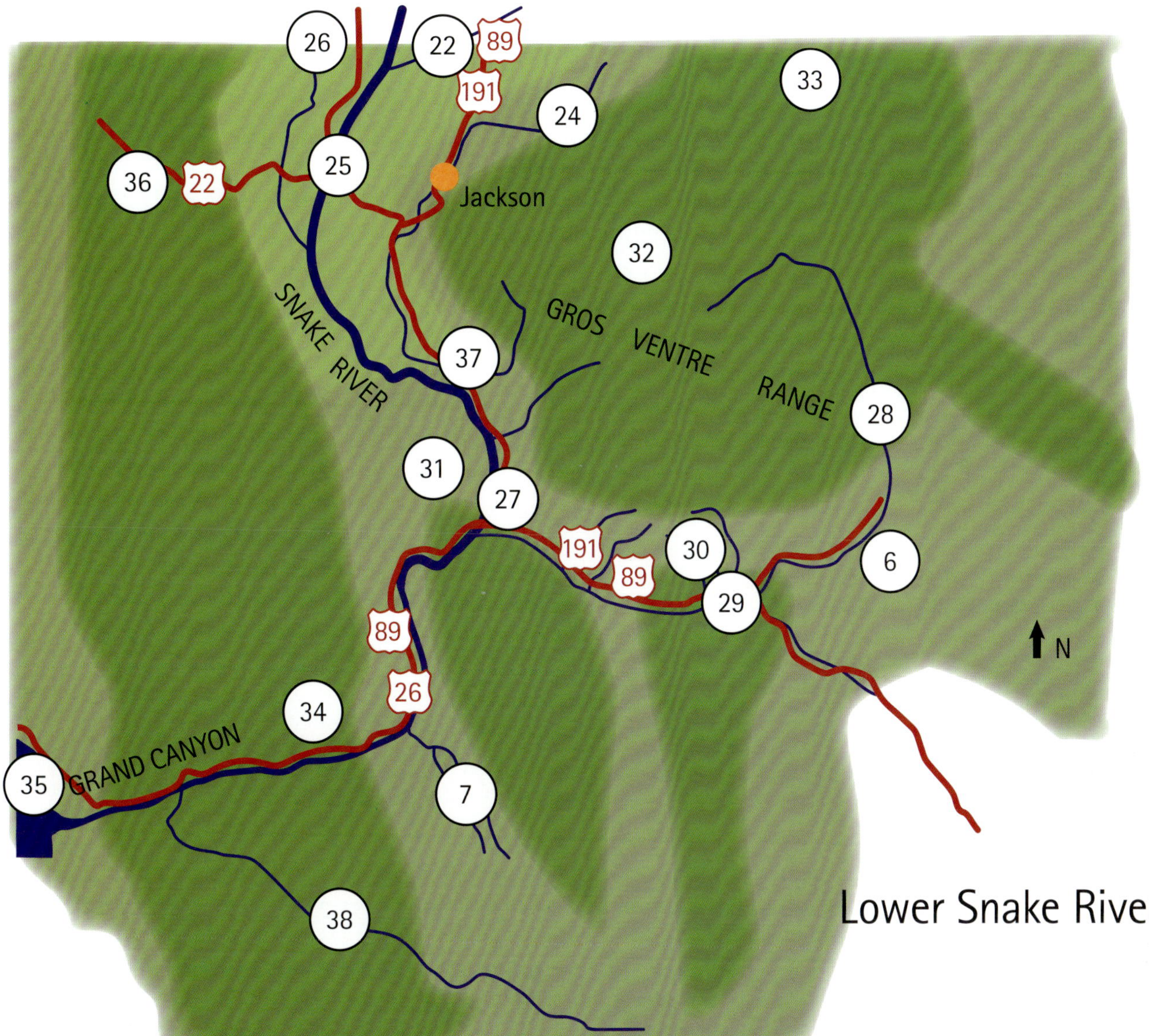

Lower Snake River

1. Yellowstone National Park
2. Teton Wilderness
3. John D. Rockefeller, Jr. Memorial Parkway
4. Grand Teton National Park
5. Gros Ventre Wilderness
6. Hoback Drainage
7. Bridger-Teton National Forest
8. Mt. Moran (12605)
9. Grand Teton (13770)
10. Lewis Lake
11. Heart Lake
12. Mariposa Lake
13. Jackson Lake
14. Jackson Dam
15. Buffalo Fork
16. Moran Junction
17. Leigh Lake
18. Jenny Lake
19. Grand Teton National Park Inner Loop Road
20. Moose, Wy./Moose Bridge
21. Pacific Creek
22. Gros Ventre River
23. Moose Junction
24. Flat Creek
25. Wilson Bridge
26. Fish Creek
27. Hoback Junction
28. Granite Creek
29. Hoback River
30. Hoback Canyon
31. Munger Mountain
32. Jackson Peak (10741)
33. Sheep Mountain (11190)
34. Snake River Canyon
35. Palisades Reservoir
36. Teton Pass
37. South Park Bridge (Von Gontaard's Landing)
38. Greys River
39. Heart River
40. Lewis River

Part I: Upper Snake River, Wyoming

Will Dornan

The Snake River flows through the beautiful but seismically active valley of Jackson Hole.

Geology, Human History, & the Development of a Fly-Fishing Heritage

The Upper Snake River begins as a series of small streams draining valleys deep in the backcountry of Yellowstone National Park and the Teton Wilderness. At one time, and for a very long time, the headwaters were thought to be either Lewis Lake or Heart Lake, both located in the southern part of the Park. In fact, when Lt. Gustavus Doane made his ultimately failed attempt to navigate the entire Snake River in 1876, he and his company of frontier soldiers began their journey at Heart Lake. In 1971, Paul Lawrence and Joe Shellenberger, a local river enthusiast and park ranger respectively, explored the upper reaches of the Snake River above the Heart River confluence and are thought, by some, to have discovered the true source of the stream. And yet to this day, the actual headwaters are murky and a topic of debate among anglers, geologists, and geographers. All one needs to do is look at a shaded relief or topographical map of the area to realize why.

Throughout the Teton Wilderness and the southeast portion of Yellowstone National Park exists an almost impenetrable puzzle of valleys and ridges, each acting as its own drainage basin. It is difficult to determine which of the small streams coming from these basins is the actual headwaters for the Snake River. Some feel that a body of water named Mariposa Lake, a high plateau lake found almost exactly on the southern boundary of Yellowstone, is the Snake River's true point of origination. No one really knows, and probably no one ever will. At the very least, it can be said that the headwaters are somewhere in the Teton Wilderness, near the Yellowstone border.

From its point of origination in the Teton Wilderness, the Snake River runs toward the west along the southern border of Yellowstone National Park, picking up the Heart River from Heart Lake, the Lewis River from Lewis Lake, and several other smaller tributaries. The Snake turns to the south just as it enters Flagg Canyon and then flows out of Yellowstone National Park, into and out of Jackson Lake in Grand Teton National Park, and through the entire length of the valley of Jackson Hole and the Snake River Canyon before emptying into Palisade Reservoir near the Idaho border.

Despite its location below Jackson Lake Dam, the Snake River looks much more like a classic freestone stream. Those characteristics that define freestone streams—fast currents, braided channels, variable seasonal flows, heavy stream-bound structure, and a plethora of tributaries—are more than apparent. As it flows through Jackson Hole and the Snake River Canyon, the river drops an average of 16 feet per mile. The massive basin it drains contains mountains that stand well over 13,000 feet in elevation. The Teton Wilderness, the Teton Range, the Mount Leidy Highlands, the Gros Ventre Wilderness, the Hoback Range, the Snake River Range, and the Salt River Range all surround the Snake River. The snow these mountains hold can reach depths of 10 feet before spring melt begins. All this snowmelt culminates in a massive runoff on the Snake River. The sustained onrush of swift-moving water changes the character of the river every year, creating new channels in some places, flooding old channels in other places, and drying up previously reliable channels to the point that they are not navigatable.

The dramatic landscape surrounding the Snake River in Jackson Hole is the result of millions of years of tectonic and glacial activity. The Teton Range, to the west of the Snake River, began to rise from the valley floor between 30 and 35 million years ago, and only within the past nine million years have these peaks made their most dramatic upward thrust. Two tectonic plates, one making up the valley floor and the other the Teton Range, lay against each other on a fault line running in a north-south direction. The valley plate extends to the west in a sinking action, while the Teton plate extends eastward in an uplifting action. The effect is a constantly sinking valley and a constantly rising mountain range. This process continues to this day, or in other words, the Tetons are still growing. From time to time, this movement causes earthquakes, some of which have been quite severe, so it is not uncommon to feel several small tremors in the valley each year.

A series of glaciers have covered Jackson Hole over the past 2 million years, helping to create large alpine lakes along the Teton Range as well as several buttes dotting the valley. At times, the glacial ice in Jackson Hole is believed to have reached a depth of 2,000 feet. As these glaciers began to recede, the melting ice found a path to the south of the valley along what is today the Snake River, but this is not to suggest that the path of the Snake is the lowest point within the valley. In fact, the lowest point of Jackson Hole is directly along the fault line that runs down the base of the Teton Range. The Snake River flows along its present path because several ice dams and glacial debris forced melt water away from the mountains. Over several thousand years, the river has eroded its own path through the glacial outwash plain that makes up the valley floor. This erosion is deepest in the Snake River Canyon, which begins at the extreme southern end of Jackson Hole. The most recent glacial periods—Bull Lake (80 to 140 thousand years ago) and Pinedale (15 to 20 thousand years ago)—never actually reached as far south as the Snake River Canyon. Instead, the canyon was the recipient of the first flow of melting glacier water. The river has had much more time to erode the rock and sediment in this part of the valley. The result is a deep, dramatic, and quite beautiful canyon.

The human history of the Snake River and Jackson Hole is relatively short in comparison to the natural history. Native American tribes, particularly the Blackfoot, Shoshone, and Gros Ventre, have frequented the valley during the summer and fall seasons for approximately 10,000 years. The harsh winters in Jackson Hole, which is over 6,000 feet at its lowest elevation, made permanent residence undesirable. However, there is evidence suggesting that a small and very primitive band known as the Tukudikas—or Sheep Eaters—did reside in the area on a year-round basis.

It is believed that John Colter, a former member of Lewis and Clark's Corps of Discovery, was the first European to venture into Jackson Hole during the winter of 1807. He was followed over the next few decades by a handful of American and French-Canadian trappers. Many of the contemporary names of the main geographic features in the valley came from them. French-speaking trappers, viewing the Teton Range from the west in Idaho, imagined the peaks to be reminiscent of a woman's voluptuous chest and name them *Les Trois Tetons*—the Three Breasts. (Let's remember, these men were alone in the mountains and, for the most part, were womenless for months, or even years, on end).

In the late 1820s, David Jackson, a partner in the Rocky Mountain Fur Company with Jedediah Smith and William Sublette, began frequenting the valley to trap beaver. His partners named the area Jackson's Hole—a *hole* was the term mountain men gave to a deep valley surrounded by high mountains. It is uncertain though when the Snake River received its name or who exactly named it. Ethnologists believe that members of the Shoshone Nation living in southern Idaho used hand signs to describe themselves as either, "the people who live among the big fish," or, "the people from the river of many fish." They used a curving S-shape with their hand to make this sign, and Europeans must have misinterpreted this to mean the sign for a snake. This branch of the Shoshone became known as the Snake Indians and the stream became forever known as the Snake River. Originally, its first European handle was Lewis' River, named by the Lewis and Clark Expedition in honor of Meriwether Lewis. Ironically, the only part of the Snake River drainage that retains this name is a piece that the party never saw, that being the small section running from Lewis Lake to the Snake River in Yellowstone National Park.

Photo Courtesy of Tom Carmichael

Pioneering fishing outfitter Bob Carmichael at his Jenny Lake operation in 1940.

Permanent settlement of Jackson Hole by European-Americans was spotty throughout much of the nineteenth century. It was not until the early 1890s that actual towns—primarily Jackson, Wilson, and Kelly—began to take root, becoming the commercial centers for the ranching trade that was developing throughout the valley. Being in a region with long, intense winters, short growing seasons, and miles from any type of national transport system meant that Jackson Hole ranchers had a very tough go of it. Many of them turned to dude ranching and hunting outfitting to supplement their incomes. By the 1920s, these activities had become the primary source of revenue for most ranch operators. Dude ranches and hunting lodges soon found it profitable to offer guided fishing trips on the Snake River as well as area lakes to guests. Ben Sheffield's ranch, near the mouth of Jackson Lake, became a popular destination for the few turn-of-the-century anglers who ventured to Jackson Hole.

In the 1930s, a handful of non-ranch-affiliated guides and outfitters became involved in the game, tapping into the increased flow of tourists and visiting anglers. Most notable were Bob Carmichael, who operated the area's first fly shop on the banks of the Snake River in Moose, and Leonard "Boots" Allen, a Bureau of Reclamation employee who guided clients on the Snake River, Jackson Lake, and streams in southern Yellowstone. After WWII, as travel to Jackson Hole continued to increase, others joined Carmichael and Allen in the growing guiding and outfitting trade. Dick Boyer offered fishing trips from a small fishing shop in the Wort Hotel. Well-known tiers such as California's Roy Donnelly and West Yellowstone's Don Martinez supplied Carmichael's shop with popular Variant and Quill patterns, and Allen sold nail keg barrels full of Humpies to anglers every year out of his Fort Jackson Fishing Trips shop in the town of Jackson.

Carmichael, Allen, and Boyer were soon hiring a number of local fishing enthusiasts as guides during the summer and fall seasons. By the early 1960s, long-time area resident Vern Bressler was leading fishing expeditions out of his base of operation at Crescent H Ranch in Wilson, Wyoming. Bressler offered trips not only on the Snake River and its tributaries, but also on the Green and New Fork rivers as well as backcountry excursions into the Gros Ventre Wilderness and the Snake River Range. But Bressler's greatest contribution to fly-fishing in the Upper Snake River drainage was the development of the spring creeks feeding into Fish Creek on Crescent H Ranch. These waters today act as a major refuge for Snake River cutthroat and are one of the Yellowstone region's handfull of true spring-creek fisheries.

By the late 1960s, Jack Dennis had established himself as a reputable guide and outfitter in Jackson Hole. He appeared several times on Kurt Gowdy's *American Sportsman* television series, which helped expose the high-quality fishing found on the Snake River to the greater angling community in the United States. Dennis was also known for his tying abilities. In 1974, he published *Jack Dennis' Western Trout Fly Tying Manual*. The first tying instruction book of its kind, it set the standard in fly-tying manuals and remains the best-selling fly-tying reference book of all time. Throughout the 1970s and 1980s, renowned tiers such as Howard Cole, Jay Buchner, Joe Allen, and Scott Sanchez would join Dennis by offering several patterns that are now synonymous with the Jackson Hole area.

Today, fly-fishing on the Snake River in Jackson Hole is more popular than ever. Several full-service shops and outfitting services exist throughout the valley, many of which employ world-renowned guides. Some of the greatest names in fly-fishing today earned their reputations on these waters. The local industry owes a lot to the pioneering individuals who helped develop this incredible fishery, but it owes even more to the fishery itself, which continues to attract thousands of anglers from around the world each year.

Trout of the Upper Snake River

To say that the Upper Snake River is an unadulterated native cutthroat fishery would not be entirely true. But, on possibly no other stream in the continental United States will one find as strong of a native trout population as on the Snake River in Wyoming. Yellowstone and Snake River fine-spotted cutthroat make up well over 90% of total trout abundance on average. On most days, cutthroat is all one will catch. But other trout call the Upper Snake River home too. Following is a detailed description of each trout species found in the drainage, including their distribution, abundance, and importance to the fishery.

Yellowstone and Snake River Fine-Spotted Cutthroat Trout (*Oncorhynchus clarki bouvieri* and *O.c. behnkei*)

To understand the importance of Yellowstone and Snake River fine-spotted cutthroat to the Snake River, one must first understand the history of cutthroat trout in the Rocky Mountain West. It is an incredible story of adaptation and survival spanning millions of years. Cutthroat started as a genus group close to the Pacific Ocean and closely linked with Pacific salmon. About five million years ago, this group split to form another that consisted of both rainbow and cutthroat. Two million years later, this group split to form two separate groups of rainbows and cutthroat. The rainbows stayed along the Pacific Coast. Cutthroat, however, setting a standard of almost unmatched exploration and infiltration, began working their way upstream to invade the waterways of the interior landmass.

Geological and climatological processes determined the distribution of this new species group across the West. Advancing and receding glaciers, lava dams, and the rising and falling of ancient inland lakes created pathways into new drainages while cutting off access to others. These tumultuous processes resulted in the natural development of several cutthroat species uniquely distinct from one another. This includes the westslope cutthroats in northwestern Montana and northern Idaho, the Bonneville cutthroat in the Great Salt Lake drainage, the Colorado cutthroat in the Green River and Colorado River drainages, and the greenback cutthroats in the South Platte and Arkansas River drainages in eastern Colorado. By the time the first humans were working their way into North America from the Eurasian landmass, cutthroats had claimed residence throughout the West, from Alberta and British Columbia to southern New Mexico.

Roughly 12,000 years ago, the single species that colonized the Snake River was the Yellowstone cutthroat. At that time, they did not exist in the Yellowstone River drainage on the east side of the divide. An ice sheet, a remnant of the Pinedale Glacier that was entering its last era of existence, blocked the Yellowstone Plateau and prevented farther migration. As this ice sheet began to melt, a path opened that allowed Yellowstone cutthroat to cross from the Snake River on the west side of the Continental Divide to the Yellowstone River on the east side of the divide. This path is called Two Ocean Pass and it still exists today. At this point, a small creek—Two Ocean Creek—runs for approximately two miles off the north flank of the pass and then splits to form two streams. The east branch becomes Atlantic Creek and flows to the Yellowstone River. The west branch becomes Pacific Creek and flows to the Snake River. Other than the westslope species, the Yellowstones are the only cutthroat to reside in streams on both sides of the Continental Divide.

The Snake River fine-spotted cutthroat is considered a subspecies of the Yellowstone cutthroat. They differ in subtle, but significant, ways. The most noticeable of these differences is the size and distribution of spots along its flanks. Unlike the large, rounded black spotting patterns found on the Yellowstone cutthroat, the Snake River fine-spotted cutthroat has small, irregularly shaped spots that have been described in many fishery texts as, "finely ground pepper." These spots are distributed liberally over the body and on the caudal, adipose, and dorsal fins. The large spots on the Yellowstone cutthroat are found in a higher concentration toward the caudal fin rather than on the rest of the body. Both species have the distinguishing red slashes underneath the lower jaw.

A less noticeable but more important difference between the two are their behavioral traits. Evidence based on observations of certain strains of Snake River fine-spots in both hatchery and wild environs by Wyoming fishery biologists suggests Snake River fine-spotted cutthroat are tougher and more adaptable trout than their Yellowstone counterpart. Anglers typically agree, and consider Snake River fine-spots to be the strongest fighter of all the cutthroats. For both of these reasons, they are the most widely stocked cutthroat species outside of their original habitat, finding homes in alien but very hospitable streams like the White River in Arkansas and the Green River below Flaming Gorge in Utah. On these rivers, where the feeding environment is far more ideal than anything found on the Upper Snake River

Will Dornan

A Snake River cutthroat caught above Deadman's Bar.

and its tributaries, it is possible to hook into fine-spotted cutthroat exceeding 25 inches.

Taxonomists have not yet officially recognized the Snake River fine-spotted cutthroat as a distinct sub-species. This is because current genetic analysis has been unable to find consistent differences between the two. However, many fishery biologists agree that an obvious genetic distinction must exist to explain the divergent spotting patterns and behavioral traits. These differences have turned political, and various fishery management bodies in the West currently find themselves on different sides of the debate. For example, the Idaho Department of Fish and Game does not officially recognize the fine-spotted subspecies, instead clustering them together with the Yellowstone cutthroat. In Wyoming, the state Game and Fish Department classifies the two as separate subspecies.

How this closely connected but obviously very different set of subspecies came into existence remains a biological mystery. Some theorize that ice dams during regionally specific glacial periods cutoff Yellowstone cutthroats from one another. These periods of isolation could have lasted several hundred to a few thousand years. When the glaciers melted, two very different sets of subspecies emerged. Those that had been cutoff are believed to have developed the behavioral and physical traits that we now see in fine-spotted cutthroat. There is only sparse evidence of actual interbreeding between the two, despite the fact that they occupy much of the same territory. Today, Yellowstone cutthroat reside in the entire Snake River drainage above Shoshone Falls in Idaho. Fine-spotted cutthroat are most abundant from below Jackson Lake to Palisades Reservoir and minimally abundant above Jackson Lake. Their numbers are minimal in upstream tributaries like the Buffalo River and Pacific Creek, but abundant in downstream tributaries like the Gros Ventre and Hoback rivers.

The harsh environment of Wyoming's Snake River—a short feeding season, limited nutrients, and heavy currents—makes it difficult for any kind of trout to survive. Cutthroat have had success here for two primary reasons. First and foremost is their ability to adapt to changes in their ecosystem. These are not just changes that have occurred over several millennia, but those that occur from decade to decade, or even year to year. Violent spring runoffs, drought, scorching summers and brutal winters are common to Jackson Hole and can take their toll on trout populations. This is to say nothing of the man-made destruction to the Snake River ecosystem. Jackson Lake Dam, the 25-mile-long levee system on the river, and streamside development have altered trout habitat and severely degraded vital spawning and feeding beds. But while non-native species introduced to the Snake River in Wyoming have struggled, if not perished altogether, Yellowstone and Snake River cutthroat continue to thrive.

The second reason cutthroat thrive on the Upper Snake River is because the stream possesses an uncountable number of spring creeks and tributaries. These nutrient-rich parts of the river system give young cutthroat ample feeding ground and refuge from the heavy flows experienced on the river during spring runoff. More importantly, spring creeks and tributaries are where thousands of Snake River and Yellowstone cutthroat primarily spawn (see Table 1, page 27). John Kiefling, former fishery management director for the Wyoming Game and Fish Department, was fond of saying, "As the spring creeks go, so goes the Snake River cutthroat." No statement better describes the importance of such water to the Snake River and its native trout.

On several occasions I have flown into Jackson Hole on commercial flights in May and June. This is the time when

Spring creeks like this are the lifeblood of Snake River cutthroat, providing both prime spawning and feeding grounds.

Cutthroat caught below the Gros Ventre River confluence.

the spring runoff is at its most intense and the river and its primary tributaries are swelling with debris and tens of thousands of cubic feet of water. When looking down at the valley floor, I have seen intermixed with the rolling strip of chocolate mud that is the Snake River several dozen slivers of light blue and green. These are spring creeks! Some are several miles long while others seem to be only a few hundred meters in length. They are everywhere, providing ample feeding and spawning water at a time of the year when cutthroat need it most.

Immediately after the runoff subsides, it sometimes seems as if young cutthroat ranging in size from six to eleven inches are doing all the feeding. Much of this is due to the fact that the tributaries still have plenty of holding water to sustain a considerable number of large cutthroat. These trout, ranging in size from 12- to 19-plus inches, run up tributaries in the spring to spawn. The vast majority of these return to the main river as water levels drop. When these large trout return is dependent on the duration of the spring runoff. During drought years, it can be as early as the first week of July. During high-water years, it can be as late as the middle of August.

Twenty-plus-inch cutthroat can be found throughout the drainage, though no one really knows what the largest cutthroat was to have ever been caught on the Snake. In 1993, I witnessed one of my father's clients land a 25 1/4-inch Snake River cutthroat across the river channel from Munger Mountain, approximately two miles upstream from South Park Bridge. It was certainly an impressive trout. But I doubt it was the largest ever landed by an angler. I have seen cutthroat that I could say with confidence were larger than 25 inches working in certain pools and runs a few times since I started guiding on the river.

The size cutthroat can reach on the Snake River is impressive when one considers the harsh environment in which they live. This *may* be due to a survival/adaptation trait that has earned them a rather unsavory reputation with many "sporting" anglers until very recently. Some fly-fishers contend that cutthroat rarely feed selectively, a behavior associated more with trout like rainbows and browns. Trout that feed selectively generally key in on one trait or a set of traits for a food type. Then they will feed only on food types displaying this trait or traits, even if there are multiple food types available. For anglers seeking a more "sporting" variety of trout, this is one of the best characteristics a fish can exhibit. It forces the fly-fisher to not only match the identity of the insect, but perhaps even a specific trait of that insect. This could be its color, size, behavior on the water, or a specific stage of its life cycle.

Cutthroat on the Upper Snake River behave in what fly-fishers call an opportunistic manner. Simply put, they tend to feed on whatever is available. Even during a mahogany dun hatch, a fly-fisherman can cast out a Stimulator or a Royal Wulff and do well. Those who prefer more "sporting" trout find this to be an undesirable characteristic. But I feel this behavior stems less from what some call a dumb-gene, and more from a necessity for survival in an unforgiving environment. On a stream where food is scarce, trout can ill afford to let any form of potential nutrients escape. They will feed on most anything, they have to, and cutthroat have survived because they are opportunistic feeders.

It is a contentious question as to what is a better characteristic for trout to exhibit, selective or opportunistic behavior. In my opinion, it all comes down to how one defines the word "sport" when referring to trout. At the 2003 Federation of Fly Fishers' International Symposium a British friend of mine (who will remain nameless here) expressed his utter disdain for cutthroat and described them as, "The most unsporting trout he has ever cast a line to." When I asked him how he defined *sport*, he exclaimed, "To be challenged by a fish and forced to use your wits in everything from fly selection to presentation." He then asked me how I would define *sport*. I said, "Simply fishing for native trout in their native environment, where they are forced to display their natural behavior."

But arguing over the virtues of selective versus opportunistic feeding is really a moot discussion when it comes to cutthroat on the Snake River. The truth is, I and many an angler, have had our hats handed to us by these trout. This most often occurs on the spring creeks or on slow-moving tributaries like Flat Creek. In fact, that British friend of mine came up blank during his first-ever excursion onto Flat Creek a couple of years ago. Yet, this happens time and time again on the Snake River, proper, as well. I get quite a kick out of watching hotshot fly-fishers with a poor opinion of cutthroat (an opinion usually developed while fishing for other sub-species on different waters) lose their minds casting fly after fly, after fly, at a fish that continually refuses their offerings. It is a lesson in humility and one that generally creates greater respect from individual anglers for Snake River cutthroat. As Paul Bruun is fond of saying, "I can show you cutthroat on the Snake River that are going to be pretty darn selective about what they are *not* going to be selective about."

Rainbow Trout
(*Oncorhynchus mykiss*)

Between 1933 and 1964, over 300,000 rainbow trout were stocked throughout the Upper Snake drainage. Most rainbows were planted in the streams and lakes of the tributaries feeding the main river, primarily the Gros Ventre, Salt, and Buffalo Fork river basins. At that time, the philosophy of the Wyoming Game and Fish Department was that managing a fishery simply meant stocking trout. This is a far cry from the proactive management plan of the agency today, which calls for maintaining existing native trout species and limiting the introduction of non-native species. Rainbows were once the stocking trout of choice for fishery managers because the species was readily available, desirable, and one of the easiest to raise in hatcheries.

The Snake River drainage proved to be inhospitable for rainbow trout. The limited nutrients and heavy spring runoff are not conducive to the species, which requires a strong supply of nutrients and more moderate flows. Despite the years of heavy stocking, it is now very difficult to find rainbows in the river system. In my most recent season of guiding on the Snake, I caught a total of two. The one shining spot for rainbow trout in Jackson Hole is a small but self-sustaining resident population that exists on the Gros Ventre River. They are found in their most abundant numbers from just below Lower Slide Lake down to the Park Service campground on the river, a length of only five miles. It is possible though to find rainbows farther downstream. The largest rainbow I have caught in the Upper Snake River basin was a 20 1/2-inch hen on the middle reach of the Gros Ventre River. How this population of rainbow has survived while most other stocked populations have perished, remains a mystery to fishery biologists.

At one time, rainbows made up a greater abundance of the total trout population in Jackson Hole. In J. Edson Leonard's 1950 book *Flies,* Bob Carmichael tells of how 20% of creeled trout in the southern part of Jackson Hole were rainbows. Guides who float-fished the Snake River in the 1950s and 1960s also tell stories of a heavy concentration of rainbows between the Wilson Bridge and the southern extreme of Grand Teton National Park. This is in the same vicinity as the confluence of the Gros Ventre and Snake rivers. It is difficult to say if the abundance of rainbows in the south end of Jackson Hole was due to the heavy stocking that occurred in the drainage, or if it can be attributed to the even heavier stockings that occurred on the South Fork of the Snake River in Idaho. It may have been due to a combination of the two. Until 1957, when Palisades Reservoir was completed, the two streams were connected and fish could move freely throughout the entire river system. Rainbows from the South Fork could have easily migrated up the Snake River Canyon and into Jackson Hole. But based on conversations that I have had with officials from the Idaho Department of Fish and Game, this theory is debatable. As early as 1983, despite heavy stockings, rainbows made up a negligible percentage of the total abundance of trout on the South Fork. They doubt those numbers were any more plentiful before that date. A stronger theory is that the heavy stockings that occurred on the Salt River (150,000 over a very short period of time) were partly responsible for the populations that existed on the Snake River. Regardless, the rainbow population in the Upper Snake drainage has almost all but disappeared.

The rainbows that existed on the Snake River above Wilson Bridge were no doubt due to the stockings that had occurred in the Gros Ventre drainage. Their demise, as

Loch Leven brown trout make up a small percentage of total trout abundance on the Upper Snake River below Jackson Lake Dam.

with the demise of the species that existed on other parts of the Snake River, has not been properly analyzed and is a source of debate. My uncle, Dick Allen, guided on the Snake River in the 1950s and 1960s, when the abundance of rainbows here was at is greatest. He recalls their numbers beginning to fall off dramatically in the early 1960s, after the completion of several irrigation diversions on the lower half of the Gros Ventre. This may explain the drastic reduction of rainbows on the lower Gros Ventre and the Snake River above Wilson Bridge. However, this does not seem to have had a substantial negative impact on the small resident population below Lower Slide Lake, which still exists.

Loch Leven Brown Trout

(*Salmo trutta levenensis*)

Brown trout were not as heavily stocked in the Jackson Hole area as rainbows were. My research of Wyoming Game and Fish stocking documents has turned up less than 80,000 total. Much heavier stockings occurred further upstream in Yellowstone National Park, primarily in Shoshone and Lewis lakes, during the 1890s. Both of these stocking locations together did not result in brown trout making up a significant percentage of the trout population in the drainage. Why brown trout have not taken to the drainage in higher numbers is a source of debate. Clearly they are hardy enough to endure. Many believe a key determinant is their spawning behavior, which might not be conducive to the Upper Snake River. One theory is that flows and gradient on the main river, where browns typically spawn, are not suitable for the creation of sustainable redds and for proper gestation. Others believe that sediment size within the riverbed is far too large for females to create a productive redd. The truth is probably somewhere in the middle.

Although their total numbers are quite small, brown trout are found throughout the drainage and populate a variety of different waters. In Jackson Hole proper, brown trout can be found throughout the length of the Snake River itself. Their abundance is greatest though in Snake River Canyon, as well as the first few miles below Jackson Lake, near the confluence of the Buffalo Fork. Their strength on these sections of the Snake can be explained in part by brown trout numbers on nearby tributaries. Downstream of Snake River Canyon, the Salt River flows into Palisades Reservoir. This stream has a strong brown trout population. Browns from here can migrate into the nutrient-rich reservoir, and some years, depending on water levels and the degree of drought, migrate up the Snake River. Every now and then I catch brown trout well above the canyon in the vicinity of South Park Bridge.

Brown trout found below Jackson Lake are a result of the relatively abundant population on the Buffalo Fork. These trout will work their way into the Snake to feed on baitfish including small suckers, whitefish, minnows, and cutthroat. Again, there are not many of them, but it is possible to catch brown trout exceeding 20 inches. In 2003, Kasey Collins, a guide for Worldcast Anglers in Jackson, Wyoming, landed a 24-inch brown at the outlet of Frustration Creek, below Deadman's Bar.

The highest concentration of brown trout in the system is found above Jackson Lake. This is in close proximity to Lewis and Shoshone lakes, the original waters where brown trout were stocked at the turn of the twentieth century. The Lewis River, which drains both lakes, is the primary tributary of the Snake River above Jackson Lake and has an abundant population of browns that exceed 18 inches. The largest browns are found on the lakes themselves. Lewis, Shoshone, and Heart lakes contain brown trout between 18 and 25 inches. In autumn, generally in the second half of October, browns will make their annual spawning run into the channel connecting Lewis and Shoshone lakes. (This highly anticipated event is drawing an ever-increasing number of anglers wishing to cast streamers and small dry flies to brown trout that easily exceed 20 inches.) Sediment size within the channel is ideal for the creation of redds.

Brown trout also run up into the Snake River in Yellowstone National Park from Jackson Lake. The run is typically brief, lasting only two to three weeks maximum, but it is an important run and one that is thoroughly enjoyable to fish if an angler times it right.

Within Jackson Hole, the lake with the strongest concentration of brown trout is undoubtedly Leigh Lake, at the base of Mount Moran and roughly 1.5 miles north of Jenny Lake. Brown trout here reach sizes that are seriously competitive with browns above Jackson Lake. During a fishing trip in 1993, a party I guided landed two brown trout that each measured 31 inches.

There is often confusion over the lineage of the brown trout found in the Snake River drainage. All too often, I will hear someone on the Buffalo Fork or Lewis Lake say, "I hooked into a good-sized German brown." In reality, these trout are not German browns at all. Brown trout stocked in the Snake River drainage, particularly those in Lewis and Shoshone lakes, are descendents of the Scottish Loch Leven. Hence the scientific name *Salmo trutta levenensis.* In fact, it is still possible to hear local anglers call these trout *loch lavens* or *loch levens.*

According to fishery biologist Robert Behnke, the most likely place to still find a pure population of Loch Leven trout is on the headwater lakes of the Snake River drainage. Browns on the other side of the divide, on streams such as the Firehole and the Madison, are descendents of Von Behr brown trout (*Salmo trutta fario*). They are named after the late-nineteenth century president of the German Fish Culturalists Association, Baron von Behr. These are the actual German browns. They can be distinguished by subtle differences in their spotting distribution and by the shape of the spots along their flanks.

Lake Trout

(*Salvelinus namaycush*)

Other than native cutthroat, no game-fish species has had a longer residence in the Snake River drainage than the lake trout, also known as mackinaw among sport fishermen. Lake trout were first introduced from the Great Lakes region to Heart Lake in the mid-1880s, and then to Shoshone and Lewis lakes in 1890. Stockings later occurred on the lakes of Jackson Hole, mostly in Jackson, Jenny and Leigh lakes. Nowadays, for the most part, the stocking of lake trout has been discontinued.

Lake trout are voracious predators that feed primarily on other fish. This has had a devastating impact on native trout. On Lewis and Shoshone lakes, the effect has been minimal, as these lakes historically contained no trout until the stocking of mackinaw and brown trout (Lewis Falls and the turbulent waters of Lewis River Canyon prevented upstream migration of native trout.) On Heart, Jackson, Leigh, and Jenny lakes, however, cutthroat populations have continually declined. On Leigh Lake, they are virtually nonexistent, but this has not necessarily translated to a threat for cutthroat populations on the Snake River. Lake trout certainly migrate out of Jackson Lake through the Jackson Lake Dam and can work their way several miles downstream, but for the most part, lake trout remain in the lakes.

A serious sport fishery has developed around mackinaw on the lakes in Yellowstone and Jackson Hole, where they can clear 50 pounds. Most of this fishing is done with steel- or lead-core trolling line with dead baits at depths of 100 feet or more. The record lake trout in the state of Wyoming is a 50-pound, 0-ounce monster caught on Jackson Lake by local resident Doris Budge in 1983. On the Snake River, sizes are much smaller, but can still be impressive. In 1995, a client I was guiding landed a 25-inch egg-ladened female on an olive bead-head zonker. It was caught 30 miles downstream from Jackson Lake Dam!

Lake trout can offer a challenge to fly-fishers. The larger variety feed well below the surface. Even with the most extreme full-sinking lake lines, it is difficult to fish for them effectively. I have heard of anglers having success at depths of 60 feet, but 30 to 40 feet is a better bet for most. In the evening, lake trout will come to the surface to feed on select hatches, primarily caddis and midges, and smaller fish feeding on the same. Fly-fishermen equipped with Elk Hair and Goddard caddis, and baitfish patterns like Clouser Minnows, Double Bunnies, and Woolly Buggers, can have luck right through sundown.

Jackson Lake, Lewis Lake, and Jenny Lake are among the best waters for anglers targeting mackinaw whether fishing with dry flies or streamers. While the Snake River can hold lake trout almost anywhere, the only location where an angler can actually count on landing one is immediately downstream of Jackson Lake Dam. Mackinaw work their way out of the lake through the dam and feed on the rich supply of aquatic invertebrates and immature fish that exist in the cool, temperature controlled water. Dry-fly patterns can be effective, but I find mackinaw in the river to retain the feeding habits that they developed while residing in the lake. For this reason, I prefer to use streamers and wet flies when I target lake trout below the dam.

Trout Foods & Fly Patterns on the Upper Snake River

In discussing trout on the Upper Snake, I have briefly eluded to the limited nutrient supply that exists on the river. Perhaps I should retract. The Snake River and its tributaries have plenty of nutrients for trout, but there is a serious difference between what is found on the Snake versus other area streams. All one has to do is turn over a stream-bound cobblestone on the Snake River and compare it to one on the Madison River or Henry's Fork. On the latter two, the cobblestone can be covered with a multitude of aquatic insects in their nymphal stages, caddis cocoons, and leeches. On the Snake, the cobblestone may have a couple of caddis cocoons and a few mayfly nymphs crawling about. This is not necessarily true of the spring creeks and tributaries in the drainage. These waters are critically important to cutthroat trout for spawning purposes. But they are important for feeding purposes as well. The cooler temperatures and gentler flows mean greater insect activity on these waters. The Blacktail Pond Creek, which flows into the Snake River above Moose Bridge in Grand Teton National Park, is a good example. Overturn a cobblestone on this creek, and one will find the same wealth of aquatic insects as on the more nutrient-rich streams of the Yellowstone region.

All of this has an impact on those events which, on mythical trout waters, all fly-fishers tend to read about, analyze, study, and wait impatiently for: hatches.

The Upper Snake River has nothing like the green drake hatch on the Henry's Fork or the salmonfly hatch on the South Fork of the Snake River. The one exception might be the June caddis hatch, which I will address later. But the Snake River has somewhat of an advantage to other streams in that, while it does not have thick hatches, it does have strikingly broad hatches. This is something that many fly-fishers new to the Snake realize after their first couple of times on the river or one of its tributaries. At the same time that large stoneflies are coming off, so too might be little yellow stones, pale morning duns (PMDs), gray drakes, and a variety of caddis, not to mention the fly ants and large grasshoppers found along the banks. It can at times be quite amazing to witness, so many different insects on the water with not one seemingly dominating another.

This feature has significantly influenced the development and use of dry-fly and nymph patterns on the Upper Snake River. Attractors—those patterns that do not imitate anything inparticular but are suggestive of a number of different insect food types for trout—are debatably the most popular type of dry flies on the Upper Snake. These patterns do not just represent multiple food types, they also act as agitators and curiosities to trout. Trout will attack them because they are taken as a threat to territory or an object of interest. Attractors such as Humpies, Variants, the Madam X, Turck's Tarantula, and Willie's Red Ant were either developed in Jackson Hole or popularized by local anglers. Renowned attractors originating from other western streams, most notably the Chernobyl Ant and Kaufmann's Stimulator, have gained a serious following on the Snake River too. These patterns can be used to fish almost any hatch, or no hatch at all, on the waters of Jackson Hole.

I do not mean to imply that more imitative and realistic patterns do not work. Don Martinez, Jay Buchner, Scott Sanchez, Howard Cole, and Will Dornan are renowned tiers who have contributed to a long but underappreciated history of imitative, hatch-specific patterns in the Jackson Hole area. Such flies can be just as productive as more suggestive patterns, yet despite this fact, attractors tend to dominate the scene.

The broad hatch factor is not the sole reason why attractors work so well on Snake River trout. Another reason is the nature of the stream and its tributaries. Trout residing on a freestone stream do not have the luxury to study all possible food choices coming at them. For the sake of argument, let's give Snake River trout the gift of speech, or at least the ability to speak for themselves. Trout cannot sit in holding water and wonder, "Is that a little green stonefly

Anglers often employ large attractors when fishing the Upper Snake River.

Table 1. Hatch Chart for Upper Snake River*

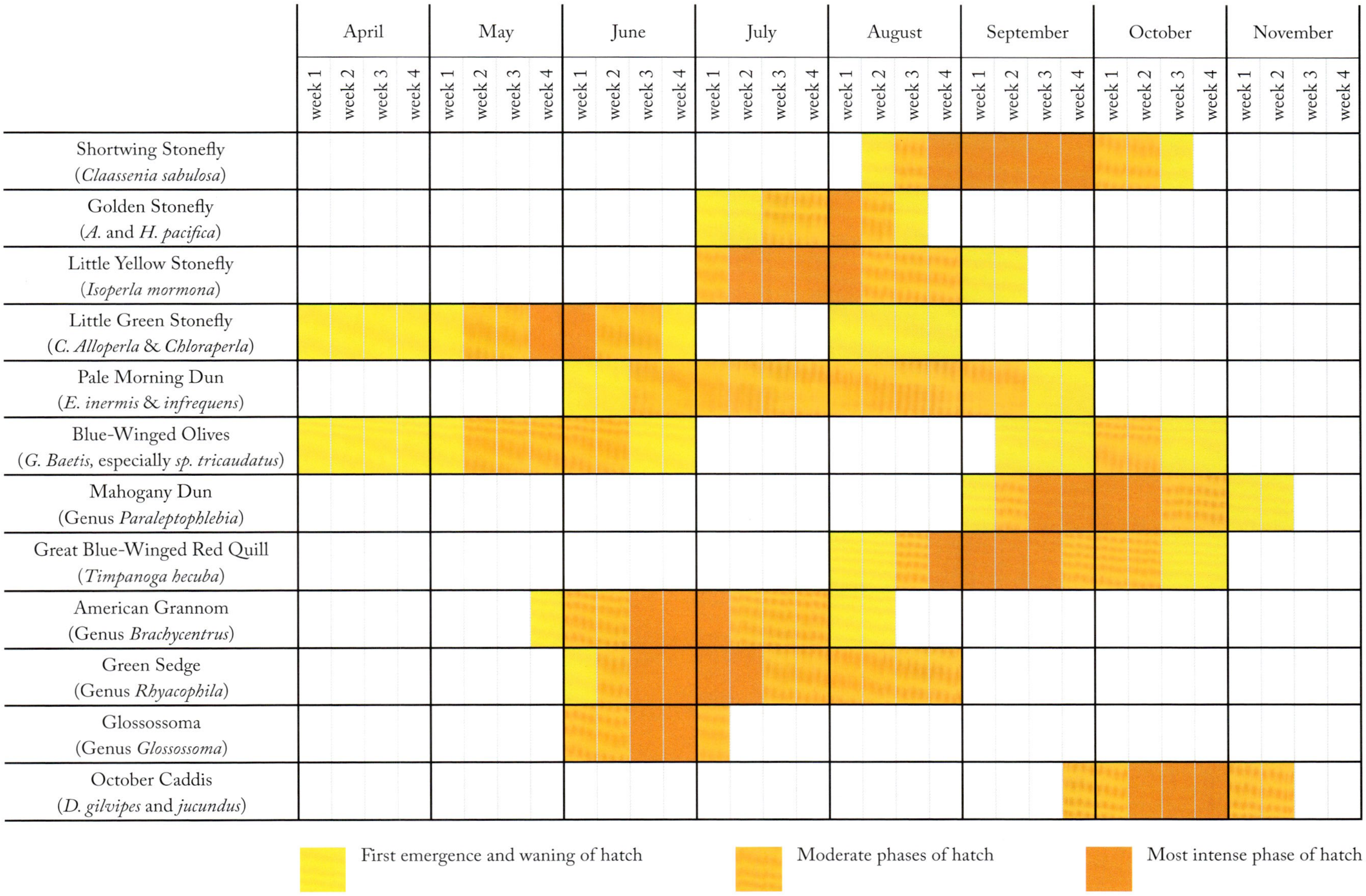

* This chart's information should be considered generalization of the hatches that occur on Upper Snake River and the South Fork of the Snake River. The hatches displayed here vary throughout the year based on climatological and hydrological patterns. Do not make the mistake, as so many do when they turn to hatch charts, of taking this information as literal gospel handed down from the heavens.

coming at me in this fast-moving current line, or is it a *Glossossoma* caddis? Wait, maybe it's a small grasshopper." In the time it takes trout to think this, the insect will have already passed them by. They must eat when they have the chance, or die from over-analyzing their options. It is for this reason that suggestive patterns representing a variety of insects tend to be the most popular types of flies for fishing the Upper Snake River.

Having heard all of this, one might begin to think that fly-fishing on the Snake River in Wyoming is a piece of cake. Simply grab any fly in your box, cast it out, and wait for the cutthroat to start rising. Nothing could be further from the truth. Successful fly-fishing in Jackson Hole requires an understanding of the different insects and baitfish that make up the diet of Snake River trout. I will deal with those that are the most important next.

Stoneflies

Like many streams in the Yellowstone area, stoneflies play an overly important role among anglers and trout on the Upper Snake. Little green stones (*Chloroperlidae alloperla*), shortwing stoneflies (*Claassenia sabulosa*), golden stoneflies (*Acroneuria* or *Hesperoperla pacifica*), and little yellow stones (*Isoperla mormona*), are popular not only because of their continual presence, but also because of their sheer size. Stoneflies such as the shortwing stonefly can reach up to 35 millimeters in length. The emergence of stoneflies on the Upper Snake throughout a given season does not necessarily follow the typical hatch schedule found on most western streams. Medium brown (*Isoperla patricia*), and little yellow stones generally emerge from July through September. However, I have seen these insects as early as April on the Upper Snake River. Golden stoneflies can emerge late into September and October in Jackson Hole, even though typical emergences on other western streams end by late August.

The shortwing stonefly (Claassenia sabulosa).

In my opinion, the most frequently occurring large stonefly on the Snake River is the shortwing stone (*Claassenia sabulosa*). They populate the river and its tributaries from the headwaters all the way down to Palisades Reservoir. Most western streams that have shortwing stoneflies experience the hatch in May and June, but on the Snake they generally begin to make their appearance in late July. Few fly-fishers actually see them because of the insects' propensity for emerging nocturnally. When I camp on the Snake River in Yellowstone National Park or on the Hoback River in late summer, I often inspect the banks at night with a headlamp, and almost always find golden-bodied shortwing stoneflies crawling from their exoskeletons. The shucks that litter the cobblestones throughout daylight hours are a sure sign of the presence and relative abundance of *Claassenia* stoneflies.

There was a time when large stoneflies like the salmonfly (*Pteronarcys californica)* contributed greatly to the overall biomass in the Snake River and its tributaries. Some claim that the salmonfly hatch in Jackson Hole was once as prolific as those found on the Henry's Fork, the South Fork of the Snake River, and the Madison River. Tom Carmichael, son of pioneering tier and outfitter Bob Carmichael, related to me a story of the annual emergences that occurred in the vicinity of Moose Bridge in the 1940s. "Me and the Dornan kids would stand on the bank with our arms outstretched," he said, "while the bugs would crawl all over our legs and chests and eventually up our necks and onto our faces. The first one to flinch and jump in the Snake was declared the loser, although after a couple of minutes all of us would end up in the river."

These kind of emergences mysteriously disappeared in the late 1950s and early 1960s. Blame has been placed on everything from pesticides to the introduction of exotic insects. Carmichael and many others contend that it is the result of habitat destruction along the middle sections of the Snake River, where a levee system now exists. Whatever the case may be, the shortwing stone is the only large stonefly found throughout the entire drainage today, though salmonflies and golden stones exist in isolated pockets.

Stoneflies have contributed greatly to the use of oversized foam-bodied flies and large attractors constructed of natural material. Among the most popular patterns on the Upper Snake River include the Chernobyl Ant, Turck's Tarantula, the Double Humpy, Willie's Red Ant, Kaufmann's Stimulator, Scott Sanchez's Convertible, Doug

Swisher's Madam X, and the Tara X. Rubber-legged flies have the edge over legless patterns in terms of popularity when it comes to imitating stoneflies. Much of this stems from the realistic look rubber legs give a fly. In addition, rubber legs can give a fly a more animated quality when twitched along the surface. This is especially true of flies like the Chernobyl Ant and Willie's Red Ant. When these flies are twitched and skirted along the surface, they can draw strikes even several feet away from a feed line. Recently, tiers have been substituting the standard medium-rubber used for legs with Flexi Floss, which tends to move in an even more animated fashion.

This does not mean that legless patterns are obsolete. When tied with the right combination of materials, they can be just as effective. The Double Humpy is a prime example of this. A Double Humpy tied with light mule deer hair from the neck and facial region, with several wraps of grizzly hackle (16 per segment!), produces a very high-floating, buoyant dry fly. When twitched along the surface, it creates a wake similar to that created by a golden stonefly or a male *Claassenia* stone when it crawls along the surface of the stream. This is a quality that generates as many strikes as twitched and skirted rubber-leg patterns. Rubber legs may be more imitative, and they may give a fly an animated quality, but they get in the way of the realistic wake that a legless pattern creates.

More and more, anglers and guides in Jackson Hole are turning to stonefly nymphs. I think the original avoidance of these kind of flies stemmed from two factors that plagued the popularity of most subsurface patterns. First, the blazing fast current of Snake River, coupled with the heavy amount of debris in the stream, makes snags highly probable and the recovery of the fly very unlikely. Second, the emergence of stoneflies often occurs late in the evening or very early in the morning. Not actually being able to see the hatch take place has kept many anglers from concentrating on this stage of the lifecycle. More recent local research on stoneflies and their consistent subsurface activity has given rise to a new interest in stonefly nymphs.

Dave Brackett, creator of first-rate flies for the Snake River.

Attractors such as the Double Humpy and the Turck's Tarantula are key patterns Snake River fly-fishers use to imitate stoneflies.

There is a whole range of effective stonefly nymphs for the Upper Snake. Many anglers are partial to classic patterns like the Bitch Creek Nymph in #4 to 8 and Kaufmann's Golden Stone Nymph in #6 to 8. But several new patterns have carved a niche of popularity among fly-fishers on the Snake as well. The giant bead-head Crystal Creek Stone Nymph is one of my personal favorites. I use gold or chartreuse flash chenille in #8 for golden stonefly nymphs and black ice flash chenille in #6 for giant black stonefly nymphs. Davies' Lightning Stone can be tied in a variety of colors to match several different large stonefly nymphs.

Veteran Wyoming tier Dave Brackett has established a reputation for creating simple yet highly effective stonefly nymphs. His Fore and Aft Nymph is constructed with tungsten beads mounted on both the front and rear of a #8 hook. This guarantees a deep, yet even ride near stream bottom, where most stonefly nymph activity takes place. Many tiers will blend orange and brown colored dubbing for the body. Doing this gives the pattern a golden brown color and allows it to be fished as both a golden stonefly and a giant black stonefly nymph. Brackett's LBS (little black stone) is another "go-to" stonefly pattern for anglers on the Snake River. Fished with a #14 to 18 hook, the LBS is highly popular during the early little black stonefly emergences that occur in April on the Snake and its tributaries.

Howard Cole, renowned Jackson Hole tier and part owner of High Country Flies in Jackson, Wyoming, has been at the forefront of creating emerger patterns. This includes small stonefly emergers. Unlike salmonflies and golden stoneflies, which emerge by crawling out of streams and shedding their shucks on shore, many smaller stoneflies of the Perlidae family emerge while still in the water. This makes them available to feeding trout. Cole's Sally Emerger is the best emerger pattern for little yellow stoneflies on Jackson Hole streams.

Mayflies

A variety of mayflies—pale morning duns, blue-winged olives, mahogany duns, brown drakes, *hecubas*—can all be found emerging on the Snake River at different times throughout the year. These insects will hatch throughout the season, but will be most noticeable to the angler in late summer and early fall. When a hatch is on it typically is not thick. Still, these insects are an important food source for trout on the Upper Snake and should not be overlooked when selecting a fly.

A favorite mayfly for many Snake River anglers is the mahogany dun (*Paraleptophlebia debilis* and *packi*), which generally appears around the first part of September and then continually emerges throughout the fall. It is a favorite for two reasons. First, mahogany duns tend to hatch with a greater degree of abundance than other mayflies in the upper reaches of the Snake River. They will by no means cover the surface in a carpet-like manner, but when a mahogany dun hatch is on, it is easy to spot. Second, the mahogany dun is almost exclusively a fall hatch fly in Jackson Hole. This is a time when fly-fishing on the Upper Snake River is unmatched. With winter approaching, cutthroat are trying to make the most of the short feeding season. The river is low, and trout will be concentrated in every available type of holding water. Competition among them can be fierce. The continual drifting and movement of mahogany duns over a riffle pool can entice voracious feeding behavior from trout below.

The *hecuba* (*Ephemerella hecuba* or *Timpunoga hecuba*) is arguably the most popular mayfly for area fly-fishermen. Few on the Snake River recognize this mayfly by its common name, which is the great blue-winged red quill. The *hecuba* is often confused with the brown drake, which the Snake River lacks great numbers of due to the limited amount of heavily silted beds where these burrowing nymphs can live. *Hecubas* are crawler mayflies, which fare easier on a cobblestone and gravel-bottomed stream like the Snake. Silted beds are important for *hecubas*, but not nearly as much so as for brown drakes. *Hecubas* typically emerge between the end of August and the middle of October. Hatches are most intense during cool, wet weather. It is an impressive sight to see individual *hecubas* drifting down a narrow side channel after a long thunderstorm with their upright, sail-like wings. Hatches tend to be greatest in the lower half of Snake River Canyon as well as in the heavily braided sections of the river between Deadman's Bar and Wilson Bridge. Individual adults range in size from 20-30 millimeters in length. Tiers often use a #10 or a small #8 (for example, a Dai-Riki #8, number 300) hook to imitate *hecubas*.

To match the Snake River's various mayflies, traditional patterns like the Humpy and the Parachute Adams are among the most popular. Because hatches are more broad than thick on the Upper Snake River, and because the dominating cutthroat rarely get the chance to feed selectively, there is no real need to fish a hatch specific pattern. However, such patterns are effective. During the fall season, I will often use imitative patterns such as a Mahogany Dun Thorax or Mahogany Comparadun to match the natural. A traditional PMD and a Rusty Spinner will work for the different stages of the pale morning dun. The most productive fly to fish during *hecuba* hatches is unquestionably a #10 to 12 Parachute Hare's Ear. When tied with brown flat-wax thread as ribbing for the body, it is a knockout pattern.

There are several locally created mayfly emerger and nymph patterns that have garnered a following. Jay Buchner's Humpback Emerger is effective as an emerging blue-winged olive when tied in #16 and 18 or as a pale morning dun in #12 and 14. Howard Cole alters the color of materials in his CDC Split Wing Cripple to imitate a wide variety of emergent and challenged *Callibaetis*. The most popular mayfly nymph imitations, however, remain traditional patterns like Prince, Hare's Ear, Copper John, and Pheasant Tail Nymphs. Flashback and bead-head versions of these stand-bys tend to be the overwhelming favorites among Snake River anglers.

Caddis

I have talked somewhat extensively about the broadness of hatches on the Upper Snake and how there is a lack of thick hatches. While I stand by this claim, there is still one aquatic insect that challenges this trend, and that is caddis. An almost uncountable variety of caddis—the spotted sedge (*Hydropsyche occidentalis*), American grannom (*Brachycentrus occidentalis* and *americanus*), *Glossossoma* (too many to even count), and green sedges (genus *Rhyacophila*)—will appear

The Upper Snake River in Wyoming has an impressive emergence of multiple species of caddis in June.

Caddis patterns are as important to Snake River fly shops as they are to their patrons.

throughout the season. But the first appearance of caddis, generally in mid and late June, is almost always a massive hatch that, in my experience, measures up to any of the other great caddis hatches on western streams. Caddis emerge and take flight in incredibly thick waves. All reaches of the river, from Jackson Lake Dam and on down through the canyon, not to mention most of the tributaries, are effected. The physical characteristics of the Snake River—higher gradient, riffles, and a scoured, cobblestone bottom favor caddis habitation over other types of aquatic insects like mayflies as well.

Unfortunately, this is also the time when the Snake River and its tributaries are in the middle of the spring runoff, making the fishing of the caddis hatch virtually impossible. But there are a few exceptions. At times, serious drought conditions, characterized by very low overall snowfall, low-water-content in the snow pack, and low precipitation in the spring, can leave the Snake River with a short runoff that peaks well before normal and ends sometimes weeks before it usually does, in early July. It is not a common occurrence, but it does happen. When it does, the water can be clear and relatively low during this massive caddis hatch. As impressive as it is to see, it is even more impressive to fish. The two 100-plus days of fishing I have had on the Upper Snake River were during this early season caddis emergence. If the chance arises to fish this hatch when conditions are right, you should do so by all means.

Based on my observations, I believe that the June hatch is comprised of more than one species, and might be as many as five. I admit that it is difficult to distinguish one species of this hatch from one another. Surely the American grannom (*Brachycentrus)*, with its greenish-black body and dark wings, comprises a significant portion. In his highly influential classic *Caddisflies* (The Lyons Press, 1981), Gary LaFontaine related to his readers that the massive caddis hatches reported throughout the Rocky Mountains in April and May are *Brachycentrus occidentalis.* This confirms my assumptions, as the April and May hatches that occur on other waters would equate to a June hatch on the Upper Snake River, which generally experiences later hatches because of its more extreme ecosystem. But another significant portion of the hatch is composed of *Glossossoma traviatum.* This particular caddis is a grayish-tan and brown with gray wings. They are about two to four millimeters smaller than grannoms. A few species of net-spinning Hydropsychidae—in particular *Parapsyche* and *Arctopsyche*—make up a portion of this hatch as well.

The Upper Snake River can also experience an exciting hatch of fall caddis (genus *Dicosmoecus*) in September and October. These are also called October caddis or giant orange sedges. The size of the hatch pales in comparison to what occurs in June, but fall caddis are much bigger, 30 millimeters on average in comparison to 10 to 15 millimeters for most of the caddis found on Jackson Hole streams. Through late summer, you can examine the floor of the riverbed closest to the confluence of spring creeks and find a gathering buildup of a fall caddis larva encased in a long cylinder of sediment. Peel this case open and you will discover a plump, yellowish orange body. This should clue you in on the size and type of pattern you will want to fish to imitate the larva, pupa, or adult. I hate to beat a dead horse, but I must cite LaFontaine once again. He lists the fall caddis ahead of the salmonfly in terms of opportunity for catching big trout.

Drop into any fly shop in Jackson Hole, and you will find as many caddis patterns as you will attractors. Deer or Elk Hair Caddis dominate the scene. This is due primarily to their versatility. A simple change of color to the hair, hackle, and thread will modify the pattern to imitate the different genera of caddis. An Elk Hair Caddis tied with orange or yellow thread on a #8 hook will imitate the color and size of a fall caddis as readily as any other fly. The Goddard Caddis is popular due to its buoyancy, but dyed deer hair is needed to match the color of most caddis. Scott Sanchez, one of the most innovative tiers in the sport today, created a Goddard Caddis off-shoot using foam as the wing material. This Foam Wing Caddis is more durable and just as buoyant as the original.

There are also several effective caddis larvae and pupae patterns. Legendary Jackson Hole tier Jack Dennis created a simple yet innovative pattern that imitates the cocoon of a tube-case caddis. The pattern is constructed of discarded tying material and is known as the Trash Can Nymph. Rob Water's Chamois Caddis Pupa incorporates buckskin or chamois to match the color of a fall caddis pupa. Howard Cole's U-Con incorporates a glass bead to imitate a bubble shuck common to most caddis. In addition to all of these, patterns such as the Serendipity, October Emerger, and Skip Morris' Brick Back Caddis can work well.

Terrestrials

Beetles, winged and wingless ants, and grasshoppers all make up a portion of the diet of Snake River trout, but grasshoppers deserve special attention. The number of hoppers in a given hatch is not as great as what I have seen on the Green River or the South Fork of the Snake River. However, as with stoneflies and fall caddis in Jackson Hole, their size can be impressive. They have *beefy* dimensions, with full-bodied heads and thoraxs and tapered—yet still large—abdomens.

The number of grasshoppers that appear in Jackson Hole during the summer season is dependent on many factors, not least of which is weather. Hopper hatches are more prolific during hotter, drier summers and weaker during summers with cooler, wetter weather. They typically begin to show up in late July and early August, but this also is dependent on weather. If the earlier part of the summer is wetter and cooler than normal, grasshoppers may not begin to appear in meaningful numbers until well into August.

Like stoneflies, the large size of hoppers in this area requires sizeable artificial flies as well. Traditional patterns such as Joe's Hopper, the Whitlock, and Jay-Dave's Hopper, when tied with a #8 or 6 hook, are still old standbys on the Upper Snake and its tributaries. Newer terrestrial and attractor patterns, in particular the Chernobyl Ant, Sanchez's Foam Wing Hopper, and Ken Burkholder's Club Sandwich© are pushing the size limit and might be even more productive. These three patterns all originated on waters outside of Jackson Hole but have found an everlasting home among area anglers. Consummate attractors such as Guy Turck's Tarantula, the Tara X, the Double Humpy, and Willie's Red Ant, also work well.

The old and the new: Jay-Dave's Hopper and the Foam Wing Hopper.

A typically overlooked terrestrial insect on Jackson Hole streams is the carpenter ant or flying ant. They deserve much more attention than they receive. Carpenter ants are not numerous, and their *hatch* is by no means predictable. But hatches do happen a few times each season, and you should be prepared. I have observed these insects on a wide variety of waters in the Jackson Hole area. They make an appearance everywhere from lakes deep in the Gros Ventre Range to the main stretches of the Snake River. Favorite patterns to match these terrestrials include Guy Turck's Power Ant—which also works well as an attractor—and Doug Gibson's Flying Ant.

Baitfish

Like trout everywhere in the world, most of what comprises the diet of large trout on the Upper Snake River is other fish. Trout here will feed on other trout but also mountain whitefish, chubs and sucker fingerlings. Mottled sculpins, redside shiners, longnose and speckled daces, and rock minnows are all native to the Snake River drainage and important food for trout.

The Upper Snake is thought of primarily as a dry-fly stream, but with well over 90% of what trout eat coming from below the surface, streamers and other types of wet

Traditional streamers used on the Snake River.

flies are obviously productive. Two of my all-time favorite streamers for Jackson Hole streams were developed by local tiers. One is Scott Sanchez's Double Bunny. This heavy, super-sized wet fly continually brings in some of the largest trout on the river and its tributaries. Its true origins are on the South Fork of the Snake River, and therefore I discuss it in greater detail in Part II.

My other all-time favorite is the J.J. Special, a pattern created by Jim Jones of High Country Flies. I generally tie this rubber-legged streamer on big # 6 to 4 hooks, almost matching the size of Sanchez's Double Bunny. Like many other fly-fishermen, I think of the J.J. as a suckerfish imitation, and fish it as such too: heavy and deep. During early-season fishing, when waters are high and often off-color, the J.J. Special is my go-to subsurface pattern. It is one the most effective streamers in use on the Snake River today. Of course, many other streamers are productive. Woolly Buggers, Wet Muddlers, Zonkers, Girdle Bugs, and sculpin patterns are all standard wet flies that will work on the Upper Snake during almost any part of the fishing season.

About the Flies on the Upper Snake River

The flies used to match Snake River trout food deserve more coverage than I have given them in this section. In Part IV, I will provide a selection of popular patterns, along with material requirements and a brief bit of history and tactics used to fish each fly.

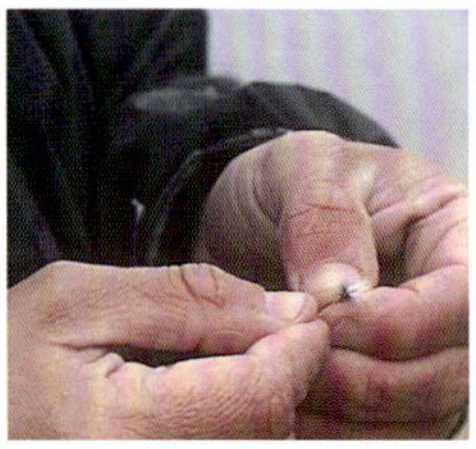

Fly-Fishing Strategies & Tactics for the Upper Snake River

I have heard it more than once. A client in my boat who, upon taking a long look at the fast-moving current carrying us downriver with seemingly no place for trout to feed whatsoever, will turn to me and ask, "Can trout actually live in this kind of water?," or, "So when does the river slow down enough to fish?" Many of these anglers have visions of classic trout water such as Hat Creek, Silver Creek, or the Harriman section of the Henry's Fork dancing in their head. It is difficult for them to imagine that the swift currents of the Upper Snake can hold a marlin, let alone a trout. They begin to doubt the stories they have heard about the size and number of trout on the Snake River. One fishing trip, however, usually does the trick. They become true believers in the productivity of the Snake and the tenacity of the trout that occupy it.

The Upper Snake is indeed different from many other rivers. It even bares little resemblance to neighboring trout streams such as the Madison, Green, or Teton rivers. But in all actuality, the Snake River has a reputation among more experienced anglers as being relatively easy to fish. One just needs to understand that reading the water on the Snake is different than reading the water on most other streams. As such, fishing it will involve different strategies than what one might be used to.

Current Breaks and Holding Water

Although the vast majority of the Upper Snake River is below Jackson Lake Dam, it can be classified more as a freestone stream than a tailwater. Those attributes that define a freestone stream—fast currents, braided channels, and stream-bound structure—can be found on almost every section of the river. These features can be intimidating for some fisherman, as the places a trout can hold seem miniscule, sometimes even non-existent. Therefore, it is important, for an inexperienced fly-fisher to familiarize him or herself with the types of subtle current breaks—also called breakwater, holding water or pocket water—that exist all along the Upper Snake River.

In general, current breaks provide three elements that are critical to the survival of trout: (1) a place where trout can hold and expend a limited amount of energy; (2) a position near a main current, which will act as a food source for trout by bringing nutrients to them; and (3) protection from predators, primarily birds of prey like eagles and ospreys. The first two elements are the most important. On a stream like the Snake River, trout feeding directly in the main current can never consume the nutrients required to sustain themselves. Trout need to position themselves in water that provides as little current as possible. At the same time, they need to be in a position where there will be food. This means near the main current of a channel where most of its nutrient supply will be drifting. If a trout positions itself in a dead back channel, the extreme tailout of a run, or in a flat, there will almost certainly be no current but there will also be very limited nutrients. Snake River trout tend to avoid feeding in such water. The idea is to find breakwater that exists near main currents.

There are four primary types of current breaks that I consider important targets for those who are fly-fishing the Upper Snake River. These are: (1) riffles—including downstream runs and upstream shelves; (2) stream-bound structure; (3) confluence points; and (4) side channels. I will go through each of these current breaks separately and explain the strategies and tactics you should use for fishing them.

Riffles

Riffles are a quintessential feature of most trout streams. On the Snake River, they are typically characterized by a deep hole extending off the downstream end of a submerged shelf or bar. This deep hole acts as a current break for trout, and on the shelf itself, river water has a chance to oxygenate and eject built-up gases. This is beneficial for the growth of trout food such as aquatic insects and freshwater mollusks like snails. However, the current is generally too fast for trout to hold. As the current moves downstream off the shelf, it still carries the same amount of momentum, but a pool is created as the shelf floor drops off abruptly. The current on the surface might be substantial. Beneath the subsurface portion of the run or pool, however, the current is minimal.

It is in this subsurface portion of the pool that trout lay in wait for nutrients moving with the current coming off the upstream shelf. As trout food moves off the shelf, either on the surface, in the surface film, or below the film, trout waiting in the pool will come up from the depths to feed. They are in the current for only seconds, and thus will only expend a negligible amount of energy for the nutrients they are taking in.

Riffles on the Upper Snake River are small or moderately sized. One will notice a big difference between the shelves and riffles on the Upper Snake and those on the

Working a riffle below Mt. Moran.

South Fork, which tend to be much larger. Still, riffles on the Upper Snake vary greatly in terms of length, width, and depth.

Holding Water on a Riffle: Upper Snake River

1. Shelf forming the upstream edge of the riffle pool. This shelf creates dissolved oxygen important for the growth of aquatic insects.
2. Riffle pool. The depression creates ideal holding water for trout and a prime area to feed on aquatic insects coming off the upstream shelf.
3. Upstream portion of the riffle pool. Trout will direct their attention here, waiting for aquatic insects to drift off the shelf. The dominant trout in this pool will typically hold in this upper portion of the pool.
4. Downstream portion of the riffle pool. Trout that are not dominant feeders in this pool will hold and feed in this position. But many times one can find large, dominant trout holding here as well.

For the most part, the entire riffle is a feeding zone for trout. The larger the riffle, the more trout it can generally hold. But it is the head of the riffle pool, at the point where the shelf drops off into the pool, which acts as the primary feeding position for trout. The dominant feeders will be in these positions, and it is important that you lay your fly where these trout will be focusing their attention. When guiding, I invariably instruct my clients to cast their fly onto the shelf at least three to five feet upstream from where it drops off into the pool. My experience suggests that feeding trout in riffle pools are typically focusing on the current at the immediate point where it comes off the shelf. By laying a fly a few feet upstream from where the riffle pool begins, you are giving trout a chance to see it move naturally with the current off the shelf. Strikes typically occur just as the fly moves off the shelf, in the first six feet of the pool.

Do not make the mistake of disregarding the rest of the riffle. Once your fly has moved six feet into the pool, go ahead and continue to let it drift. It is very possible that trout in the middle and downstream portions of the pool and run will come up and take your fly. Even so, it is important that casts be concentrated on the downstream edge of the shelf. If your casts are only a couple of feet downstream from the edge of the shelf, you will likely be casting downstream of the focus point of the dominant feeders. It is likely then that these trout will never see your fly.

Structure

On most streams, structure receives a lot of attention from anglers. The same is true for the Upper Snake River. I define structure simply as stream-bound material—logs, trees, brush, and boulders. Structure provides excellent holding water and protection for trout. It also creates a nutrient-rich source for trout, as many aquatic insects will use structure to crawl from a stream to emerge.

Stream-bound structure of any size can form numerous current breaks for trout. I will use as an example a fallen tree laying approximately 12 feet into the stream from the bank from which it has fallen. It is partially submerged, with the root ball facing upstream and its crown facing downstream.

The most obvious breakwater for trout is the pool that forms just at the downstream edge of the root ball on either side of the trunk. These pools are typically the largest current breaks formed around the structure. Trout hold in these pockets without expending energy and dash out to the edge of the main current to take any food passing by. Less obvious current breaks are located along the trunk of the tree. The branches extending off the tree will form holding water for trout, though these are difficult to fish due to the potential snags surrounding it, but a properly placed fly can be rewarded with a strike from a large trout.

Holding Water Along Stream-Bound Structure

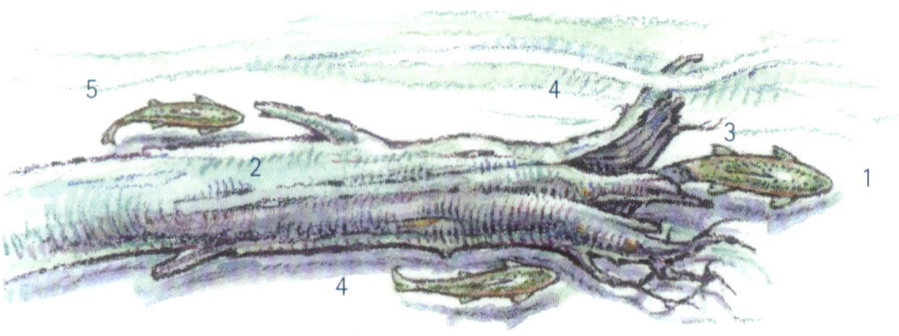

1. Channel of river bed.
2. Stream-bound structure in the form of a fallen tree with the root-ball facing upstream.
3. Pillow at the upstream portion of the structure. A depression is formed here that creates excellent holding water. Dominant trout will typically hold here. They will have the first opportunity to feed on nutrients moving downstream with the current.
4. Upstream flanks of the stream-bound structure. Holding water in this example is formed by the root-ball and lower trunk of the tree. Dominant feeding trout will typically hold here. Non-dominant feeding trout can also hold here as well.
5. Downstream flank of the stream-bound structure. Holding water in this example is formed by the limbs of the tree extending from the trunk into the current. Typically less-dominant trout will hold and feed in this position. Dominant trout can also hold and feed here as well.

This fly-fisher is fishing productive structure below the Pacific Creek boat launch.

One of my favorite pieces of holding water is a current break formed at the head of the structure, where the current flows directly into the extreme upstream piece of the structure. Using the example of the fallen tree, this would be where the current flows into the root ball. It is referred to by many fly-fishers as a *pillow*. The force of the current literally digs a hole through the cobblestone bed and creates both a shelf and a pool. The surface current flows at a fast rate into the structure, but the current in the pool below is minimal, allowing trout to hold and feed without expending a lot of energy. Depending on the force of the stream and the amount of time that the structure has been in a particular spot, these pools can be anywhere from a foot to several feet wide. In this situation, I would lay my fly three to five feet upstream of the edge of the shelf and let it drift into the pool. From an upstream position, whether float-fishing or wade fishing, you can easily control the drift of the fly with the fly line. An angler can strip the fly away from the root ball and pull it off to either side of the tree to fish the current closest to the pools along the trunk.

The same strategy can be used to fish stream-bound boulders. Holding water can form on the upstream edge of this type of structure, but better current breaks are formed on the downstream edge and, to a lesser degree, along the flanks.

One complaint of many float-fishermen is that, because of the fast river current, it is near impossible to get a decent drift when floating by most kinds of structure. The current many times negates the possibility of effectively wade fishing much of this structure. A very effective tactic that I employ is to swing the bow of the boat into the structure just as I pass it, and then continue to point the bow upstream as I float by. This allows the angler positioned at the front of the boat to have a much longer drift with his or her fly. It also allows the fly to lie in the downstream pools created by the structure for a longer time period than if it was simply cast to those pools from the boat while drifting by. This method should be performed with caution, however, as the boat may be out of position to navigate around obstacles immediately downstream. If you perform this maneuver, make doubly sure that you have read the water downstream properly and that it is clear of potential obstacles.

Holding Water at Stream-Bound Structure

1. Direction of the stream current.
2. Stream-bound structure in the form of a large boulder.
3. Pillow formed at the upstream edge of the structure. A depression is formed here that creates excellent holding water. Dominant trout will typically hold here. They will have the first opportunity to feed on nutrients moving downstream with the current.
4. Holding water formed downstream of the stream-bound structure. The current break here creates ideal holding water. Both dominant and non-dominant trout can hold and feed here.

Confluence Points

A confluence point is exactly what it sounds like—a point where two different channels come together to form one channel. On a heavily braided stream like the Upper Snake, where channels are constantly splitting and converging, confluence points are everywhere. In my opinion, they remain the most overlooked type of breakwater that holds trout.

Confluence points are generally found at the downstream end of an island. The island typically ends as a tapered point. Depending on the rate of flow of each current, and the physical makeup of the downstream end of the island, a pool of variable size will be formed where the two channels meet. This pool represents a current break where trout can hold and feed, and what is advantageous for trout holding in confluence points is that they have two channels bringing food to them, in effect, doubling the amount of available nutrients.

Confluence points are not strictly about islands. They can be found where creeks and small tributaries join the river as well. Typically, the best holding water where tributaries flow into the river is at the extreme upper end of the confluence and at the pool that forms at the extreme lower end, between the bank and main current.

I employ two types of strategies when fishing confluence points. The first can be done by either wading or float-fishing. You should lay your fly upstream approximately six to ten feet from the confluence point and no more than three feet from the bank of the channel. This should give you a decent drift down to the pool and allow trout enough time to focus in on it. Due to the speed of the Snake River, focus times for trout are not long, sometimes only a split second, with trout hitting the fly as it rides the inside edge of the current alongside the pool.

Another strategy is best employed when float-fishing and is the same one used when fishing structure. As you pass by the end of the island at the confluence point, turn the bow of the boat to the point and keep turning upstream as you pass it. The front angler in the boat will be able to cast a fly directly into the pool and the upstream turning motion of the boat will allow the fly to lie in the pool for several seconds, giving trout more than enough time to focus in on it and strike it.

There is another confluence point that is quite different from the ones described above. This is the line created between the main river current and a back channel with little or no current. Most anglers call this a *seam line* or a *seam*. The current break at a seam line is large in comparison to other types of holding water because it involves the entire back channel. Feeding trout congregate here because it's where the current is minimal, yet their food is easily accessible as it moves with the main channel.

Fishing a seam is relatively simple in comparison to other confluence points. For float-fishermen, the best strategy is to position the boat just inside the back channel. The angler can cast his or her fly upstream onto the seam line and allow it to drift down to the point where the seam line ends, which typically is along the downstream bank. This tactic can be done whether using a nymph or a dry fly. The current tension between the seam line and the water in the back channel can cause the fly to drag in an unnatural manner, but mending your line will help maintain a natural drift. A wading angler can best fish a seam from the point where the back channel and main channel meet. It is best to cast your line directly from this point onto the seam, doing so with a significant amount of slack line on the water. This allows the fly to drift downstream along the seam with minimal drag. Another option is to cast your line into the main channel, allowing the current to carry the fly to the seam line. This requires that the angler mend the line to keep the fly from dragging.

I consider seams to be more important to fly-fishing on the South Fork, so I will deal with them in greater detail in Part II.

Holding Water at a Confluence Point

1. Side channels.
2. Island splitting two side channels.
3. Confluence point. The convergence of two side channels creates holding water for trout. Dominant trout of this confluence will typically hold and feed near the point of the island, but this is dependent on the depth of the holding water. By being positioned here, trout will have the first opportunity to feed on nutrients moving downstream in the two side channels.
4. Downstream portions of the confluence point. Larger confluence points will form holding water several meters downstream from the point of the island where trout will feed.
5. Upstream flanks of the confluence point. Larger confluence points will create holding water in this position. If that holding water is created, the dominant trout of the confluence point can feed in this position, as it will allow them to have the first opportunity to feed on nutrients moving downstream in one of the two side channels.

Side Channels

Except for a couple of sections of river, side channels exist seemingly everywhere on the Upper Snake. Many are large enough that one can float a large driftboat down them, but the best side channels are those that are small and narrow and must be fished from shore. For wading anglers, this should be no problem, as they are on foot to begin with. For float-fishermen, this really shouldn't be a problem either. Most side channels are within sight of the main river channels, so other than having to cross loose cobblestones and debris such as fallen logs, are a relatively easy walk to get to. Yet, I still see many anglers disregard side channels altogether. Some float-fishermen will stay only in the main river channels, and when they do exit the boat to fish, it is only to hit riffles and structure within the main channels. Some wading anglers head straight for the main channels, bypassing the side channels that they may have had to cross to get to the river. Side channels deserve much more attention than this.

The advantage for trout in side channels is that the current is much slower than in the main channels, meaning that they do not expend significant amounts of energy. Essentially, a small side channel can be considered one, long, current break. This does not mean that one can cast a fly anywhere on a side channel and expect a strike.

A fly-fisher works a confluence point in Snake River Canyon.

Trout still need protection, minimal current, and holding water in order to survive.

What you should target in side channels is the same as what you would target in the main channels. Riffles, structure, and confluence points are found throughout most side channels. The difference is that the current breaks they create are smaller than what is found in the main river. Because they are small, they will hold fewer fish, but not necessarily smaller fish. Some very large trout can dominate small riffles and pools alongside fallen trees in side channels. This is a good rule for most of the Snake River. The size of the water one fishes does not automatically dictate the size of the fish.

Nymphing a side channel below Pacific Creek on the Snake River.

Side channels fish well throughout the season, but they can be a lifesaver anytime there are high flows on the Snake River, such as early in the season after the runoff ends or when the floodgates at Jackson Lake Dam are open. Fishing on the main channels can be excruciatingly slow at these times and I almost invariably concentrate on side channels, where currents are slower and trout will not have to kill themselves trying to take my fly.

A Word About Banks

I did not purposely omit the possibility of fishing banks on the Upper Snake River. They are important and create excellent holding water for trout. In my experience, however, they are less important than the other types of holding water I have outlined above. This stems from the hydrologic nature of the Snake River. As a high-gradient stream with flows dictated by runoff and upstream dam releases, holding water along banks is extremely difficult to fish properly. Those who wet wade find it difficult to position themselves in the stream current. For those fishing from watercraft, the speed of the current makes precision casting difficult.

These fast currents also make a decent drift problematical to maintain. Furthermore, because of the high gradient, and relatively high fluctuation of flows during a given season, and from year to year, the configuration of a particular bank might be advantageous for the creation of holding water at one level, but completely unfavorable at another level. Thus banks are inconsistent as locations for break water.

Nonetheless, banks are important targets for anglers. They can provide protection for trout, current breaks and can be sources of food. I have my favorite banks on every section and will concentrate on them when guiding and fishing personally. The holding water is usually extremely close to the bank. Current breaks are often created by undercut portions of the bank or by small bank outcroppings. I fish these current breaks closely, usually with my dry fly or nymph within two to three inches of the bank. The fly you use will be passing by the breakwater fast, but remember that natural trout foods are traveling by the banks at a similar pace, so trout will not study their options too long. They will make quick decisions as to whether or not to eat or strike what is passing by. A strike will occur fast, so be prepared to react and set the hook just as fast.

Dry-Fly Tactics

Dry-fly fishing is the dominant form of fly-fishing on the Upper Snake River. The speed of the river's current can be intimidating if one is looking for the perfect drift, but it is important to remember that one does not always need that perfect drift. Nutrients that make up a trout's diet are limited, and the river is carrying those nutrients by at a pretty fast pace. These trout do not have the time, or energy reserves, to study potential prey for a specific trait. This includes movements such as a natural drift. What is more, insects such as stoneflies, caddis, and grasshoppers—important parts of the trout diet on the Snake River—are movers to begin with. A moving dry fly can oftentimes elicit a strike more readily than a naturally drifting fly.

Intentionally moving dry flies such as large attractors, stonefly imitations and grasshopper imitations is a very popular tactic on the Snake River. Many anglers will purposely twitch both rubber-legged and legless attractors, to imitate the movement of stoneflies and grasshoppers on the surface. But even flies that are moved in a manner other than twitching and skirting—for example, ones that are dragged just under the surface by the current—can generate strikes. One very effective tactic I use with attractors, especially Double Humpies, Turck's Tarantulas, and Tara Xs, is to purposely let the fly drag, and then go wet, while fishing structure and banks. I believe trout see this as a small baitfish or an emergent stonefly. Trout will many times hit these with more vigor than dead-drifted or twitched flies on the surface.

In those instances when a natural drift is called for, I will employ a reach cast to minimize the amount of drag created by swift currents. The reach cast is achieved by changing the direction of the rod tip by approximately 90 degrees during the power stroke. In other words, I cast my fly in the direction of the target, then swing my rod tip 90 degrees upstream before the fly and line lands on the surface. The result is a straight line cast with the line, leader and fly all landing on the surface at the same time. What is created is essentially a mid-cast mend. With the line and leader well upstream of the fly, the fly will be able to drift drag-free for several feet before the line and leader are pushed downstream of the fly by the current.

Nymphing Tactics

Despite its reputation as dry-fly water, the Snake River and its tributaries are becoming more and more popular for nymphing. This stems in part from local tiers taking a greater interest in these subsurface patterns. There is also a greater understanding among the local fly-fishing community of the larval and pupal stages of aquatic insects and the techniques required to fish their imitations.

Many fly-fishermen use a dry fly/nymph combination commonly called a *dropper system*. This type of rigging uses a large dry fly, usually an attractor or a grasshopper imitation, as an indicator on the surface. A nymph is connected to this indicator with a length of tippet material tied around either the bend of the hook of the surface fly or its eye. The length of the tippet is entirely dependent upon the type of water being fished and the depth at which most subsurface feeding is taking place. This system has three advantages. First, it allows the angler to fish to trout feeding both above and below the surface. Secondly, it gives the angler a way to control the depth at which the nymph is fished. Lastly, the surface fly acts as an indicator. When a fish strikes the nymph, abrupt movement is put into the surface fly, much like what would occur with a bobber. This lets the angler set the hook on sight, rather than by touch or feel.

There are certain disadvantages though to fishing nymphs with an indicator or combined with a surface fly in a dropper system. In high winds, even the best of casters can wrap the nymph and tippet in a hopeless tangle around the indicator fly. It can also give the fallacy that depth is actually controlled, while in truth, it only allows the nymph to be fished at one range of depth. For example, if the tippet coming off the indicator fly is two feet in length, then the nymph cannot be fished any deeper than that.

For these reasons I often fish nymphs without an indicator. I get far better depth control with a free-drifting nymph because it is not limited by the tippet and indicator fly. More importantly, a free-drifting nymph forces the angler to use the sense of touch, which I feel is an important and often underappreciated sense that anglers

This rainbow was caught on the Gros Ventre River with a Black Zonker.

can lose connection with by solely fishing dry flies or only nymphing with an indicator. Even the subtlest of strikes can be felt on a high-quality line and rod. It is also beneficial for the fly-fisherman to feel the difference between hook-ups on the bottom and actual hook-ups with fish. What is more, fishing indicators on high-gradient freestone streams like the Snake River and its tributaries losses much of its intended effectiveness. The variable currents and speed of the streams will naturally put movement into the nymph, tippet, and indicator, and often this movement can be taken to be strikes when they actually are not. Fishing without an indicator relieves the angler of this problem and forces fly-fishermen to use the much more reliable sense of touch.

Whether one chooses to fish with an indicator or a free-drifting nymph, certain tactics can go a long way to increasing nymphing success on the Snake River. The most basic is to cast the nymph far enough upstream so that it will have time to sink to the depth at which trout are feeding. This can range anywhere from just under the surface film to right at the bottom of the stream. For trout feeding just under the surface, casts will not have to be placed too far upstream. However, a heavily-weighted nymph can sink well below the feeding zone of trout as soon as it enters the water. You can remedy this by having un-weighted or lightly-weighted nymphs ready in conjunction with the more popular weighted variety. Un-weighted nymphs, especially Prince, Pheasant Tail, and Hare's Ear nymphs, can represent a wide array of emergent mayflies and caddis. Fishing these in the surface film and shallow riffles can be more effective than weighted nymphs.

The swift currents of the Upper Snake River require a nymphing angler to be constantly ready to mend the fly line. If you are wading, you should place your nymph upstream from your target and allow it to drift down to where the trout are feeding. As the nymph drifts, send a series of upstream mends (typically two, but no more that four) into your line and then strip in the remaining slack. The mends allow the nymph to sink to a proper depth while the stripping in of the line allows one to be ready to set the hook when a strike occurs. If the nymph is sinking below the feeding zone or directly to the bottom, you can either raise your rod to bring the nymph back up to the proper depth, or simply re-cast upstream. If you are fishing from a boat, the same technique will work except that the casts will be directed downstream from the boat. In addition, the reach cast that I described above can be used to allow nymphs to drift naturally.

Streamer Tactics

Streamer fishing is one of my all-around preferred methods of fishing on any river. Many more anglers are casting wet flies on the Upper Snake than when I was growing up, but it still isn't as popular as it should be. There are numerous reasons for this. One is the simple appeal of dry-fly fishing, of seeing trout rise to a floating imitation. Another is that streamer fishing a river as fast and jam-packed with structure as the Upper Snake can be intimidating. These are acceptable reasons, but ones that should not keep you from missing out on how good streamer fishing can be. With more experience in streamer fishing will come more confidence. The reward can be the largest trout on the river. Just remember, well over 90% of what trout eat is subsurface.

The Upper Snake is by no means a deep river. Yet trying to get your streamer as deep and as near the bottom as possible can be difficult with the swift current. Most of the time the current grabs the line and drags it in front of the fly, which in turn forces the fly toward the surface. You can remedy this problem by employing a tactic I already mentioned when discussing dry-fly and nymph-fishing tactics: the mend.

From a boat, I cast downstream toward my target and immediately throw two to three upstream mends into my line. The slack that this creates will cause the streamer to sink because it takes longer for the current to carry the line past the fly. I then strip in the slack until I have a tight line, drop my rod tip to the surface, and continue to strip in. The stripping motion gives streamers an attracting (some have described it as pulsating) movement. Eventually, the current dragging the line will force the fly back up toward the surface. But the important thing is that the fly has made it down to a depth where large trout are holding and feeding. This tactic works when wade fishing as well. Instead of casting downstream, cast upstream to your target, then throw in the two to three upstream mends, drop your rod tip, and begin stripping.

Simply trolling a streamer by a target is a tactic that often works. However, stripping in a streamer tends to generate far more hook-ups. I believe much of this is due to the action produced in the body of the fly by the stripping motion, but stripping in a fly can be overdone. I see many anglers retrieving their line right up to the leader joint. Typically, strikes on streamers occur after only a few strips once the fly has passed by a trout. Instead of bringing in all that line and then having to waste time and energy working the fly back out to the optimal position, I will retrieve only eight to ten feet of line with four to six successive stripping motions before recasting. This allows the angler to cast the streamer back immediately, with minimal effort, to the most productive water.

The increasing popularity of streamer fishing is in large part due to advances in tackle. Specialized sink-tip systems, density-compensated tips, and simple lead-core line has allowed anglers to put their flies into waters that were difficult to fish a couple of decades ago. I fish my streamers and wet flies with a floating line the majority of time on the Snake River. But there are places, times, and situations when I prefer to use a sink tip.

I use sink tips on the Snake River not because of the river's depth but because of its velocity. The speed of the river is fast enough to force even the heaviest of streamers to the surface when fishing downstream from a stationary position. If trout are not feeding in the top water column, it is difficult to get much action. A sink tip that is 15 to 24 feet in length can make a big difference. My favorite sink-tip system is Rio Products' VersaTip system, which I use with a 7-weight rod, and big #4 to 2 wet flies. A type 3 (three-inch-per-second sink rate) and a type 6 (six-inch-per-second sink rate) gives me the opportunity to fish every piece of each water column in most pools or runs. Comparable to this is Jim Teeny's Teeny 200 and Teeny 300 sink-tip lines. The disadvantage here is that the sink tips are not interchangeable.

Some waters in the drainage, however, require heavier tips that can sink faster and deeper. In Snake River Canyon, for example, there are several holes and pools that are 20 feet deep or more. In such situations, I switch to a sink tip that is more customized and allows for fishing deep water. Borrowing tactics I learned while steelhead fishing in British Columbia, Oregon, and Washington, I have recently started using 20- to 25-foot coils of 420-grain sink-tip material. Rio Products markets this material under the name T-14. Myself and many others also use 10- to 15-foot lengths of lead core line to achieve the same result. With all these sink-tip combinations, I prefer to use four to six feet of level leader between 10- and 15-pound test. This allows one to better turn over large streamers and wet flies while casting.

Jason Sutton

River Log: The Snake River & its Tributaries from Yellowstone National Park to Palisades Reservoir

River Safety

Before introducing the reader to the different sections of the Snake River and its tributaries, I would like to talk about the swiftness of the Snake River, with an emphasis on safety. The Snake River is not a deep river, but on every stretch you will experience very swift water. The Bureau of Reclamation regulates and records stream flow for the Snake River. They measure stream current by the volume of water carried past a point of reference in one second, and use the term *cubic feet per second (cfs)*. It is almost useless to try and determine an average flow for the Snake in a given year. Flows can vary widely due both to the degree of runoff being carried by its tributaries and the release from Jackson Lake Dam.

The heaviest flow period is typically during the spring runoff between the first part of May and the first part of July. After this, flows begin to decrease throughout the entire drainage, with the exception of those times when the Bureau of Reclamation opens the gates at Jackson Lake Dam. While many tributaries reach levels low enough to wade entirely across safely, this is almost never the case on the Snake River itself at any time of the year. The swift current, matched with the heavy amount of debris and streambound structure, make it a very dangerous river whether you are a boater or a wader. Every year there are accidents and, unfortunately, almost every year there are deaths. At many boat launches, warnings are posted notifying boaters of the dangers that exist and that watercraft should be piloted only by experienced individuals who are familiar with the river. Please heed this warning. None of the cutthroat on the Upper Snake River are worth a human life.

These two photos, taken from Moose Bridge in June and September respectively, illustrate the dramatic changes that occur on the Snake River during and after spring runoff.

The Snake River Above Jackson Lake, Yellowstone National Park

The Snake River inside Yellowstone National Park is a difficult but very rewarding part of the stream as a whole. The difficulty is primarily one of access. No watercraft of any kind is allowed on rivers within the Park. Only wade fishing is allowed. Access is limited further by the distance between trailheads and most of the river. Only a small portion is within close hiking distance from the South Entrance Road. To reach some of the best fishing on the upper reaches of the stream, a hike of five miles or more may be required. Horseback trips are a better way to go for those who wish to fish 15 miles or more from a trailhead.

The reward for those who fish this area is unparalleled solitude since few anglers attempt to fish it. Geyser basins are found all along the Snake River. Abundant wildlife is present. Elk and moose feed in riparian areas close to streams, as will the occasional bison. Cutthroat and brown trout dominate much of these waters. The latter originated from stockings that occurred in Lewis and Shoshone lakes. Above Lewis River Canyon, only brown trout and lake trout exist. Browns tend to be in their greatest numbers around the confluence of the Lewis River. Upstream of here, their numbers begin to decline and cutthroat trout are found in greater abundance.

I have guided several backcountry trips into Heart Lake and the headwaters of the Snake River over the past 15 years. I find the best fishing for both size and number of trout to be below the confluence of the Heart River and the Snake River. The Heart River is not a very large stream.

There is consistent beaver activity along the entire length of the Snake River.

It originates at the mouth of Heart Lake and flows approximately three miles to the Snake River. Generally, the Heart River carries more water than the Snake after the spring runoff subsides (one of the reasons why early explorers believed Heart Lake to be the actual headwaters). I have caught several cutthroat over 18 inches on this short stretch of river. The Snake River above the confluence contains plentiful pockets of holding water year round. These pockets can hold cutthroat trout up to 19 inches. However, I find the water below the confluence is more suitable trout habitat.

Note: Fishing in Yellowstone National Park requires a Yellowstone National Park fishing license. Wyoming state fishing licenses are not valid. A license can be purchased at the South Entrance. At the time of writing, park fishing license fees were $15.00 for three days, $20.00 for seven days, and $35.00 for a season.

Bison near the Snake River in Yellowstone National Park.

South Gate Launch to Flagg Ranch

(Approximately 3 miles)

The South Gate Launch is the first launch from which one can legally put a watercraft on the Snake River. The launch slip is primitive at best. A wooden slide structure built several decades ago is used to slide watercraft down to the river. If you are floating this section of the Snake River, you will have to portage your boat to the stream edge. The primary geological feature on this stretch is Flagg Canyon. The Snake River here is surrounded by steep walls of volcanic rock. These walls, along with large boulders that litter the river, are serious obstacles for float-fishermen. Sufficient experience can go a long way in helping one successfully navigate this section of river.

Flagg Canyon has excellent holding water for cutthroat and brown trout, especially around the plentiful amount of structure found in the river. In autumn, brown trout make their annual spawning migration out of Jackson Lake and up the Snake River. Flagg Canyon is among the best areas to fish for these large trout that have fattened up through the summer in the nutrient-rich lake. The brown migrations through this section of the Snake River is blazing fast. It typically ends two to three weeks after it starts.

At the lower end of the canyon, Sheffield Creek enters the Snake River just before it makes a turn to the west. This confluence represents the best piece of trout water on this section of the river. It can be easily accessed by wade fishermen from Sheffield Creek Campground, located on the southwest side of the U.S. Highway 89/191 Bridge. Sheffield Creek can fish well from its mouth up to 400 meters upstream, after which holding water becomes sparse. At the mouth, large cutthroat can hold at the confluence point and in the riffle pool below a shelf created by the merging of the two streams. The Flagg Ranch boat launch is less than 100 meters downstream from the mouth of Sheffield Creek. The launch can be accessed from the west side of U.S. Highway 89/191 on the north side of the bridge.

Flagg Ranch to Lizard Creek

(Approximately 7 miles)

The launch at Flagg Ranch is a simple gravel rock launch suitable for most types of watercraft. The upper part of this float is inside Rockefeller Memorial Parkway and is maintained by the National Forest Service. The lower part enters Jackson Lake and Grand Teton National Park. If floating this section, or anywhere else within the Park, be sure to have a Grand Teton National Park boat permit. A motorized permit is required if you wish to use a motor on the lake. In order to take out at Lizard Creek, float-fishermen will have to cross three miles of Jackson Lake. Unless using a canoe, a motor is a good idea.

This section of the Snake River receives far less pressure than the rest of the stream. I have fished it several times by boat in my life, but I believe it is much better for wade fishing. One can easily access the stream at either the Flagg Ranch or Huckleberry Hot Springs campsite. The channels here are more braided than upstream and contain more structure. This creates plentiful holding water for trout on this section of the Snake River. Fishing is further enhanced by a wealth of high-nutrient tributaries, including Glade Creek and Polecat Creek (flowing out of Polecat and Huckleberry Hot Springs). These two creeks receive a rather large portion of the brown trout population that run up the Snake River from Jackson Lake to spawn in the fall. This is a rather unique feature, as brown trout are generally known as main-stem spawners. The size of sediment on these two creeks is ideal for spawning brown trout, but whirling disease has been identified among cutthroat trout in Polecat Creek. Fortunately, it has not shown signs of spreading to other parts of the drainage.

There is abundant wildlife on this portion of the river. Moose and deer are plentiful, as are beavers, otters, sandhill cranes, and pelicans. Grizzly bears are beginning to frequent this area again more and more. (The Rockefeller Memorial Parkway is squeezed between the Teton Wilderness and the northern extreme of Grand Teton National Park, both of which are prime territory for grizzlies.)

Like the river further upstream, cutthroat and brown trout dominate. There will also be chances here to catch the occasional mackinaw lake trout that works its way out of Jackson Lake. Brown trout will work their way upstream from the lake in autumn to spawn. Next to the spawning run of browns that occurs in the Lewis River channel between Lewis and Shoshone lakes, this one is the most popular that occurs in the Snake River drainage. It draws a loyal following of anglers from the Jackson Hole area annually. The brown runs here generally occur in late October and early November, but can take place well into November and even December.

Grand Teton National Park

Unlike Yellowstone National Park, one can fish Grand Teton National Park (GTNP) with a Wyoming state-issued fishing license. Non-resident licenses cost $14.00 a single day or $92.00 for a season. Resident licenses cost $6.00 for a single day and $24.00 for a season. A donation to Wyoming Search and Rescue can be made with the purchase of either license.

All watercraft are required to have a GTNP boat permit. Permits can be purchased at the Visitor's Center in Moose, Wyoming. A non-motorized permit costs $10.00 and a motorized permit costs $20.00. Be advised that only non-motorized crafts are allowed on the Snake River within Park boundaries. You can only use motorized watercrafts on the lakes within GTNP.

Jackson Lake Dam to Pacific Creek

(Approximately 5 miles)

This is the shortest and safest section of the Upper Snake River for fly-fishers. Most boaters wishing to float this part of the river launch at Jackson Lake Dam. There is no actual slip down to the water, so all watercraft has to be dropped onto the man-made gravel bank and dragged down to the river.

Jackson Lake Dam

Fishing guides will do this several times in a season. If you have a reliable raft, skiff or driftboat, you should not worry too much about hull damage.

There are several access points along this stretch where wade fishermen can reach the river, including Jackson Lake Dam, the Meadows, Oxbow Bend, Cattleman's Bridge, and Pacific Creek. Mt. Moran is within constant view on the first half of this stretch of river. The stunning backdrop, easy access, short distances, abundant wildlife (especially moose and eagles) and relatively safe wading and floating, makes it one of the most popular sections of the Snake River in GTNP for both anglers and sightseers. So be prepared for crowds.

This stretch offers very little by way of stream-bound structure, and there are only a handful of riffles to speak of. As such, it is not one of my favorite pieces of water to float fish or wade fish. But its closeness to Jackson Lake Dam means a relatively constant supply of freshwater and nutrients. Regulations require that the dam at least be kept at a natural minimum flow of (280 cfs), meaning that there is never a complete shutdown of water flow from the dam. In addition, because there are no serious tributaries on this stretch, it remains less impacted by the spring runoff and heavy seasonal rains compared to stretches farther downstream. It is a reliable stretch for fly-fishing year around.

The most prominent riffles on this stretch are found just above and below Christian Creek. If they are not occupied, I highly recommend that you fish them as they offer the most productive holding water found above Pacific Creek. I have luck here with everything from soft hackles to small streamers. Cutthroat that hold in these riffles are often small, only about eight to ten inches. However, I have caught some cutthroat on dry flies here that will go up to 15 inches.

All anglers should be aware of the boundaries of an eagle-nesting zone found on this stretch. The river cannot be fished by wading anglers one-half-mile above and below the nests between February 1st and August 15th. Float-fishermen can fish this area from boats, but no stopping, anchoring, or even back paddling, is allowed. The zone itself moves as the eagle nests move. Some years the best fishing water on this stretch will be directly in the middle of these zones. Fines can run anywhere from $50 to $200.

Its location immediately below Jackson Lake makes this stretch of river the closest thing to a tailwater found on the Upper Snake. Heavy midge and Trico hatches occur throughout the year. Blue-winged olives and PMDs are also plentiful. In the beginning of July, golden stoneflies and little yellow stoneflies begin to make their appearance. Snake River and Yellowstone cutthroat abound throughout the entire stretch. The occasional brown trout can be caught here as well. The proximity of Jackson Lake also makes this stretch a prime spot to catch mackinaw lake trout. Immediately below the dam is one of the best places to target this species. It is often crowded, sometimes to the point where fishing here may seem unappealing. But seeing others bringing in large lake trout usually causes anglers to have a change of heart.

Below the Cattleman's Bridge access area, the river slows significantly as it passes through Oxbow Bend and a wide, mile-long channel above Pacific Creek. It is often described as a slack-water section that offers very slow fishing. However, there are two noteworthy targets that typically produce trout. The first of these is the long bank on the north side of the river. PMDs, blue-winged olives, midges, and Tricos can be plentiful along this bank in the early evenings. In the middle of the day, I have used Foam Wing Hoppers and Schroeder's Parachute Hopper with a high degree of success. The largest cutthroat I have caught on this stretch of river—18 1/2 inches—was on a Foam Wing Hopper in 2002.

On the south bank of the channel, a set of four springs enters the river approximately half-a-mile above Pacific Creek. These springs supply nutrients and fantastic feeding opportunities for trout. Targeting trout with mayfly nymphs and adults along the seam of these springs can give anglers some of the best fishing on this piece of the river. Sparkle Pupas and Copper Johns in #16 to 18 have been consistently productive over the past several years at the mouths of these springs.

Pacific Creek to Deadman's Bar

(Approximately 10 miles)

Pacific Creek landing is situated 50 meters downstream from where Pacific Creek, the first major tributary below the dam, enters the Snake River. This marks the point at which the Snake begins to take on more freestone characteristics. The gradient of the river increases and the river starts to braid heavily, forming several islands, cobblestone bars, and riffle pools. Stream-bound structure is abundant on this stretch and will be for almost the entire length of the river until it reaches Snake River Canyon.

One mile downstream from Pacific Creek Landing is the confluence of the Buffalo Fork and the Snake River. The Buffalo Fork is a haven for the small population of brown trout that exist in the Jackson Hole area. For this reason, brown trout are not uncommon on this section of the Snake River. Still, the Pacific Creek to Deadman's Bar stretch is dominated by cutthroat. Both Yellowstone and Snake River fine-spotted cutthroat are plentiful here.

For anglers wishing to wade fish, there are several access points. The primary access opportunities are either at the extreme upstream (Pacific Creek Landing) or downstream (Deadman's Bar) portions of the stretch. This section of the river can also be accessed near its center point via the RKO road, a dirt road built and used by RKO Studios when they filmed Hollywood westerns in the area between 1929 and 1960. It runs along the west bank of river. A small dirt parking lot in the vicinity of the east face of Signal Mountain serves as the best place to prepare gear and make the short walk to the stream. The water closest to the parking area is a long flat stretch of water and it does not present the best fishing. Guided fishing trips often use this part of the river as a lunch stop, as it offers good views of the Teton Range from the east bank and a canopy of tall spruce and fir trees on the west bank to protect parties from the elements. For wading anglers, it is best to work downstream from here. You will find more riffle pools and stream-bound structure where trout can hold.

This stretch of the Snake River has decent hatches of PMDs, blue-winged olives, and *hecubas*. The riffles and structure on this stretch hold some very large cutthroat that rise readily to mayfly imitations like Parachute Adams, Parachute Hare's Ears, Compara-duns, and Rusty Spinners. Nymphs are equally productive. I generally use Pheasant Tails, weighted Sparkle Pupas, and Cole's LOF. I fish them deep, at least two feet beneath the surface. They can be fished with a dropper system or independently with equal success.

Pacific Creek to Deadman's Bar is one of my favorite stretches on the Snake River. I enjoy the relative solitude of this section, with little wading and boat traffic. I like watching the river change from a slow-moving stream with tailwater characteristics, to a fast-flowing stream with several pools and natural structure where trout can hold. This is also one of the most beautiful stretches of river found anywhere in the West. It is the only section that allows a complete and full panoramic view of the Teton Range, with Mt. Moran forming the major peak in the north and the stunning cathedral peaks of Teewinot, Mt. Owen, and the three Tetons to the south. North American bison and moose are common during most of the summer and autumn.

A driftboat works the bank below Deadman's Bar.

This stretch is on a major migration route for elk and deer in autumn. It is possible to hear bugling throughout the day. In addition, there is a healthy population of eagles and ospreys. These are all added bonuses to a day of fantastic fishing from Pacific Creek to Deadman's Bar.

Deadman's Bar to Moose Landing

(Approximately 8 miles)

Deadman's Bar to Moose Landing is debatably the most famous section of the entire Snake River. If you have seen a photo of the Grand Teton with the Snake River in the foreground, it was most likely taken somewhere along this reach. No other reach of river runs as close to the range as this one. It is wildly popular for scenic rafting trips. With the exception of the whitewater section in Snake River Canyon, Deadman's to Moose has more rafting traffic on it than any other stretch of river in Wyoming. It might also be the most popular stretch for both visiting and resident anglers as well.

The freestone characteristics that begin to take form upstream become even more pronounced on this section. If any stretch is meant to be an indicator of the power and strength of the annual runoff, this is the one. Roughly four miles downstream from Deadman's Bar, a maze of channels splinters off from the main channel to both the east and west banks. These often become clogged with debris that enters the river as banks erode during each spring runoff. This can create severe hazards for inexperienced boaters. No other stretch in Grand Teton National Park experiences more accidents than this one.

But it is these hazardous conditions that make the fishing spectacular. The stream-bound structure creates natural breakwater and protection for trout. Each fallen tree, logjam, and brush pile represents a possible feeding position for cutthroat. The amount of structure on this stretch is unmatched, which means the number of possible feeding positions for trout is unmatched as well. Anglers have ample opportunity to fish a countless array of islands, riffles, confluence points, seams, and structure.

Deadman's Bar is the primary launching point for most scenic float trips in the Park. A single scenic guide can float up to five trips in a given day. As a result, the slips at Deadman's Bar and Moose Landing can be congested throughout the day. It tends to be worse before 10 a.m. and after 5 p.m., as fishing boats are also putting-on and taking-off the river. Deadman's Bar can seem a bit chaotic at times, but remember that a type of common-sense etiquette exists at launch sites in the same way that it exists on the river. It is not so much, "First come, first serve," as it is, "First ready, first serve." Once you have your boat prepared to launch, you can back it down at one of the two available slips. After it is off the trailer and in the water, you should move your craft so that it does not obstruct the slip for the next boat to be launched. No preparation of the boat should be done at the slips themselves. This is one of the major causes of congestion at the landings causing frustration among scenic guides, who are often on a very tight schedule. After securing the boat with an anchor or tie-down system, pull out of the slip and park your vehicle so that it too does not obstruct boat and trailer traffic at the landing.

This code of etiquette should be used at landings when you are preparing to take your craft from the river. You should secure your boat so that it does not obstruct the slip for boats being put onto trailers. When the slip is clear, back your vehicle down to the water, then bring your boat to the slip and load it onto the trailer. Here, you should secure the craft to the trailer and then pull out of the slip so that others may load their boats. No disassembling of the boat or equipment should be done in the slip itself. This can be done in the parking area where both your boat and vehicle will be out of the way. I mention this piece of etiquette in this part of the journal because Deadman's Bar and Moose Landing experience heavier than average use. But this is a general code and should be adhered to at every launch site on the river.

High boat traffic is only a small inconvenience on what is one of the better sections to fish. It may seem congested at the landing, but once on the water, the crowds seem to disappear. The numerous river channels present fishing boats with the chance to get away from those areas that appear to be a bit more crowded. I have my favorites channels for sure. But in reality, one is just as good as the other. Each will have its own set of riffles, structure, confluence points, and banks to fish.

Access to the river on this reach is as good as that found upstream. Wade fishing downstream from Deadman's Bar can be good. At Moose, it is better to access the river from the east bank, which can be done at the small village of Dornan's. There is more than enough parking at this location. In addition, there is also a general store and a full-service fly shop, Will Dornan's Snake River Angler. It's a perfect place to start a day of fishing on the river.

Easy access is also available at two prime spring-creek locations. On the east side of the river, approximately two miles north of Moose Junction, is a turnoff for the Blacktail Ponds. It is only a short walk to the river from this location and the fishing on the creek itself is fantastic. On the west bank, the river can be accessed by taking the RKO road, just north of the Cottonwood Creek turnoff, and driving approximately five miles to the steep bluff overlooking the river. You can walk down from this point to where Frustration Creek enters the river. Like the creeks at the Blacktail Ponds, the fishing here can be superb.

While the fishing on the numerous spring creeks is exceptional in the Jackson Hole area, most of them are private or, in the case of Grand Teton National Park, strictly regulated. Fishing on the spring creeks between Deadman's to Moose is not allowed until August, after spawning has subsided. For some anglers, this is frustrating.

Table 2. Trout Population Estimates for the Upper Snake River between Deadman's Bar and Upper Bar BC Ranch

Size Group (Inches)	*Number per Mile*					
	1990	1999	2001	2003	2006	Mean
5.0-8.9					525	
6.0-8.9	272	209	307	149	415	270
9.0-12.9	190	214	353	220	329	261
≥13.0	72	138	353	143	102	162
Combined	534	561	1013	512	846	693

*Combined for SRC ≥ 6 in.

Size Group (Inches)	*Pounds per Mile*					
	1990	1999	2001	2003	2006	Mean
5.0-8.9					77	
6.0-8.9	37	27	40	21	65	38
9.0-12.9	95	108	192	114	162	134
≥13.0	79	159	425	177	124	193
Combined	211	294	657	312	351*	365

*Combined for SRC ≥ 6 in.

Source: Wyoming Department of Game and Fish

*These estimates include all trout species within the measurement parameters. Non-cutthroat species represent less than one percent of total abundance.

Levees have severely impacted the riparian habitat in the middle section of the Snake, but the fishing is among the best found on the river.

But these are very important waters. As I mentioned in the earlier section dealing with trout on the Snake River, spring creeks are the lifeblood of cutthroat trout and the primary reason they thrive in this harsh environment. They deserve protection. I think it wise to only dedicate a small part of any excursion on the Snake to fishing spring creeks. Trout there should experience as little disturbance as possible. Besides, the fishing on the Snake River is just as good. (If you do decide to fish any creek or tributary, be advised that the regulations can be very different than those for the river. Check Wyoming Game and Fish and Grand Teton National Park regulations before going.)

One other excellent access point to the river is Schwabacher's Landing, located approximately five miles north of Moose Junction on Highway 89/191. When water levels are high enough, or if there has been strong enough runoff to force a permanent channel for the season to the landing, Schwabacher's offers an excellent launching point for a short, half-day-long float-fishing trip down to Moose. Wade fisherman need only follow the riverbed upstream from Schwabacher's to reach the main channel.

In my opinion, the reach of river running from Deadman's Bar to Moose Landing represents the perfect habitat for Snake River cutthroat. The plethora of structure, islands, and channels form an uncountable number of breakwater pockets that cutthroat seek out for survival on streams like the Snake. The cutthroat here can grow incredibly large—as can the small number of brown trout. Despite the crowds, Deadman's to Moose rarely disappoints.

Middle Sections

Moose Landing to Wilson Bridge

(Approximately 15 miles)

At approximately 15 miles in length, the stretch of water running from Moose Landing to Wilson Bridge is the longest on the Upper Snake River. About one quarter of its length is within Grand Teton National Park. The rest is surrounded by privately owned property and small parcels of land maintained by the Bureau of Land Management (BLM). Public wade-fishing access on this stretch is very limited. Unless given permission by private landowners, wading anglers are restricted to the part of the river within Grand Teton National Park below Moose Bridge and the small piece of public access above Wilson Bridge.

Eagles are a common sight when fishing below Moose Bridge.

The south boundary of Grand Teton National Park marks the beginning of a 24-mile-long levee system on both banks of the Snake River. It was constructed by the Army Corps of Engineers in the late 1950s and early 1960s. The original purpose for the levees was to control flooding, especially around the town of Wilson. But it also created additional riverfront property. Today, multi-million-dollar homes on huge parcels of land dot the river on both sides.

While local public opinion was originally in favor of a levee system, this is not the case now. The levees are viewed by many as a prime example of the destruction man can cause in his effort to control the environment. Riparian habitat along the river has been negatively altered. Close to a half dozen major islands have been destroyed due to the increased rate of flow in this channelized section of river. Colonies of cottonwoods have disappeared. It has also had a significant impact on cutthroat habitat. The levee system has contributed to the buildup of silt in traditional spawning beds. Many of the best side channels that existed on the river are gone. I have walked many times through the original riverbed now blocked by the levee. The old channels are still there to this day, minus the water from the river. In some places, these channels swing as far as a half-mile from where the river's flow is permanently restricted today. I often contemplate how wonderful the fishing must have been in these places before being destroyed by ill-conceived plans for flood control and streamside development.

Despite the negative impact of the levees, the fishing on these middle sections is some of the best found on the river. This is a testament to the adaptability of the cutthroat and the benefit of proactive management policies by the State and local organizations. While some spring creeks have been forever altered, many are protected so that cutthroat can still make their spring runs and spawn effectively. Moose to Wilson has one of the highest concentrations of spring creeks in the entire drainage. As a result, cutthroat here are as abundant and as large as in any other section of water in the area (See Tables 3 & 4, pages 50 & 51).

Like Deadman's Bar to Moose Landing, this stretch is full of structure and has numerous side channels, both of which contribute to the abundant pockets of breakwater for feeding trout. These side channels converge with the

Table 3. Trout Population Estimates for the Upper Snake River between R Lazy S Ranch and Wilson Bridge

Size Group (inches)	*Number per Mile*						
	1993	1994	1998(a)	2000(a)	2002	2004(b)	Mean
6.0-8.9	415	652	594	161	279	215	386
9.0-12.9	168	128	432	192	311	96	221
≥13.0	137	136	183	500	170	94	203
Combined	720	916	1,209	853	760	405	810

Size Group (inches)	*Pounds per Mile*						
	1993	1994	1998(a)	2000(a)	2002	2004(b)	Mean
6.0-8.9	55	97	73	19	33	29	51
9.0-12.9	84	69	205	100	137	45	107
≥13.0	202	176	248	601	222	114	260
Combined	341	342	526	720	392	188	418

Source: Wyoming Department of Game and Fish

(a) The high estimates experienced in 1998 and 2000 are most likely the result of favorable water conditions that occurred between 1994 and 1999, when the Snake River drainage encountered above-average annual moisture and annual cumulative snowfall.

(b) The decline in total trout abundance that occurred between 1998 and 2004 is most likely the result of unfavorable water conditions between 2000 and 2005, when the Snake River drainage encountered a severe drought cycle characterized by below-average cumulative snowfall and annual moisture.

* These estimates include all trout species within the measurement parameters. Non-cutthroat species represent less than one percent of total abundance.

main channel to form ideal confluence points for trout to hold. Small but productive riffles abound on almost every turn that the river makes on this section. And while the levees are a detriment to the ecosystem, they actually fish incredibly well. The boulders that form the levee create ideal breakwater and protection for trout. All of this combines to create some of the best habitat offered on the Snake River. In my experience, no other piece of the river fishes as consistently as that flowing from Moose Landing to Wilson Bridge. It is perhaps my favorite section of river.

One of the most appealing aspects of this stretch is the light traffic it receives. Only one scenic outfit is permitted by Grand Teton National Park to float below Moose Landing. If you happen to float this section, the only scenic boats you will see will be during the midday lunch trip, and this will only be three boats at the most. The limited public wading access lessens shore traffic. And while this stretch is popular among local fly-fishing outfits, its length and number of channels mean that you rarely feel crowded by other boats.

I also find this section to be extremely beautiful, despite the levees and smattering of trophy homes. From Moose Landing, the river moves south from the Cathedral Peaks to Buck Mountain, Death Canyon, Granite Canyon, and then along the southern part of the Teton Range, which includes Rendezvous Peak and the Jackson Hole Mountain Resort. To the east, the peaks of the Gros Ventre Range, most notably Sheep Mountain and Jackson Peak, are in full view. There is much by way of wildlife as well. Moose and deer roam the banks during most of the year and elk become plentiful in fall as they move from the high country down to the valley floor for winter. You will find more eagles and ospreys here than on any other stretch in the Park.

The principal tributary on this stretch is the Gros Ventre River. Upstream diversions significantly cut the actual flow most years. Much of the water that does enter the Snake from the Gros Ventre comes from a number of spring creeks that enter just upstream from the confluence. Wyoming Game and Fish recognize this area as one of the prime spawning and feeding areas for Snake River fine-spotted cutthroats. In fact, a small creek known as lower Bar BC Creek (not to be confused with the Bar BC creeks above Moose Landing) is designated as a home spawning ground for one of the purest and wildest strain of cutthroat in the West. They are known as Bar BC strain cutthroat and are heralded by fishery scientists for their fast growth and fighting ability. The large Snake River cutthroat now stocked on the Green River in Utah and the White River in Arkansas, some of which are reaching over 27 inches in length, are direct descendents of this race of cutthroat.

The cutthroat that spawn in Bar BC spring creek and nearby Three Channel Creek contribute to the large trout found on this part of the Snake River. One of my clients landed a pair of 20- and 21-inch cutthroat at the upstream confluence point of the Snake and Gros Ventre rivers in September of 2001.

The Gros Ventre confluence is also one of the few parts of the river where rainbow trout and cutthroat hybrids exist. Members of the resident population of rainbows that live below Slide Lake in the Gros Ventre drainage will at times migrate downstream to the Snake. Like the cutthroat here, they can grow large. If you are float-fishing on this stretch, don't be surprised if you spend two or three hours fishing the Gros Ventre River confluence.

Table 4. Summary of Total Estimated Spawning on Spring Creeks at and above the Gros Ventre River Confluence, 1995-2004

Year	*Number of Redds Mapped*	*Minimum Pairs*	*Maximum Pairs*	*Total Trout*
1995	662	840	1,063	1,903
1996	692	904	1,233	2,137
1997	710	996	1,364	2,370
1998	834	1,150	1,597	2,747
1999	1,073	1,238	1,558	2,796
2000	1,089	1,219	1,572	2,791
2001	1,011	1,215	1,636	2,854
2002	915	1,186	1,577	2,763
2003	517	754	1,018	1,772
2004	851	1,026	1,384	2,409
Mean	***835***	***1,053***	***1,400***	***2,454***

Source: Wyoming Department of Game and Fish

Wilson Bridge to South Park Bridge
(Approximately 11 miles)
This stretch is the only part of the Upper Snake River not fully regulated by federal or state agencies. This section is surrounded by private land and small parcels of BLM land. It is almost completely channelized by the same levee system. Both Wilson Bridge and South Park Bridge are within close proximity to the population centers of Jackson, Wilson, and Teton Village. These sites tend to be very crowded. On weekday evenings and weekends, scores of local fishermen flock to these relatively close access points. Adding to the crowds is the number of scenic and guide fishing trips that use it without having to worry about the quota regulations in Grand Teton National Park and Bridger-Teton National Forest. On top of all this, Wilson Bridge is the start of less restrictive regulations in terms of tackle usage with bait-fishing allowed downstream of the bridge.

The memorial to Joe Allen at Wilson Bridge.

Table 5. Trout Population Estimates for the Upper Snake River between Wilson Bridge and Fish Creek

Size Group (Inches)	*Number per Mile*							
	1994	1995	1996	1998	2000 (a)	2002 (a)	2005 (b)	Mean
5.0-8.9							728	
6.0-8.9	933	190	313	412	333	1345	595	589
9.0-12.9	279	178	156	255	414	447	158	270
>13.0	113	56	76	101	227	138	127	120
Combined	1325	424	545	768	974	1966	880	979

Size Group (Inches)	*Pounds per Mile*							
	1994	1995	1996	1998	2000 (a)	2002 (b)	2005 (b)	Mean
5.0-8.9							93	
6.0-8.9	111	24	35	81	36	181	83	79
9.0-12.9	141	85	77	130	200	181	59	125
>13.0	152	78	103	143	278	224	184	166
Combined	404	187	215	354	514	586	326	370

Source: Wyoming Department of Game and Fish

(a) The high estimates experienced in 2000 and 2002 are most likely the result of favorable water conditions that occurred between 1994 and 1999, when the Snake River drainage encountered above average annual moisture and annual cumulative snowfall.

(b) The decline in total trout abundance that occurred between 2002 and 2005 is most likely the result of unfavorable water conditions between 2000 and 2005, when the Snake River drainage encountered a severe drought cycle characterized by below-average cumulative snowfall and annual moisture.

* These estimates include all trout species with the measurement parameters. Non-cutthroat species represent less than one percent of total abundance

The consequence of all of these factors is that the trout on this stretch are under more pressure than any other on the Upper Snake. One would think that the fishing from Wilson Bridge to South Park would be subpar, or at least on the decline. This is not even close to reality. I am still baffled by the health of the trout population on this stretch of river (see Table 5, page 52). Despite the levees and the most intense fishing pressure in the valley, this reach continuously produces some of the largest trout on the Upper Snake River. Once again, it is a true testament to the toughness and adaptability of the area's native cutthroats. While non-native trout species have declined to negligible numbers, cutthroat trout continue to thrive.

The strength of the cutthroat population here is in large part due to a high concentration of nearby spawning water. More tributaries enter the river on this section than anywhere else on the Upper Snake. While float-fishing, anglers will pass by Fish Creek, Mosquito Creek, Spring Creek, Taylor Creek, Cody Creek, and Blue Crane Creek, just to name the most well-known tributaries. There are still a number of smaller creeks whose names I don't know, and some may not even have names. But they are there, and contribute significantly to healthy spawning on an annual basis (see Table 6, page 53).

Like so much of the river above it, this stretch is characterized by an intense amount of structure, islands, shelves, and riffles. Some of the most productive side channels on the entire river are found here. I have run a small portion of my trips between Wilson and South Park Bridge every year since I started guiding. It is an incredibly consistent stretch for dry-fly aficionados. The spring creek and freestone-like habitat here is ideal for a variety of aquatic

This cutthroat is an example of the large members found between Wilson Bridge and South Park Landing.

Table 6. Summary of Total Estimated Spawning for Spring Creeks between Wilson Bridge and South Park Bridge, 1998-2007

Year	*Number of Redds Mapped*	*Minimum Pairs*	*Maximum Pairs*	*Total Trout*
1998	278	437	660	1,097
1999	246	336	508	844
2000	365	527	782	1,309
2001	240	312	455	767
2002	184	204	255	459
2003	152	194	274	468
2004	287	352	489	841
2005*	231	293	391	684
2006**	59	87	115	202
2007***	221	371	445	816
Mean**	**245**	**336**	**473**	**809**

Source: Wyoming Department of Game and Fish

*Estimate does not include May or Fish creek redd counts.
**Estimate does not include May, Flat or Fish creek redd counts.
*** Estimate does not include Cody, Flat or Nowlin creek redd counts.
****Mean calculated without 2006 estimate.

insects. Shortwing stoneflies and little yellow stoneflies are abundant as are PMDs throughout summer and mahogany duns in the fall. This stretch has one of the best hatches of October caddis in the Upper Snake River.

Snake River Canyon

South Park Bridge to Pritchard Landing
(Approximately 11 miles)
South Park Bridge is the unofficial beginning of the canyon section of the Upper Snake River. From this point, and continuing downstream, the river loses much of the characteristics that defined the middle section and those stretches in Grand Teton National Park. Gone for the most part are the braided channels, islands, and stream-bound structures. The streambed narrows as it becomes confined by dramatic granite walls. Despite the absence of structure and islands, Snake River Canyon holds its own when it comes to the number and size of trout. At times, it can fish better than any other portion of the Snake River.

The landing at South Park Bridge is not a public access point. It is a private landing owned by longtime Jackson resident Paul Von Gontard. Many locals call it "Von Gontard's Landing". Von Gontard has continually kept this landing open every season, despite his concerns about congestion during the summer season and some littering. (The latter of which has been significantly reduced in recent years due to the installation of a garbage container and portable toilet, thanks to support provided by The Snake River Fund and Wyoming Department of Game and Fish.) If you use this access point for either float-fishing or wade fishing, please remember that your personal courtesy and respect goes a long way in ensuring that it will remain open to the public in the future.

Because of the increased volume of the river flowing into a more restricted channel, this stretch, and the sections below it, run deeper than what is found upstream. For this reason, I am a big fan of using deep-sinking streamers and wet flies here. My favorites patterns include Double Bunnies, J.J. Specials, olive and silver Zonkers, Tequillies, and earth-tone colored Woolly Buggers. Sometimes I will even go so far as to use a 20-foot sink tip. Dry-fly fishing and light-weight nymphing can still be pretty good on this stretch. There are fewer riffles, but the ones that exist are prominent, typically long with subtle drop-offs into downstream pools. During PMD and *hecuba* hatches in the fall, large trout will hold in these elongated pools and feed on emergers and adults. A Rusty Spinner and traditional PMD patterns are simple flies that can be highly productive on these riffles.

South Park Bridge to Pritchard Landing will take on far fewer tributaries than what is found upstream. The ones that do flow into the river here, however, are vital to the health of the lower river. The three major tributaries—Flat Creek, which enters the river just below South Park Bridge, the Hoback River, and Fall Creek—contribute a lot of water. On a stream where flows are impacted by a dam and miles of levees, Snake River Canyon mimics natural flow closer than any other part of the river. According to hydrologists and fishery specialists from Bridger-Teton National Forest and the Wyoming Department of Game and Fish, this is a prime reason why the cutthroat population in the canyon is so healthy. Despite the lack of tributaries and spring creeks, trout abundance here is as strong as anywhere else.

Dog Creek to West Table
(Approximately 10 miles)
The ten-mile section of water between Dog Creek (commonly called Pritchard Landing by local river enthusiasts) and West Table Boat Launch is one of the most beautiful pieces of river on the Upper Snake. The stunning Snake River Canyon truly begins to take shape here. Granite and limestone walls rise steeply on both sides of the river. To the west, they help to form the Snake River Range, and to the east, they form portions of the Wyoming and Hoback ranges. Colonies of cottonwoods, swamp maples, and chokecherry bushes line the river banks. These turn a brilliant gold and red in the fall. Wildlife is abundant here, especially moose, deer, and black bear. This stretch also contains a healthy concentration of eagles and ospreys.

The majority of the land adjacent to this piece of river is maintained by Bridger-Teton National Forest. However, there are some private parcels. Immediately at the head of the section, and directly across from Prichard Creek, lies the new Snake River Sporting Club golf course development. It is constructed on the site of an old swimming complex that utilized the natural hot springs flow into the river from Johnny Counts Flats. The golf course has become a major

Fall colors upstream of West Table boat launch.

A Snake River fine-spotted cutthroat taken in the canyon.

source of concern for environmental groups and river users who are fearful of potential riparian degradation. River users and conservation groups worry that levees will be constructed to protect the golf course, which runs directly along the river bank. There is also the possibility that nearby eagle nests will be disturbed.

I am often asked what this section of river's best attributes are in terms of fly-fishing. One trait is that the river here closely mimics natural flow, a factor that is beneficial for native cutthroat. But Pritchard Landing to West Table, as well as the canyon section below it, offer another special trait for anglers. Several years ago, the Wyoming Department of Game and Fish stocked Palisades Reservoir with hard-fighting Bar BC strain cutthroat. Late in the season, as Palisades Reservoir drains to meet irrigation demands, these cutthroat begin to run upstream into the Snake River. I have typically noticed that these runs occur as the reservoir hits 70% capacity. As the reservoir drops to 60%, then 50%, then 40% capacity, the appearance of these trout become even more pronounced. They are among the hardest fighting cutthroat found in the upper Snake River. One can tell when they hook into these fish by the mercurochrome coloring along their sides, a physical trait developed from their more variable diet (including zooplankton and crustaceans) in the reservoir. I have heard some describe them as *steelhead cutthroat*. This label comes as much from their fighting ability as it does from their unique coloring. In my opinion, the appearance of these cutthroat in the canyon, typically starting in mid to late August, is this section of river's best attribute for fly-fishers.

To the uninitiated, bank fishing on this section of river will appear to offer terrific possibilities. The water here is deep, and allows trout plentiful feeding room and protection from predators. However, I find that hugging banks closely with either dry flies or nymphs is not nearly as productive as it is upstream of the canyon. My experience suggests that targeting one's flies off the bank by several feet is a much better tactic. Trout on this section have a lot of midstream holding water that is not necessarily evident to fly-fishers. I often position myself as far out into the current as I can safely wade and then cast my fly upstream and away from the bank. Many times my fly will be as far as 40 to 60 feet from my position, which is already 10 to 15 feet from the bank. The targets I choose are primarily submerged structure and midstream foam lines. This tactic can produce fantastic results.

Large stonefly patterns, both nymphs and adults, can be very effective. Chernobyl Ants, Plan Bs, Double Humpies, Crystal Flash Stone Nymphs, and Kaufmann's Golden Stone Nymphs are excellent flies to use when stonefly emergences are taking place. But this is a great stretch for the June caddis emergence when flows and clarity permit. The hatch is often more prolific than anywhere else. In 2001, a drought year when the runoff peaked before Memorial Day, anglers were blessed with low, clear water. This was when one of the most intense caddis emergences in recent memory took place. I experienced two consecutive days of 100-plus fish days floating between Moose and Wilson. Other guides, however, experienced even better fishing from Dog Creek to West Table. In retrospect, that incredible week of fishing was probably best on this section of the Upper Snake.

Dog Creek to West Table has relatively more tributaries in comparison to the rest of the canyon. Several small creeks drain the flanks of the adjacent Snake River and Wyoming ranges. Key among these are Bailey Creek and Pine Creek. The fishing in the vicinity of Bailey Creek is exceptional. An island splits the river here and the channel where Bailey Creek enters is characterized by classic riffle pools that can be productive. The largest cutthroat I have caught in the canyon, a 20-1/4-inch Snake River fine-spot, was in the Bailey Creek channel. I have also caught several brown trout in the vicinity of these creeks. Brown trout make their way up the Snake from Palisades Reservoir and the Salt and Greys rivers. They make up only a tiny portion of the total trout number in the canyon, but they can reach impressive sizes.

Additional landings and launches exist on this stretch. All of these are located on the west bank and are easily accessible from Highway 26/89. Two miles upstream of Dog Creek is Astoria Boat Launch. Key downstream landings include Elbow Campground and East Table. These two access points are ideal for those wanting a shorter float or for those who want to avoid the crowded landing at West Table, which is the primary staging area for the Snake River's whitewater outfitters. They are maintained by Bridger-Teton National Forest and act as great access points for wade fishermen. However, while West Table is a developed landing with paved slips leading down to the river, East Table and Elbow generally require four-wheel-drive vehicles.

West Table to Sheep Gulch

(Approximately 8 miles)

This is the world-famous whitewater section of the Upper Snake River. Everyday at the height of each summer season, scores of rafts will depart the West Table boat launch, their passengers ready to run rapids with names like "Kahuna," "Ropes Rapid," "Cottonwood Rapid," and "Lunch Counter." Kayaks depart from here as well, the paddlers (river speak for kayaker) often attacking the different rapids over and over again. The combination of heavy boat traffic and Class III-IV rapids turns some anglers off from the idea of fishing this section. This is a shame, as the river below West Table is a wonderful section to fish.

Although certainly crowded, the plethora of rafts and kayaks rarely interferes with the fishing. Most rafting guides and paddlers understand when they might be obstructing an angler. Generally they stay clear unless the situation warrants otherwise. It's a common-sense piece of river etiquette that makes things on crowded sections like this go more smoothly. But it is also a two-way street. While these river users are trying to do their best at not interfering with your fishing, you should do the same for them. Before pulling out of a hole or pocket to enter the main current of the river, always look upstream beforehand to ensure that you are not cutting off another boater or paddler making their way downstream. This is good advice on all stretches of river, but it is doubly important on more congested stretches like this one.

Safety is a serious concern from West Table to Sheep Gulch. It is not just the well-known rapids that one must keep an eye out for. Several spots on this stretch look deceivingly harmless, and you may not get a chance to react to a potential situation until it is too late. Back currents can swing a boat hard and fast into canyon walls when one is attempting to pull into an eddy, cracking the sides of fiberglass driftboats, tearing holes into rubber rafts, or flipping a craft. Several midstream obstructions exist as well, including pour-overs, also known as *keepers*, that move water back upstream to fill a hole created by surface turbulence. Some of these can prove almost impossible to get out of. One of the most infamous keepers is called "Three-Oar-Deal," so named because an unlucky whitewater guide broke three oars attempting to pull out of it. One should always be mindful of what lay downstream and use extra caution when floating this section.

My favorite time to fish this section is late fall, generally from the last half of September until the end of October. Crowds have generally dispersed by this time and flow levels are low enough that I am less concerned about the rapids. The Canyon is also stunningly beautiful at this time of year. The cottonwoods that cover the steep banks turn a crisp gold and red. This section is famous for its deep holes and the extremely large trout that they hold. During the 2003 One-Fly Tournament, Mike Janssen took High Point Guide honors by scoring 1,510 points on this stretch. Fishing heavy #2 streamers—J.J. Specials, Tequilleys, and Girdle Bugs—can result in violent strikes from large cutthroat. Pools on this section are deep. I am a big fan of using sink tips (type 6 and type 8 generally) and lead-core line to fish this water. But dry-fly fishing can also be good. October caddis are plentiful here in the fall, as are mahogany duns.

A view of the canyon just above Sheep Gulch.

Sheep Gulch acts as the last official landing on the Upper Snake River. It is possible to float and wade fish the last three miles from Sheep Gulch to Palisades Reservoir. Heavy rapids still exist on this stretch, including The Narrows—a tightly walled constriction that almost becomes a waterfall when the river reaches certain levels. You should use extreme caution on this stretch, much the same as you would above Sheep Gulch.

The last mile on this part of the river slows considerably as it begins to enter Palisades Reservoir. If you are float-fishing, you might be required to do some fairly heavy rowing to move downstream at a suitable speed. A landing exists on the west bank of the river, just below the mouth of the Grays River.

Area Lakes and Tributaries

The Jackson Hole area has a wealth of fishing opportunities in addition to the Snake River. At times, especially during the spring runoff, the lakes in the valley and some of the tributaries offer the only reliable fishing in the valley. They will fish well for most of the season. There are more of these opportunities than I can count, and I certainly can't cover all of them here. Instead, I offer some of my favorites and some of those that should be mentioned strictly on their reputation for great fly-fishing.

Head Water Lakes and Rivers: Lewis and Heart

Lewis Lake and Heart Lake contribute the majority of water to the Snake River above Jackson Lake. Both are deep lakes and have strong populations of lake trout, which were first introduced in the 1890s. On Heart Lake, they can reach extreme sizes. In fact, the Park record lake trout, 42 pounds, was taken from this lake in the 1930s. While growing up I would accompany my father on a number of pack trips he would guide on Heart Lake. Lake trout that exceeded 35 pounds were not uncommon on these expeditions. Some of the boat-dragging, hour-plus fights with fish we eventually lost suggests to me that there are lake trout exceeding 50 pounds in Heart Lake. There are also some very impressive cutthroat on both Heart Lake and the Heart River.

Heart Lake is not easily accessible. The main trailhead is adjacent to Highway 89/191 and requires an eight-mile hike, plus an additional five miles to reach the Heart River, which exits the lake from the east. Only non-motorized craft are allowed on Heart Lake and must be packed in either by horse or on foot. The latter may seem impossible, but I have seen some do it. In 1990, Jackson Hole outfitter Bob Barlow packed in a 12-foot rubber raft, complete with break-down oars and seats, when he could not secure a horseback permit for a guided expedition. His back was never quite the same again.

One word of caution when fishing the Heart Lake Basin: It is prime grizzly bear habitat. One should be on guard when venturing into this region. Carry bear spray as a deterrent and obtain information from Park authorities about recent bear activity in the area.

Will Dornan works the shallow beds of the Lewis River Channel.

A nymph-caught Loch Leven brown landed below Lewis Falls.

Lewis Lake and the Lewis River are easily accessible from Highway 89/191. Lewis Lake has a boat ramp on its southeast shore from which motorized craft can be launched. It contains healthy populations of both brown trout and lake trout. I like to fish with full-sinking lines along the west shore of Lewis Lake, using Zonkers and Woolly Buggers in black, olive, and, on bright days, silver and white. Many anglers also use Clouser Minnows and Mohair Leeches in olive or purple. The flats along the northwest shore offer the chance to sight cast to cruising brown trout. In evenings throughout the summer and early autumn, caddis and brown drake hatches can cause these flats to erupt with surface-feeding brown trout. Even the lake trout get into the mix.

The Lewis River is most accessible below Lewis Falls—easily within sight of the Highway 89/191 Bridge. Downstream of the bridge, the river flows slowly through a lush meadow frequented by moose and elk. The meadow experiences brown drake hatchs starting in late June and early July that produce some very good fishing. The brown trout respond to large drake nymphs primarily, but in the evenings, they will rise slowly to adults as they emerge and while females deposit eggs. By late August, this hatch and the milder stonefly emergences become rare. Most anglers focus on nymphing and streamer fishing on the Lewis River during the fall. Through the season, it's a great place to try a hair mouse in the evening.

The legendary Lewis Channel, flowing out of Shoshone Lake, enters Lewis Lake from the north. Beginning in late September, browns will make an annual spawning run up the channel. The fishing on this structure-filled body of water can be spectacular. It has drawn an ever-growing group of loyal followers for decades. Floating and density-compensated sink-tip lines with a six- or seven-weight rod are standard tackle. Zonkers and Woolly Buggers work as well here as they do on the lake, but my best action has occurred on dark sculpins and wet Muddler Minnows.

Mount Moran towers above Jackson Lake.

Fishing the Channel requires a hike of four miles from Highway 89/191. As an alternative, though, anglers can also row up the channel roughly two miles, anchor their boat, and make a shorter hike up to the prime fishing spots, because motorized watercraft are not allowed in the channel itself.

The weather during the brown run on the Channel can be variable. There are times when you will find yourself fishing here for browns under blue skies and in warm, 50-degree temperatures. However, it is more common to be fishing under overcast skies or in freezing rain and snow. This kind of weather can make fishing in the Channel phenomenal. Some of my most cherished Yellowstone memories are of fishing the Channel with fellow guides in October as our off-season approached, casting Woolhead Sculpins to holding brown trout in a heavy cascade of sleet. Typically, I am wearing neoprene waders, fleece gloves, and an ear-to-ear grin.

The Lakes of Grand Teton National Park: Jackson, Leigh, Jenny, and Phelps Lakes

Although found on the valley floor, these lakes are actually classified as alpine lakes. They formed between 15 and 80 thousand years ago after the retreat of the Bull Lake and Pinedale glaciers. These massive bodies of ice gouged deep depressions into the Earth's crust that were later filled as the glaciers receded and melted. The result was several large lakes that are deep and extremely cold.

Lake trout that were planted in the drainage in the early twentieth century have thrived in these lakes. They have done better than any other non-native trout species. Most fishermen go very deep with heavy trolling gear. On many of the submerged bars, fishermen will troll as deep as 100 to 125 feet of line. It is difficult to reach these depths with sinking fly line, even density-compensated versions. The deepest I can recall hooking a trout with sinking line was around 40 feet, I have heard of some anglers hooking lake trout at 70 feet below the surface. Fishing with flies is better close to shorelines and near the mouth of tributaries.

Early morning and early evening are the best times to fish these lakes. Wind during the afternoon hampers navigation on these lakes and makes casting difficult. Lake trout in the early evening will move into the shallows to feed on running baitfish and emerging insects. These fish will rise to the right kind of dry fly or emerger, and this gives an angler a great opportunity to hook into an enormous trout on the surface. Below the surface, nothing works better than a Double Bunny or a classic saltwater fly like a Clouser Minnow. However, a significant portion of a trout's diet on these lakes consists of freshwater invertebrates. Scuds fished in the shallows along islands and the lakeshore can be very productive, in addition, I also have had a lot of luck on olive, gray, and black in #12 to #16. When fishing scuds, I rely solely on a traditional sink tip.

Jackson Lake and Jenny Lake are both accessible from the inner loop road in Grand Teton National Park. Motorized craft are allowed on each. This makes fishing a whole lot easier, although you will find them more crowded, too. Leigh Lake and Phelps Lake are designated as non-motorized bodies of water and must be reached by a trail. Large lake trout, cutthroat, and browns can be caught with a fly from the shore or with a portable watercraft like a float tube or kick boat. Leigh Lake is approximately one-and-a-half miles from the trailhead at String Lake. Phelps Lake is approximately three miles from the Death Canyon Trailhead.

Crystal Creek.

Major Tributaries:
Pacific Creek, Buffalo Fork, Gros Ventre River Drainage, Hoback River Drainage, Greys River

Pacific Creek is the first major tributary below Jackson Lake. It's unique in that it is directly linked with a stream that flows east from the Continental Divide—Atlantic Creek. They are both connected by Two Ocean Creek, which straddles the Divide until it splits east and west. Some fish biologists feel that it is here that Yellowstone cutthroat first crossed the divide hundreds of thousands of years ago to populate both sides of the Rocky Mountains. Some believe that it is here, too, that the Yellowstone/Snake River cutthroat evolutionary split began.

Pacific Creek has fantastic fishing. I find it best immediately after the runoff subsides, which is generally a week or two before the Snake River clears. During this time, it generally has enough volume to hold a decent number of fish. Later in the season, volume falls off to a point where holding water for trout becomes scarce. Fishing can still be quite good on the upper portion of Pacific Creek late in the season. This section is closer to the runoff source and what some suspect to be high mountain springs. It is possible to hook into trout between 14 and 15 inches that hold and feed in these holes. Larger trout are found at the mouth of Pacific Creek, where it enters the Snake River. This is without question the most popular stretch of the creek for local and visiting fly-fishers. It has very easy access from Pacific Creek boat launch.

The Buffalo Fork, also known as the Buffalo River, enters Snake River approximately one mile downstream from the mouth of Pacific Creek. This entire stream is wonderful to fish. It is navigable and can be floated, but there are places where boats must be portaged around logjams. Most anglers prefer to wade fish it from shore. There is abundant structure creating excellent breakwater for its cutthroat and brown trout population. These fish feed mainly on baitfish, stoneflies, and caddis. Terrestrials will make up a small portion of their diet in late summer. The Buffalo Fork provides diverse fly-fishing throughout the season with excellent activity both above and below the surface. I have had my best luck on large stonefly nymphs and streamers fished close to structure.

The Gros Ventre River drainage is a fly-fishing paradise unto itself. It presents a stunning landscape and its several creeks and lakes offer several opportunities to wet a line. A well-maintained road runs along much of its length, making most of the waters easily accessible. At the same time, some of the best backcountry fly-fishing in all of Wyoming can be found in the Gros Ventre Wilderness.

Brewster Lake, deep in the Gros Ventre drainage.

East of Highway 89, the Gros Ventre River can be accessed at the Gros Ventre River Campground. It is located three miles downstream from the village of Kelly. Some of the best fishing is found below Lower Slide Lake. It's in this part of the Gros Ventre that the last remaining resident population of rainbow trout exists in its greatest concentration. Lower Slide Lake has an impressive population of cutthroat. Fishing here can be excellent during the handful of intense evening caddis hatches that occur throughout the summer.

The upper portion of the drainage offers even better fishing and generally receives less pressure. Fishable tributaries include Slate, Cottonwood, and Crystal creeks. These streams enter the Gros Ventre approximately four to six miles above Lower Slide Lake. The trout found here are almost exclusively Snake River fine-spotted cutthroat. Crystal Creek is a particular favorite among local and visiting anglers. I have had success fishing it with everything from a Zebra Midge to a Chernobyl Ant. You can access this stream from the bridge above Crystal Creek Campground. The best fishing, however, is found at a hidden access point a little farther upstream. To get to it, you take the cutoff just before the entrance to Red Rock Ranch. The road is clearly marked.

Approximately 10 miles farther up the drainage is Soda Lake, locally famous for its 20-plus-inch cutthroat. The name is derived from its high alkaline content that results from surrounding soil runoff and low water exchange rate. The high alkalinity allows for a higher than normal amount of aquatic invertebrates. The combination also allows trout to grow fast. Conversely, the high alkaline level also contributes to poor reproduction rates. It is regularly stocked by the Wyoming Game and Fish Department. The one-mile access road to Soda Lake was an absolute nightmare to drive before it was renovated in 2000. Now, almost any front-wheel-drive vehicle can navigate the road when dry. Unfortunately, many of these front-wheel-drive vehicles are now at Soda Lake on a regular basis.

At the extreme headwaters of the Gros Ventre River are Chateau and Brewster lakes. In the 1940s Wyoming Game and Fish stocked these lakes with brook trout because they are above Upper Gros Ventre Falls and devoid of native cutthroat. Thus far, the descendents of these stocked trout have not shown a significant propensity to migrate below the falls. The brook trout that inhabit these lakes can grow in excess of six pounds. They readily take dry flies, nymphs, and streamers. On Chateau Lake, they tend to be slightly more selective. A hike of eight miles is required to reach Chateau Lake, 13 miles to reach Brewster Lake. It is a hard push but you will be assured of few other anglers. The Gros Ventre Wilderness has only limited restrictions for travel by horseback. This is an enjoyable and less strenuous means of accessing one of the most beautiful parts of Snake River country.

The Hoback River is the primary tributary of the canyon section of the Upper Snake River. It drains a huge, mountainous region with truly beautiful vistas. I equally enjoy both wading and floating the Hoback. Highway 189/191 parallels the river through most of Hoback Canyon. This gives fly-fishers a lot of access.

There are a number of wonderful tributaries to the Hoback River, many of which are prime spawning springs for cutthroat. One of these is Granite Creek. A hot springs is located near the head of this stream, and a dip in these pools is a perfect way to end a day of fishing. More adventurous anglers can follow Shoal Creek, which enters the Hoback two miles upstream from the Granite Creek confluence, to its headwaters at Shoal Lake. It's a long march

Shoal Creek.

Blacktail Pond's spring creek.

up a very steep trail, and the trout are not extremely large, but casting among the cascading waterfalls is probably as good as it gets. Fishing Shoal Creek itself in early and mid-summer can produce cutthroat between 12 and 17 inches. Willow Creek enters the Hoback River approximately five miles upstream of the Hoback-Snake River confluence. This long, vegetation-lined stream is easily accessible via a well-maintained trail. It has tremendous pocket water that holds large cutthroat well into August.

The Greys River is the last major tributary of the Snake River upstream of Palisades Reservoir. This classic freestone stream has good fishing throughout. Most agree, however, that the upper portion is where the really good fishing starts, and it gets better as you move upstream. The Greys River Road runs alongside the entire length of the stream, making access very easy. Kayakers enjoy this river as much as anglers. They tend to prefer the lower section, below where the best fishing is. I try and fish the Greys at least once a year. One of my favorite excursions is to fish the river up to its headwaters, and then cross the divide and fish La Barge Creek (a tributary of the Green River) down to the town of La Barge. It is at least a two-day trip, but one that is well worth it.

Other Streams and Tributaries: Cottonwood Creek, Fish Creek, Flat Creek, Blacktail Ponds and the Salt River

Cottonwood Creek is a beautiful stream flowing out of Jenny Lake. It enters the Snake River approximately two miles above Moose Landing. I have never noticed Cottonwood Creek to receive a lot of fishing pressure. It officially opens to fishing on August 1st.Cottonwood Creek is a tough body of water to fish because of its small size and the amount of surrounding vegetation. But in several spots, the creek has decent-sized ponds where large cutthroat hold among cottonwoods and aspens that have been fallen by beaver. These beaver ponds are actually very accessible to anglers. One of the best is only a short walk downstream from where the Inner-Loop Road of Grand Teton National Park crosses Cottonwood Creek. One can park and prepare gear in the parking lot next to the bridge.

Fish Creek enters the Snake River on the west bank approximately four miles south of the village of Wilson. It is heavily influenced by a high concentration of spring creeks, the most famous of which are in the vicinity of Crescent H Ranch and River Meadow Ranch. Almost all of this is blue-ribbon trout water. Unfortunately, almost all of it is located on private land. The one exception is the small piece of public access located on Fish Creek Road, just north of Wilson. Here, one can fish this outstanding stream and experience what only a handful of landowners and their guests experience. It's not a large access point, and it is only partially marked. So make sure you are not trespassing.

World-famous Flat Creek leaves its headwaters high in the Gros Ventre Wilderness and flows down through the southern extreme of Jackson Hole before entering the Snake River above Snake River Canyon. The most popular part of this enchanting little stream is located in the National Elk Refuge. Fishing here opens on August 1st. The first two weeks are typically crowded. Very large Snake River cutthroat call this meandering stretch of creek home. The Wyoming Game and Fish Department has done an incredible job of making this section of Flat Creek what it is today. Anglers do very well in the Refuge section with terrestrial patterns, caddis (particularly Partridge Caddis and Chamois Caddis) and *Baetis* patterns. The cutthroat get very wise, very fast after the first week of August. By then I am typically down to 6X leader and am stalking trout like I do nowhere else in the region. It can be extremely frustrating, but also extremely fun.

After leaving the refuge, Flat Creek flows through the town of Jackson, where only children under the age of 14 are allowed to fish. As someone who grew up on this creek, I can tell you that the fish here are plentiful and big and it was a great place for someone like myself to hone his skills at an early age. Once Flat Creek leaves the town of Jackson, it flows through a long stretch of private ranchland and then enters the South Park Feed Grounds before flowing into the Snake River. Fishing in the South Park Feed Grounds is open during all of the general season and is far less crowded that what is typically found in the Elk Refuge. The fishing does pale in comparison, but the southern end of Jackson Hole is beautiful and it makes for a nice change of pace at times.

An alternative to Flat Creek is the Blacktail ponds and their outlet streams. These waters open to fishing on April 1st but typically receive less pressure than what is found on Flat Creek. Cutthroat in the Blacktail ponds grow to impressive sizes and, like Flat Creek, feed opportunistically until the middle of August. After that, they become a bit wiser about what they are feeding on. The access to the ponds is approximately one mile north of Moose Junction on Highway 26/89. It's a short walk down a steep hillside from the access point to the first streams that can be fished.

The Salt River is not an official tributary of the Snake River today. Before the dam at Palisades was erected in the late 1950s, the Salt was a major tributary and had a significant impact on the drainage. Today it flows directly into Palisades Reservoir and still plays an important role. Although a strong cutthroat fishery, the Salt also has one of the healthiest populations of brown trout in the Snake River drainage. There are several public access points maintained by the Wyoming Game and Fish Department. The best can be found at Auburn Bridge, Silver Stream, and McCoy Creek. To a large extent, this river is surrounded by private land, most of which is used for agricultural purposes. I have never had any kind of problem with landowners on the Salt, nor have I heard of any confrontations. Your best advice is to simply obey posted trespassing notices and stay within the actual riverbed.

Part II: The South Fork of the Snake River, Idaho

Natural & Human History of a Fly-Fishing Paradise

Upon crossing the Wyoming-Idaho border at Palisades Reservoir, the Snake River officially becomes known as the South Fork of the Snake River. The label assists in differentiating it from the North Fork of the Snake River, more commonly known as the Henry's Fork. The earthen dam that acts as the South Fork's starting point is maintained by the Bureau of Reclamation. It was constructed in the mid-1950s for irrigation demand downstream in the Minidoka region of central Idaho. In building the reservoir, the Bureau flooded 15,000 acres of prime ranchland in an area formerly known as Grand Valley. Old-timers who remember Grand Valley before the building of the reservoir tell stories of exquisite hot springs that were popular amongst local teenagers during long winters. This should come as no surprise, for the Grand Valley Fault has produced several thermal features throughout the immediate region. Old-timers also tell stories of the excellent fishing that existed here before the dam. Several major tributaries flowed into the Snake River here, including the Salt River, Indian Creek, Gear Creek, Big and Little Elk Creek, and McCoy Creek.

Palisades Reservoir acts as a convenient man-made break between the upper Snake and the South Fork. But through research I have done on the entire waterway during my lifetime, I have reason to believe that Grand Valley was a natural break even before the installation of the dam. It was a natural separation between two very different parts of the same river. Swift, freestone tributaries and spring creeks come to an end in the vicinity of Palisades for the most part. This contributes to the different abundance of Yellowstone and fine-spotted cutthroat on the two different portions of river. The slope from the mouth of Snake River Canyon on down to the confluence of the South Fork with the North Fork is considerably less than what is found upstream in Jackson Hole. The elevation is considerably lower as well—5,372 feet above sea level at Palisades Dam compared to 6,770 feet at Jackson Lake. While total volume increases, comparative flow rates decrease because the gradient is less dramatic. The South Fork is fed from the bottom of Palisades Reservoir, which leads to colder overall water temperatures. The consequence of these factors is a much more hospitable environment for trout and other fish. Holding water is more abundant, as is trout food such as aquatic insects and baitfish. For this reason, exotic trout species such as rainbows and browns have done well. And for all trout species, sizes are consistently larger on the South Fork than on most western streams.

As the South Fork leaves Palisades Reservoir, it runs northwest through a riverbed constricted primarily to one channel. Further downstream, islands will form in some places and cause side channels to break away from the main course of the stream. But for the most part, the principle feature of the South Fork is that of a channelized river with less structure and braiding than found on the Snake River in Wyoming. There are only a few tributaries flowing into the river below Palisades Reservoir. This makes the dam the primary source of water for the South Fork and the key determinant of the physical character of the river.

The first geographic feature the South Fork flows through is Swan Valley. It is flanked by three ranges: the Caribou Mountains to the south and the Big Hole and Snake River Mountains to the north. These are not massive ranges. Even their tallest summits are dwarfed by peaks found farther upstream. There are only a few streams flowing into Swan Valley from the Caribou and Big Hole But mountains. But those that do—especially Palisades Creek, Rainey Creek, and Fall Creek—contribute the majority of in-flow to the South Fork. They are vitally important to this river and the trout that call it home.

Continuing downstream, the South Fork flows though a tight draw at the northwest end of Swan Valley where thumbs of the Big Hole and Caribou ranges jut out toward each other. The only thing separating the two mountains groups at this draw is the Snake River. After leaving Swan Valley, the river runs along the northeast end of Conant Valley and then flows into one of the most dramatic physical feature in eastern Idaho: the Canyon of the South Fork. The Snake River runs between high volcanic walls composed of rhyolite and basalt before opening up onto the Great Snake River Plain. It will be joined by the Henry's Fork further downstream and then continue its journey to the Columbia River.

Eastern Idaho was Indian country. Bands of Shoshone-Bannock and Blackfoot would frequent the area during most of the year. They used the Snake River as a source for water and fish to supplement their diets. The Bannocks established a buffalo hunting route known simply as the Bannock Trail that ran into Yellowstone and Montana. Swan Valley, Conant Valley, and the Canyon of the South

Fork could have seen its first Europeans in 1811 when Wilson Price Hunt's Astorian party was traveling west to the mouth of the Columbia River. The raging currents of the Snake River Canyon in Wyoming stopped them in their tracks. They were forced to go farther north over Teton Pass. The record of the first Europeans to venture along the banks of the South Fork is sketchy at best, but no doubt, French and English speaking trappers were scouring the area for beaver through the first half of the nineteenth century.

A ferry was established in the 1860s in the small settlement of Eagle Rock—latter to become Idaho Falls. A bridge followed, and soon the growing town became the economic and social center for the increasing number of farms in the region. In the 1880s, Conant Valley, Swan Valley, and the Antelope Flats area were becoming increasingly dominated by agriculture. The Snake River and its small number of tributaries provided a direct source for irrigation water. By this time, the Utah and Northern Railroad had arrived in Eagle Rock on its path from Ogden, Utah to Butte, Montana. Known as the Yellowstone Branch of the Union Pacific, it would connect well-to-do anglers for the first time to treasured trout streams like the Madison and the Henry's Fork.

While the railroad connected wealthy eastern anglers with the fantastic waters to the north, the South Fork remained isolated. It wasn't until the 1940s that a paved version of Highway 26 replaced the dirt and gravel roads that had for decades linked the small agricultural communities along the river to Idaho Falls. For the most part, locals had the South Fork to themselves throughout the first half of the twentieth century. Resident anglers and tiers—including Thone Roos, Etsel Radford, and Ardell Jeppsen—did much to advance the sport locally during these early days. Radford's Fizzler and Jeppsen's Super Renegade (formerly known as the Hooligan) were renowned South Fork patterns.

Unmatched in her impact on fly-fishing in the South Fork area was Marcella Oswald.

She operated a sporting goods shop on First Street in Idaho Falls with her husband Harvey from the 1940s through the 1970s. A self-taught tier, Marcella developed a reputation for durable and effective flies. She and Harvey were recognized as *the* primary suppliers of South Fork patterns. In his book *Snake River Country* (1991, Frank Amato Publications), Bruce Staples claims that, "There is no food form that Marcella couldn't create a pattern for and which did not become locally popular." Among her best-known flies is Marcella's Trout Fly, which arose out of local demand for a pattern that could imitate the giant salmonflies that emerge on the river in early summer. It has remained synonymous with fly-fishing on the South Fork to this day. She dispensed her knowledge to local sportsmen through classes she taught at the Idaho Falls City Recreation Center.

Stan Yamamura was a master fly designer who met local demand for quality patterns and tying materials through his wholesale outfit—Stan's Flies. The popularity of his patterns eventually reached the waters of Wyoming and Montana. What Marcella Oswald was to East Idaho fly-tying in the 1950s and 1960s, Stan was in the 1970s. His influence extends to the realm of conservation as well. In 1972, he was a founding member of the Upper Snake River Chapter of Trout Unlimited.

Ralph Alexander's Hackle Den began in his home in Idaho Falls in the late 1970s. Ralph moved to a Second Street location to be the first full-service fly-fishing shop in Idaho Falls. Marcella Oswald was one of his employees at that location and at his expanded location on First Street. At his First Street location, Alexander featured tying demonstrations by renowned tiers including Bing Lempke, Charlie Brooks, Bruce Staples and Buck Goodrich. Alexander retired from the business in 1985.

Guiding on the South Fork was in its infancy during the first half of the century. As a national highway system developed, more visiting anglers began to frequent the South Fork. Alma Kunz's lodge in Teton Valley, Idaho, mainly hosted fishing excursions on the Henry's Fork and Teton River but offered occasional trips on the South Fork as well. They started floating it in earnest in the 1970s. The Champions of Swan Valley offered guide services through their store, the Irwin Trading Post. New England native Bob Bean settled in Blackfoot, Idaho and in the 1960s and 1970s offered tying classes and fly-fishing instruction through the Blackfoot Community Center and Lifetime Sports courses at local schools. Bob's son, Mike Bean, is today the head guide for The Lodge at Palisades Creek.

The 1980s and 1990s saw a veritable explosion of interest in fly-fishing on the South Fork of the Snake River. In many ways, it rivals the popularity of the Henry's Fork today. Wes Newman was a local angler who was at the forefront of this emerging interest. Although now residing in Kansas and far removed from the Snake River, he is still recognized as an authority on patterns and techniques for the river and area trunk streams. It was during these years that we saw the rise of premier streamside fishing lodges like the Lodge at Palisades Creek and Spence Warner's South Fork Lodge. In 1986, Jim Gabettas opened Jimmy's All Seasons Angler in Idaho Falls. This fly shop acts as an unofficial information center for East Idaho fly-fishers. Today, these operations are staffed with some of the most renowned contemporary guides, tiers, and river authorities on the South Fork—people like Bruce Staples, Brenda Swinney, Ken Burkholder, and Ooley Piram. Together, they continue the legacy of a tremendous angling heritage on one of America's greatest trout streams.

Trout of the South Fork

In the opening of this book, I spoke of the subtle differences between the Upper Snake River and the South Fork. One of these is the abundance of various trout species. Both sections of the Snake River contain cutthroat, rainbows, and browns. But while cutthroat clearly dominate above Palisades, the South Fork has comparatively strong concentrations of all three species. This can be attributed to the more hospitable environment this section of river offers. A lower elevation, more holding water, and more aquatic invertebrates make it possible for non-native species to thrive alongside native cutthroat. Current estimates by the Idaho Department of Game and Fish suggest that total trout numbers on the South Fork are well over 5,000 per mile.

Yellowstone Cutthroat Trout
(*Oncorhynchus clarki bouvieri*)

Yellowstone cutthroat are officially the only trout native to this part of the Snake River. They exist below the South Fork on the main stem of the river down to Shoshone Falls, upstream of the South Fork on the Snake River in Wyoming, and on the east slope of the continental divide in the Yellowstone River drainage. Their traditional habitat included the Henry's Fork of the Snake River. Overharvesting and the stocking of rainbow trout have led to the virtual disappearance of cutthroat from this part of the drainage. Snake River fine-spotted cutthroat do not *officially* exist below Palisades Reservoir. Idaho's Department of Fish and Game does not recognize the fine-spotted cutthroat as a subspecies, instead classifying it alongside Yellowstone cutthroat as the same trout. Nevertheless, many local fly-fishers make such a distinction and claim to catch members of both subspecies on the South Fork every season.

The completion of Palisades Reservoir effectively cut off both Yellowstone and Snake River fine-spotted cutthroat from upstream migration to prime spring creeks and tributaries. The dam also obstructed the upstream spawning migration of a particular strain of Yellowstone cutthroat that often produced extremely large individuals. This strain was centered in the upper reaches of the canyon, just below Conant Valley. There is uncertainty as to whether or not these cutthroat have perished. If they do still exist, there is no doubt that they are only a fraction of their original abundance.

Yellowstone cutthroat hold in a variety of water types but prefer riffles, riffle pools, shelves, and structure. They readily take dry flies and will also consume nymphs, baitfish, and other subsurface foods. Sizes can range from six-inch fingerlings to girthy 20-plus-inch individuals. Like their Wyoming counterparts, they spawn primarily in tributaries, the most important of which are Palisades, Rainey, Pine and Burns creeks. This typically occurs from early June to late July. Spawning of cutthroat on the South Fork also occurs from late April through mid-July, although to a lesser degree than that which occurs on tributaries. The classic spotting pattern and colored slashes under the jaw that I described in Part I of this book is also present with South Fork cutthroat. They are found in abundant numbers on all sections of the river. However, that abundance has been threatened in recent years. Habitat alteration and manipulation of natural stream flow are major culprits, but so too is the introduction of non-native species, particularly rainbow trout. Matt Woodard and the Home Rivers Office of Trout Unlimited in Idaho Falls are attempting to circumvent these threats by funding and overseeing the reconnection of Pritchard and Garden creeks to the South Fork in Conant Valley. Both have the potential now of being spawning streams for cutthoat.

Rainbow Trout
(*Oncorhynchus mykiss*)

Rainbows were first introduced to the South Fork of the Snake River in the early 1900s by the U.S. Fish and Wildlife Service, but the most intensive stockings occurred from the 1960s until the early 1980s. This was a response to the growing fishing industry on the river and concerns over harvesting and the sustainability of trout. Rainbow trout were the easiest to raise in hatcheries and readily available. They were also highly desirable among the angling community, primarily because of their fighting ability and the size they can attain under ideal conditions. The size of these trout on the South Fork is competitive with the more prestigious rainbow streams in the American West. I have caught several over 20 inches during my guiding tenure on the river. In 2004, I witnessed a client of James Osmond, head guide of Heise Expeditions, land a 24-1/2-inch rainbow in the canyon section of the South Fork. There is no doubt that bigger ones are out there.

The holding and feeding water rainbows typically access is similar to that of cutthroat. This does not mean, however, that they necessarily feed in the same way. Rainbows have

A rainbow caught on the Upper South Fork. Jason Sutton

a propensity to feed on subsurface invertebrates. Some say more so than their close cousin, the cutthroat. This makes nymphing a highly effective form of fly-fishing for those targeting rainbows. I have most luck on *Baetis* nymphs, but they tend to be highly selective when feeding on these aquatic insects. Rainbows will certainly feed on caddis pupae and stonefly nymphs, especially when these insects are preparing to emerge. The 25-inch rainbow that James Osmond's client landed in 2004 was caught on a #16 Bead Head Pheasant Tail. Count on surface feeding among rainbows during the early part of thick hatches, particularly pmds and caddis and, to a lesser degree, salmonflies and golden stoneflies.

Rainbow trout abundance is much stronger on the upper part of the South Fork than on the lower section, where they make up less than 1% of total trout numbers (see Table 7, page 68). Fishery biologists are still at a loss to explain why this is. There does not seem to be any considerable physical differences between the two parts of the river. Perhaps it is a mysterious natural barrier. If so, it is an effective one. Rainbows from the Henry's Fork, which merges with the South Fork just above Menan Buttes, have not shown significant signs of running up the South Fork and have not taken up residence there.

Rainbow trout can spawn in the main river, primarily in side channels. But they can also spawn heavily in tributaries, often in the same beds as cutthroat. This creates a situation of hybridization and the destruction of the genetic lineage of wild cutthroat. Serious concern has been raised over the introduction of rainbows to the South Fork of the Snake River and the subsequent decline of total cutthroat abundance. It is a contentious issue that has pitted guide against guide, fly shop against angler, and the State of Idaho against certain segments of the fishing public. There are those who feel that the South Fork can become a stream that sustains both types of trout and those who feel that rainbow numbers should be reduced significantly to protect native cutthroats. Others feel the South Fork would be better off as a rainbow stream at the expense of the cutthroat. The Idaho Department of Fish and Game and the Bureau of Reclamation are making a considerable, albeit controversial, effort to control the problem. These two agencies have developed a three-pronged attack in an attempt to contain the rainbow population. The plan includes the manipulation of seasonal releases from Palisades Dam to better mimic the natural flow of the river, a weir system on tributaries to prevent rainbows from spawning with cutthroat, and a no limit on caught rainbows. Jim Fredericks of the Idaho Department of Fish and Game has shown data from recent electro-shocking that shows a decline in rainbow numbers that are 12 inches or larger. This suggests that the harvesting

Table 7. Trout Abundance for the Lower South Fork*

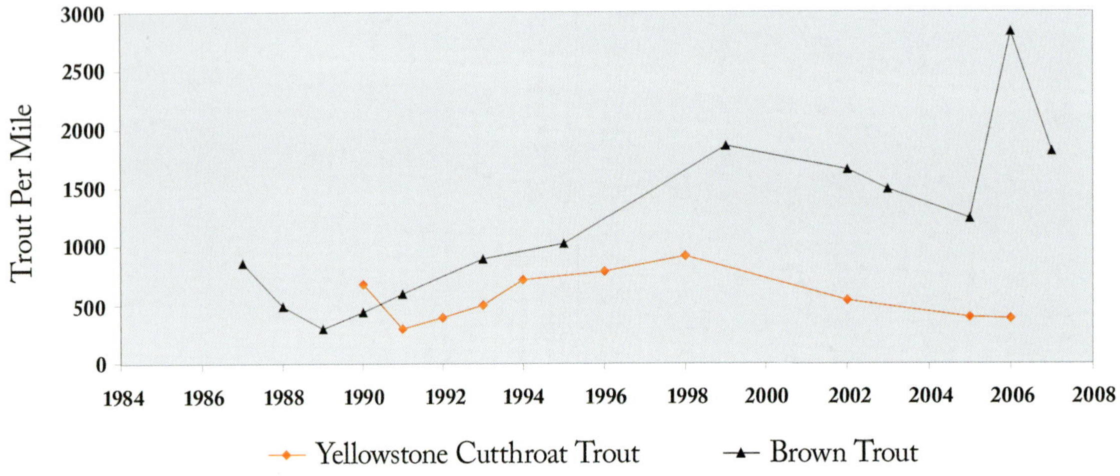

	Trout Per Mile		
Year	*Cutthroat*	*Rainbow*	*Brown*
1987	680	NA	855
1988	301	NA	484
1989	399	NA	299
1990	496	NA	439
1991	717	NA	595
1992	NA	NA	NA
1993	784	NA	894
1994	NA	NA	NA
1995	915	NA	1029
1996	NA	NA	NA
1997	NA	NA	NA
1998	NA	NA	NA
1999	540	NA	1852
2000	NA	NA	NA
2001	NA	NA	NA
2002	396	NA	1658
2003	382	NA	1492
2004	NA	NA	NA
2005	122	NA	1242
2006	187	NA	2837
2007	NA	NA	1812

*Measurements taken in the vicinity of Lorenzo Boat Launch.

Trout Abundance for the Upper South Fork *

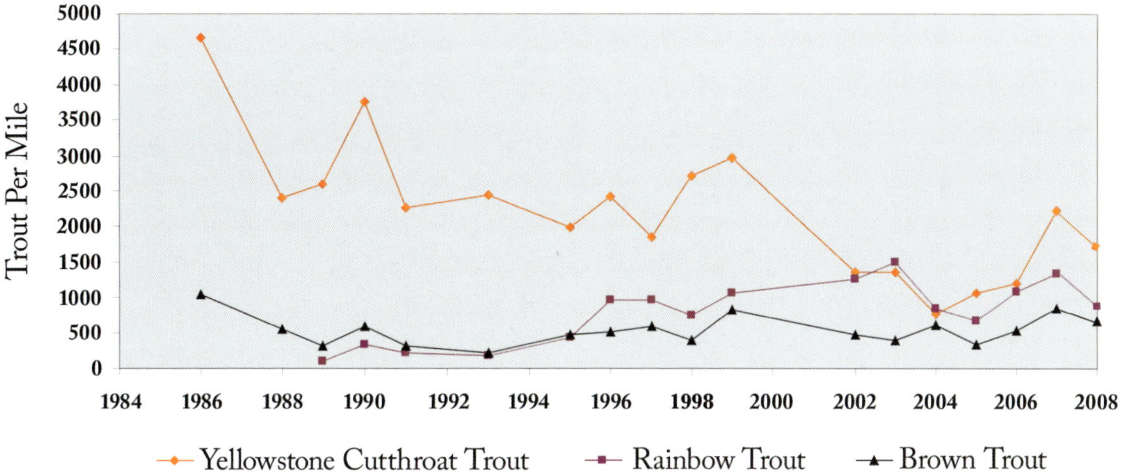

	Trout Per Mile		
Year	*Cutthroat*	*Rainbow*	*Brown*
1986	4,659	NA	1034
1987	NA	NA	NA
1988	2,404	NA	548
1989	2,595	102	308
1990	3,756	330	594
1991	2,255	216	314
1992	NA	NA	NA
1993	2,437	177	218
1994	NA	NA	NA
1995	1,983	436	474
1996	2,421	958	506
1997	1,845	974	595
1998	2,726	743	401
1999	2,977	1055	825
2000	NA	NA	NA
2001	NA	NA	NA
2002	1,355	1265	463
2003	1,353	1501	386
2004	771	854	618
2005	1,061	678	333
2006	1,207	1092	531
2007	2,224	1329	854
2008	1716	925	612

* Measurements taken in the vicinity of the Conant Boat Launch

Jason Sutton

A brown trout taken on the lower South Fork.

and flow manipulation elements of the current plan may be having an impact. Regardless, the jury is still out as to whether this program is having a positive affect.

Loch Leven Brown Trout
(*Salmo trutta levenensis*)

Like rainbow trout, brown trout were first stocked in the South Fork in the early 1900s. Stockings were far less frequent than rainbow plantings and they typically contained far fewer fish. Still, the trout friendly environs of the South Fork have allowed browns to carve out a nice niche for themselves among the total abundance of trout on the river. No efforts have been made toward the control of their population, as they do not create problems of hybridization or severe propagation so often associated with rainbow trout. South Fork brown trout have remained a popular fixture among local and visiting anglers alike. They are by far the largest trout on the South Fork. The Idaho state-record brown trout came from the South Fork of the Snake River in 1981. It weighed in at over 26 pounds!

South Fork brown trout are not big fans of swift water, which is why they typically shy away from riffles and riffle pools. In my experience, they typically favor three water types. The first of these is structure. Browns have a fondness for good cover, especially fallen trees, log jams, and brush piles, which provide them protection and current breaks where they can hold without expending energy. This desire for cover draws brown trout to a second type of water: banks, specifically undercut banks. Undercut banks, a plentiful feature along many sections of the South Fork, provides sufficient holding water for brown trout and gives them easy access to terrestrial and stonefly adults when they fall to the river's surface. Lastly, brown trout will frequent what many anglers call *skinny water*.

Skinny water is characterized by long, slow-moving, shallow cobblestone flats that stand next to featureless banks. The word "skinny" refers to the shallowness and lack of significant current found in this water type. Generally the water is no deeper than two feet. Brown trout that hold in skinny water are often larger than average—17 inches or more. This makes it a fun type of water to target with nymphs, emergers and dry flies. Several times I have witnessed a large brown, holding in a foot-and-a-half of water, move from its feeding zone to engulf a #6 salmonfly imitation. In skinny water, such a move creates an impressive wake on the surface and the trout is completely visible as it prepares to strike. It is a remarkable sight.

Brown trout are most numerous on the low sections, from the middle of the Canyon section (around Cottonwood Flats) to Menan Buttes. In fact, electroshock data in 2003 suggests that they outnumber cutthroat by more than four to one in the vicinity of Lorenzo Bridge. This is also where the largest members of the population can be found. Why browns choose the lower part of the river over the upper is surprising when one considers the difference in water temperature. On the upper section, water is fed into the river from the bottom of Palisades Reservoir, which keeps water temperatures on the river consistently in the 50s or lower 60s during the season. These low temperatures are further maintained by the inflow from tributaries on the upper section. Once the river begins to move into the canyon, median water temperatures begin to rise. By the time it reaches Lorenzo, these temperatures can be well over 60 degrees.

Research based on the observations of brown trout in wild habitats suggests that they are not highly adaptable to temperature extremes. In *Yellowstone Fishes* (Stackpole Books, 1998), Varley and Schullery provide evidence of this among the Von Behr browns in the upper reaches of the Madison River drainage. The browns here are less able to survive the extremely warm temperatures of the Firehole than the cooler temperatures found downstream on the main stem of the Madison, where their numbers are more plentiful and sizes much larger. Despite this, the browns on the South Fork favor the lower section of the river and the higher water temperatures that go with it. Perhaps the water temperatures upstream are too low. Varley and Schullery have suggested that cold headwaters in the same drainage are not preferred by brown trout either.

Like their counterparts on the upper Snake River in Wyoming, brown trout on the South Fork are for the most part descendents of the Loch Leven strain. However, there is uncertainty as to the purity of this strain. Fishery biologists speculate that a certain degree of crossbreeding between similar species occurred in American hatcheries during earlier decades.

Trout Food, Hatches, & Fly Patterns of the South Fork

The relatively low elevation and diverse riparian environment of the South Fork makes it a virtual river-of-plenty for its resident trout population. It is one of the most noticeable differences between the two sections of river in Wyoming and Idaho. In all aspects of available trout food—from aquatic invertebrates to terrestrial insects to baitfish—the South Fork is abundant. There is also a significant diversity in trout food. However, it is not as common to find as many multiple hatches of aquatic insects on the South Fork as there are on the upper Snake. In some cases—such as with several terrestrial and caddis—the individual insects are actually smaller on Idaho's section of the river. But for the most part, the South Fork has the advantage. Hatches are thicker and sub-aquatic food is plentiful year round.

Aquatic Insects

Several aquatic insects call the South Fork home, but there are four particular bugs that I will focus on in this journal. They are among the most abundant and most important to trout. They have also contributed to the development of several patterns from regional tiers. These insects are: the salmonfly (*Pteronarcys californica*), the golden stone (*Calineuria* or *Hesperoperla californica*), the pale morning dun (*Ephemerella infrequens* and *E. inermis*), and the October caddis (*Dicosmoecus gilvipes* and *jucundus*).

Salmonflies

The sheer size and number of salmonflies make them a critical food type for trout on the South Fork. On average, they are between 30 to 50 millimeters in length. Their annual emergence in early summer is feverishly anticipated by all the anglers in the area, (not to mention the hordes of visiting fly-fishermen who flock to eastern Idaho for this almost festive-like occasion). I like to think of the South Fork salmonfly hatch as more of a *bug burst*. Over a four-week period, salmonflies shed their shucks into literal piles on the banks and take to the air in thick waves all along the stream. Casting to some of the West's largest trout as they attempt to devour these enormous two-plus-inch bugs is a treat for anyone lucky enough to be on the river when salmonflies make their appearance. Salmonflies typically hatch on the South Fork between the middle of June and the middle of July. As water temperatures approach 54 to 55 degrees, nymphs will begin to crawl from the streambed to emerge. When water temperatures hit 58 degrees, hatches are typically in full swing.

The salmonfly hatch is an absolute joy to fish, but it can also be highly challenging. Seasonal runoff and demand for irrigation water downstream during the early summer months when salmonflies emerge can cause flows to vary dramatically. When flows begin to creep above 16,000 cfs, subpar fishing can result. The nature of the hatch itself is another perplexing element for the angler. Salmonflies start emerging on the lower sections of the river and work their way upstream to Palisades Dam. Once the hatch appears on a particular stretch of the stream, it will only be a matter of time before trout gorge themselves on these behemoth bugs. Stoneflies can live up to a week after their emergence. But if you hit a stretch even a couple of days after their first appearance, you might be casting to trout that are completely sated from overfeeding.

The South Fork salmonfly hatch is also notoriously inconsistent from year to year. I will use recent history as an example. 2000 and 2001 were considered two of the most prolific hatches in recent memory. From the Henry's Fork confluence to Palisades Dam, the entire river experienced tremendous salmonfly activity. 2002 witnessed a strong hatch also, but one that only made it halfway upstream, to the middle of the lower canyon section. Adult salmonflies were almost non-existent on the upper half of the river. In 2003, the hatch was noticeably weaker than usual. An angler should certainly take all of these complexities into account when preparing for this hatch. But don't be fooled by the difficulties that can arise. Regardless of high flow levels and

Evidence of the South Fork's salmonfly "bug burst".

A salmonfly during emergence.

hatch inconsistency, being prepared with the proper patterns and tactics can make fishing the South Fork salmonfly hatch worthwhile almost any given year.

There is one simple rule in pattern selection for the salmonfly hatch: go big! They offer a huge year-round meal while in their nymphal stage, and during the hatch, trout will selectively feed on these giant bugs. This does not mean that you will need a perfect imitation. The silhouette and color of your pattern are important, but they are secondary to size. A #6 hook is typical of the standard salmonfly pattern, while #4 is by no means out of the question. Attractors such as the Chernobyl Ant, Willie's Red Ant, the Double Humpy, the Rubber Legged Double Humpy, and the Taranasty are among the most popular. Marcella's Trout Fly is a classic dating back to the 1950s and is still in use today.

A pattern that has gained more recent popularity among salmonfly enthusiasts is the Tara X. This large attractor of mysterious origin is thought by many area anglers to be an adaptation of Guy Turck's famed Tarantula. The Tara X can be constructed from both foam and dubbing material. Most fly-fishermen tend to use visually stimulating orange foam or Angora. The black tips of a golden pheasant tippet will match the egg sac on an egg-positing female. A standing deer-hair and calf-tail wing gives the appearance of a fluttering wing of a salmonfly as it skirts along the surface. A Tara X that incorporates these materials together will offer one of the most visually imitative patterns for the salmonfly in use today.

Dry-fly action can be extraordinary, but many overlook the fact that there is a lot of subsurface activity as well. While salmonflies are mating along the banks and positing eggs on the stream surface, they are at the same time crawling from the riverbed to emerge. This makes fishing with stonefly-nymph imitations an effective strategy. One of my all-time favorites is the Crystal Creek Stone Nymph that I tie with exaggerated rubber legs. Bumping this big nymph along the cobblestone river bottom close to the bank can almost guarantee strikes during the height of the salmonfly hatch. Classic patterns work as well. The Bitch Creek Nymph is still a standby, as is Lawson's Henry's Fork Stone Nymph.

Golden Stoneflies

When using taxonomic classifications, local anglers often refer to golden stoneflies on the South Fork as *californica* species of the genus *Calineuria.* However, local entomologists I have spoken to claim that the golden stones on the South Fork are actually *californica* species of the genus *Hesperoperla*. Others claim that both species are present. In my opinion, the differences between the two are so minute that anglers should not care too much. I am sure the trout don't care too much either. For the sake of diplomacy, I refer to both species when discussing golden stoneflies.

Golden stoneflies generally emerge in early July on the heels of the stonefly hatch. They appear on all sections of the river. The hatch is best on the upper stretches, from Palisades Dam down to the middle of the Canyon. Golden stoneflies will emerge throughout the summer, though their hatch often reaches its climax by the end of July. This hatch is not near as thick as the salmonfly hatch and individual golden stones—at 20 to 40 millimeters in length—are not as big as individual salmonflies. But you will still notice them. The lifecycle of golden stones is similar to that of most large stoneflies. They typically live between two to four years in their nymphal stage before emerging. As mature nymphs, they crawl from the streambed onto banks, foliage, and structure, where they then split their shucks open and emerge as full-fledged adults. After mating on the banks, the females take to the air and the river to deposit their eggs. These egg-positing stoneflies, along with the hundred that will fall from banks and structure to the stream surface, are irresistibly easy pickings for trout.

Immediately following the defining salmonfly hatch season, one would think that golden stoneflies would go almost unnoticed in comparison to salmonflies. This is only partially true. Salmonflies signal the official high-intensity kickoff to the fly-fishing season on the South Fork. But upon the first sign of golden stones, we anglers are reminded that yet another stage of the fishing season has come upon us.

Table 8. Hatch Chart for South Fork of the Snake River *

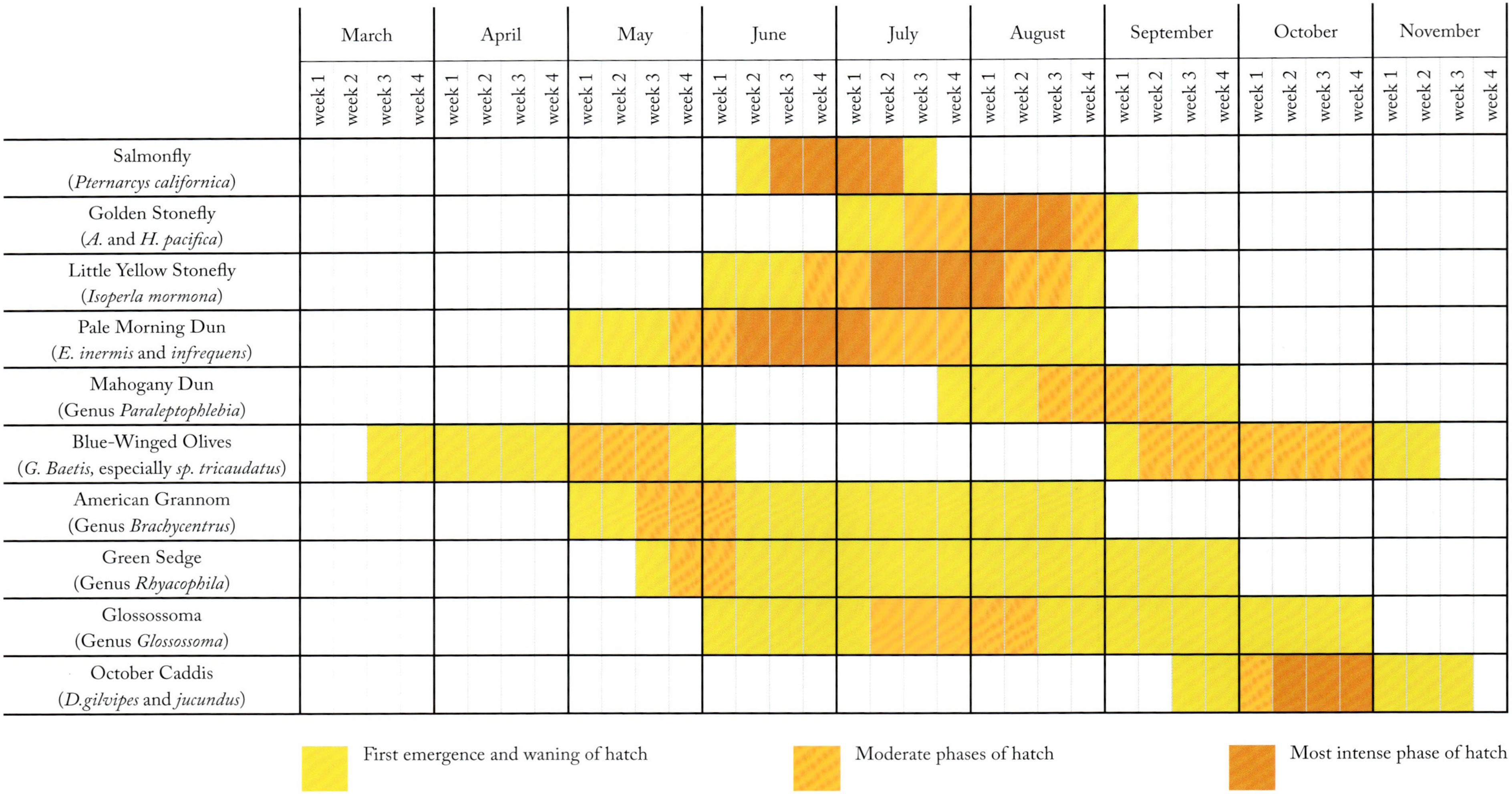

* This chart's information should be considered generalization of the hatches that occur on Upper Snake River and the South Fork of the Snake River. The hatches displayed here vary throughout the year based on climatological and hydrological patterns. Do not make the mistake, as so many do when they turn to hatch charts, of taking this information as literal gospel handed down from the heavens.

The golden stonefly hatch is more gradual and steady in comparison to the literal wave-like salmonfly hatch. They will also be on the scene for a longer duration, sometimes for six weeks or more. Golden stones do not attract the extreme number of visiting anglers that the salmonflies draws. Nevertheless, there are still quite a few who come to fish the South Fork from the middle of July through August—during the period when golden stoneflies emerge—because the fishing can be so good.

Classic attractors like the Madam X and the Double Humpy are terrific patterns to use when golden stones begin to emerge. More recent patterns such as Guy Turck's Golden Tarantula, Jack Dennis' Amy Special, and yellow foam-bodied Tara Xs are among the favorites of local anglers and guides. The title of "most popular pattern" to match golden stoneflies over the past five years probably goes to Brenda Swinney's Plan B. This foam-bodied variation of the Chernobyl Ant has an uncanny ability of attracting trout even during times of above average air and water temperatures, something that can afflict eastern Idaho when these insects are about. Tied in #8 to 10, and with a thin foam body, the Plan B is one of the most effective flies on the South Fork today.

Like the salmonfly hatch, too much attention is paid to what is happening on the surface. I am typically below the surface at least half the time when golden stoneflies are emerging. I stick to three nymphs inparticular. The classic among these is Kaufmann's Golden Stone. I will also use a Golden Rubberlegs, a pattern developed by Arrick Swanson of West Yellowstone, Montana, which is popular on the Madison River. My favorite, however, is Scott Sanchez's Spandex Stone Nymph. This nymph features two beads—one for the head and one for the thorax—for extra depth. The golden yarn or dubbing incorporated into the bodies of these nymphs around the thorax give a realistic impression of gills on the natural. I fish these no bigger than a #8, and with the extra bead head it has no trouble getting down to the bottom, where trout do almost all their feeding on stonefly nymphs.

Pale Morning Duns

The pale morning dun (PMD) is just one of many mayflies that makes an appearance on the South Fork. Having to choose one that is my favorite is a rather difficult decision. For me, it is probably a toss-up between the PMD and the mahogany dun. I like mahoganies because of their late-season emergence and the fact that there are so many patterns available that imitate their specific life stages. But due to the vastness of the hatches and the number of times that it appears during a season, the PMD takes the cake as my all-around favorite mayfly on the South Fork. It receives an unequal share of attention from most area anglers. PMDs first show up in early June and continue to hatch through the summer and early fall. They emerge in a variety of weather and temperature situations with hatches typically lasting only a couple of hours. However, when climatological conditions are ideal (cool and overcast or cloudy with light rain) a PMD emergence can last for several hours. These conditions can also trigger thick emergences that blanket slow-moving side channels.

PMDs are minute, measuring between eight and 12 millimeters in length. Several species exist on the South Fork, of which *inermis* is probably the most common. PMDs have two distinct surface stages: the dun stage, when they are fully emerged; and the spinner stage, when they are spending the last of their energy reserves mating and then positing eggs on the surface of the stream. During the dun stage, the PMD has a pale yellow color with wings standing vertically from the body. This makes it easy to spot for both fly-fishers and trout. During the spinner stage, it has a reddish or rust color and wings that either remain standing vertically or lay horizontally from the body in a spent fashion on the water. A simple PMD Comparadun and CDC Rusty Spinner are usually all one needs to match the two different stages of this hatch. I stick to these two most of the time. I fish both flies concurrently, due to the fact that the two stages can occur simultaneously on longer, drawn out hatches. But don't shy away from more general patterns like small (no bigger than a #16) Humpies, Parawulffs, White Wulffs, and Variants. These are tried and true patterns that work well when looking to imitate PMDs.

October Caddis

I spoke briefly about these large insects—sometimes called giant orange sedges or fall caddis—in the previous section about the Upper Snake River. I mention them here because they are an important trout food on the South Fork as well. The primary difference I have observed among October caddis on these two sections of river is size. They tend to be slightly smaller (three to five millimeters) on the South Fork. Caddis are plentiful here and several species emerge throughout a give season. As their name suggests, October caddis emergences begin in early autumn and continue through the month that bares their name, or perhaps vice versa. As larvae, they spend most of their lives in cases built from stream-bottom sediment. But they do a lot of moving about as they feed, rebuild cases, and find suitable water for pupation. October caddis will primarily crawl to streamside structure and foliage to emerge, although there are several species that will swim to the surface and emerge while still in water.

Mating starts almost immediately after the hatch. Egg-depositing females will do some heavy moving on the water, skirting along the surface with fluttering wings. This generally acts as a major attractant for trout. Thus, the skirting movement I described above with salmonfly imitations also works well with October caddis. Due to the close time interval between emergence, mating and ovipositing,

Large October caddis patterns are often used on the South Fork of the Snake River in the fall.

fishing a double rig with an adult and pupa imitation works well for me. A standard #8 orange-bodied Elk Hair Caddis with red hackle is one of the easiest flies one can use for a surface imitation. For the pupa, I like to use an enlarged version of Craig Mathews and John Juracek's X-Caddis. I believe Mathews and Juracek's original pattern was tied with tan dubbing in a #14 to 16 to imitate a spotted sedge or *Glossossoma* pupa. For October caddis I use a #8 hook and substitute orange or an orange-cream dubbing blend for the original tan dubbing. My favorite October caddis larva imitation is Rob Waters' Chamois Nymph, which I often color in with black and brown marker. The natural chamois color is effective for a pupa if it's lightly weighted or fished without weight. The Rock Roller, a cased-caddis nymph used on the Madison River in Montana, is gaining a strong following on the South Fork as an October caddis nymph imitation.

Terrestrials

The South Fork is *almost* famous for its grasshoppers. They do not reach the size of those found on the Upper Snake River, but they are still big and, more importantly, numerous. Above and below the Canyon of the South Fork, grasshoppers will invade the riverbanks between July and September. Many of them end up in the water where they are devoured by surface prowling trout. Several species of grasshoppers exist in this part of Idaho. For the most part, their coloration schemes are similar. The body color of grasshoppers will change from green to a pinkish cream and then to yellow and brown as they mature. In a chameleon-like manner, the hue of these colors will change to match the vegetation they inhabit at a given time. Early in the summer, hues will be close to green to match lush streamside vegetation. Later in the summer and into the fall, hues will be closer to yellow and brown to match vegetation in drier conditions. Keep these color schemes in mind when attempting to match hoppers.

Traditional patterns from other parts of the country—Joe's Hoppers, Jay-Dave's Hoppers, and Whitlock Hoppers—work well as imitations. But South Fork grasshoppers are partially responsible for one of the most detailed and innovative terrestrial patterns in fly-fishing today: Ken Burkholder's foam-bodied Club Sandwich. Burkholder is a master tier who has created several popular commercial patterns. The Club Sandwich is by far his most famous fly. This gargantuan bug with big rubber legs and an extended foam body is literally unsinkable and is quickly becoming a legendary fly. I enjoy fishing this fly with a nymph dropping three to four feet from it. Because of its size and buoyancy, I can use a larger than normal dropper nymph.

The size and success of the Club Sandwich has led some area anglers to use it as an imitation for other large insects in the trout's diet. I have fished it during salmonfly hatches with success. The variations I make to it are rather simple. Changing the color of the belly foam to a rust-orange, gray, or tannish-brown is important, but this is less important than silhouette. The size of the bug partially meets this requirement. The silhouette of a fluttering wing is the final piece. I do this by adding a large clump of calf tail or Siberian brown bear hair. Bear hair is something that Burkholder advocates using as wing material for other large patterns, particularly foam ants. It works just as well with his most famous fly.

Terrestrials such as flying ants can be found on most sections of the Upper South Fork. I have never witnessed much activity amongst these bugs on the lower sections. It has been suggested to me that much of this might be due to less hospitable habitat (they prefer naturally wooded areas) and the use of pesticides on the wide swaths of agricultural land surrounding the banks here (something which I am less certain of). An exception exists with beetles that can be found on all sections of the river. Their numbers are not strong, but they are certainly there and make up a small

The Club Sandwich. An excellent hopper imitation.

portion of the top water diet for trout. The months of July and August are typically the warmest on the South Fork. Temperatures can easily reach the upper 90s. It is during this time that pine beetles and bark beetles can appear on the river, especially in the canyon section. The canyon has strong stands of Douglas fir and Russian olive trees that beetles will infest. I mention the temperatures because often beetles and other terrestrial patterns are the only flies that can bring trout to the surface during midday fishing. Pine beetles are between 1/8- and 1/3-inch long. Foam Beetles tied on #12 to 14 hooks remain the standard imitation for these warm-weather insects. Craig Mathews' Blue Ribbon Flies, in Montana, has a pattern creatively named the Blue Ribbon Foam Beetle that works well on the South Fork. Bing Lempke's Foam Beetle, first tied in the 1970s, is a classic, although it has completely disappeared from area fly shops.

Scott Sanchez's Double Bunny.

Baitfish

The South Fork of the Snake River is a paradise for piscivorous trout. The stream has its share of the minnows and chubs that I described in the previous section. But what makes the South Fork so strong in terms of baitfish is its abundant population of whitefish. Trout will feed on the immature whitefish year around. Of course, this has a downside, as whitefish feed on newborn trout and can make for a rather miserable day of nymphing, when at times they can account for over half of the total days catch. They are native to the Snake River, but according to local fishery experts and those who fished the South Fork before 1957, their numbers have dramatically increased since the implementation of Palisades Reservoir. This is of major concern to those of us troubled by the impact that stream manipulation is having on the natural processes of the Snake River.

The abundance of baitfish on the South Fork is partially responsible for the creation of some of the Yellowstone Region's most popular streamers and wet flies. The most well-known of these is Scott Sanchez's Double Bunny. This saltwater inspired baitfish imitation started out as a massive and heavy #4 streamer that won three straight One-Fly Tournaments (1992-1994) before it became virtually outlawed from the tournament (flies larger than #8 were restricted from the contest staring in 1995. In 2005, #6 hooks were again allowed into the contest). Today, Double Bunnies in #6 and 8 can be found, but these do not work nearly as well as the original #4. If one is an experienced streamer-fisherman, the original version will not disappoint. They can be weighted with lead-free wire wrapped around the shank of the hook, with cone heads, or with dumbbell eyes. I refrain from using wire together with cone heads of dumbbell eyes because it can cause the fly and leader to twist. My preference is to use just dumbbell eyes, as this weight combined with the weight of the saturated rabbit fur submerges the streamer to the depth required to entice large, deep feeding trout. If you are tying a Double Bunny for your own personal use, you should use a dark-over-light color configuration, as this better imitates a natural baitfish. I like to use olive, black, or gray fur tied on top of white, tan, or gray. Krystal Flash chenille or Flashabou can be used too as the flank or lateral line. Dumbbell eyes should be tied underneath the shank of the hook. This will keep the dark fur riding on top of the light.

Also coming from the South Fork is the flash chenille-bodied, rubber-legged Tequilley, a pattern that builds upon the success of Jim Jones' J.J Special. The rubber legs and flash chenille pulsate when the fly is stripped under the surface. This motion generally acts as an attractant to predatory trout. I fish these with a bead- or cone-head to assist them in gaining the proper depth. Like the J.J. Special, debate rages as to whether this pattern is imitating a bottom-feeding baitfish, a crustacean, or large stonefly nymph. The Tequilley works in a variety of water conditions. During those few times when the South Fork is off-color from runoff or intense rainfall, I will rely on the Tequilley for most of my subsurface fishing.

Also popular are more traditional streamers and wet flies like Woolly Buggers, Zonkers, and muddler patterns, particularly the Wet Muddler and Kiwi Muddler. Like the Tequilley and the Double Bunny, I will weight these flies fairly heavily as well. The South Fork is a rather deep river in comparison to most other streams in the Yellowstone region. A lot of success can be gained from getting streamers down to the proper depth. I will discuss this in greater detail later.

Strategies & Tactics for the South Fork

Earlier I explained the importance of recognizing current breaks to successfully fly-fish the Upper Snake in Wyoming. The same can be said for the South Fork of the Snake River in Idaho. Shelves, riffle pools, and structure are important to this part of the stream as well. In fact, I would add to this list the importance of banks, which far outperform banks on the Upper Snake in respect to hosting trout. But this does not necessarily mean that you fish these current breaks the same way. As I mentioned earlier, the nature of the stream dictates the tactics you should use. While they are technically the same stream, the Upper Snake River and the South Fork have slight differences that warrant subtly different tactics. It is these subtly different tactics that can spell the difference between success and failure when fly-fishing on either.

Shelves and Riffle Pools

The South Fork has far fewer shelves and riffles than the wildly braided Upper Snake River. What it does have, however, is comparatively large riffles. Some of these are so well-known among South Fork enthusiasts that they have been bestowed with special names like God's Riffle and Power Line Riffle. These are large enough to accommodate several boats at one time without causing too much crowding, although at times it feels like some are pushing it.

Holding Water on a Shelf and Riffle: South Fork of the Snake River

1. Downstream edge of riffle pool. Both the dominant and less dominant trout of this riffle pool will hold and feed in this position. Note the gentler decline of the upstream shelf in comparison to shelves on the upper Snake River.
2. Shelf forming the upstream edge of the riffle pool. The gentler gradient, along with the higher concentration of aquatic insects in comparison to the upper Snake River, allows trout to hold and feed on the shelf. Both the dominant and less dominant trout will hold and feed in this position.

For the fly-fisher, a crucial difference between riffles on the Upper Snake River and those on the South Fork is not size, but rather the general location where trout hold and feed. If we recall from our previous discussion regarding holding water on the Upper Snake River, dominant trout will hold at the upstream edge of a given riffle, or the point where the shelf drops off to form the pool. This position offers trout a current break because it is within a deep segment of the pool, but it also offers them a prime spot to feed, as it is the first point where food will appear as it drifts off the shelf. On the South Fork, feeding occurs not just in the riffle pool, but *on* the upstream shelf as well. In fact, trout will actually *hold* on the shelf, where there is no real current break or protection from predators, and feed on the nutrients moving downstream with the current. This would seem to defy logic at first, especially after considering trout behavior on the Upper Snake River, but the picture becomes much clearer when one considers—once again—the subtle but important differences between the two portions of the river.

Although the South Fork of the Snake River carries a greater volume of water in comparison to the Upper Snake, it also has a much gentler gradient and wider streambed, resulting in a current that flows with less velocity. Consequently, trout on the South Fork can hold and feed on these shelves without committing the literal equivalent of suicide by exhaustion. In addition to this, the South Fork provides more nutrients to trout, meaning that trout can hold on a shelf despite a current and still have a chance to replenish the energy they lose with the nutrients that are available.

What all of this means for the angler is that the shelf, not just the pool, is a primary target. It constitutes the upper-most portion of the riffle where trout will feed, not the point where the shelf drops off to form the pool, as on the Upper Snake River. How far upstream of the riffle pool trout will feed is difficult to generalize, but a good rule is that the larger the shelf, the farther above the pool feeding will occur. On one large riffle on the Upper South Fork in Swan Valley, popularly known as God's Riffle, trout can feed as far as 15 or 20 feet above the line where the shelf and riffle pool meet. On small shelves, feeding will occur closer to the riffle pool. Regardless of shelf size, casts should be placed several feet upstream of the riffle pool, and you should be prepared for a strike anywhere on the shelf.

I must comment here about the divergent feeding behavior of the various trout that hold in shelves and in riffle pools. First of all, only two of the three types of trout on the South Fork—rainbows and cutthroat—are dominant feeders in this kind of water. Brown trout tend to favor slow-moving water with more substantial current breaks. Trout feeding on the shelf are predominantly cutthroat, although there are certainly rainbow trout that will work into this water as well. In the pool, both cutthroat and rainbow will feed. However, they typically do so in dissimilar ways. Cutthroat will primarily feed close to the surface film or directly on the surface. Rainbows will come up to the surface as well, but have a greater tendency to feed deeper. I will use small, heavily waited nymphs when I target deep-feeding rainbows here. Simple patterns work fine too. I like Copper Johns or Bead Head Prince Nymphs tied on #16 to 18 hooks. Cole Sutheimer, a South Fork Lodge guide, uses nothing more than black thread and a bead head tied onto a #18 to 20 hook. This pattern is as deadly as any of the fancy, more detailed nymphs.

Banks

Banks and structure are important features for fly-fishermen on almost any trout stream, and none more so that the South Fork. I contend that banks on this part of the stream are more important here than on the Upper Snake River. The primary reason is that the South Fork has a far more forgiving gradient and is less impacted by severe runoff. Its banks are left intact throughout most of the season and do not suffer the severe erosive effects of a long period of high and fast-moving water. This allows for more, and better, holding water to be created along banks. The comparatively thick vegetation along the banks is a clear indication of this.

Working a confluence line along a bank.

The holding water created here is of such quality that it can produce even during times of high water.

But it's the use of banks by insects such as stoneflies, caddis, and grasshoppers, which truly makes them significant features for fly-fishers. Concentrating casts close to banks and structure with large attractors during the salmonfly and golden stone hatch in June and July, and with terrestrial imitations during the heat of the season in late July and August can be very productive. These large insects are typically very animated. They are movers and shakers not just on the banks, but on the water as well. Looking for the perfect drift when fishing attractors, stonefly imitations, and terrestrials is not necessary and it may actually be counter-productive. I encourage anglers who I guide on the South Fork to actively and intentionally animate their big bugs when fishing banks. It's an established tactic among experienced South Fork fly-fishermen. Yet I see so many anglers attempt to maintain the perfect drift when fishing large dry flies that it deserves emphasis here.

Latter-day classic attractors like the Double Humpy and Turck's Tarantula have long been popular flies of movement on the South Fork. When tied with heavy hackle and the right kind of deer hair—particularly light mule deer hair taken from neck and mask—these two flies will ride high enough on the water that the wake they leave when intentionally skirted along the surface is almost identical to that of a natural salmonfly or golden stone. One of my favorite foam-bodied flies I use for the purpose of movement is Allan Woolly's Chernobyl Ant. There are several versions of this fly that imitate terrestrials, some of which I have previously eluded to. Giant foam hopper imitations can elicit very violent strikes when intentionally moved along the surface. However, I typically give movement to these flies in a different manner than I will deer-hair flies or flies that are heavily hackled. I will sporadically twitch foam patterns, as opposed to giving them a consistent skirting movement. This gives foam-ant patterns the appearance of a struggling and disoriented terrestrial on the surface.

Structure

In similar fashion to the Upper Snake River, structure on the South Fork creates plentiful holding water where trout can feed without expending energy. It is most prevalent on the lower section of the South Fork where the river is less channelized and more braided. If you are fishing a stream-bound fallen tree, holding water will be found at the immediate upstream edge of the root ball, in the pools on the downstream sides of the root ball, and all along the flanks of the tree. Larger trout typically hold in the downstream vicinity of the root ball. This is where the physical area of holding water is greatest. It is also closest to the most upstream segment of the structure. Trout holding in this pool will have access to the first nutrients moving downstream with

South Fork Outfitters guide Cole Sutheimer fishing structure below Twin Bridges on the South Fork.

the current. Structure, though, does not come solely in the form of a fallen tree. Brush piles, logjams, and boulders also characterize the variety of structure on the South Fork. It is important to remember that stream-bound boulders and trees, like banks, also act as a source of nutrients for trout. Many species of aquatic insects will use them to crawl from the river and emerge.

I have never noticed any one species of trout to dominate structure. Cutthroats, browns, and rainbows all use the holding water created by fallen trees and boulders. What I have noticed is that rarely will all three species hold and feed along one particular piece of structure. If I hook into three trout off one logjam, they will all typically be either cutthroat or rainbow. These trout typically do not hold near structure where browns are holding. If one brown is feeding in the vicinity of structure, it will either be the only trout in this position, or it will be holding with other brown trout.

Seam Lines and Eddies

I briefly talked about seam lines in Part I. I mention them again here because they are important features for anglers on the South Fork as well. A seam line separates back channels and eddies from the main current of a stream. The calm, still water of the eddy or back channel acts as a current break where trout can hold. The main current brings nutrients—in the form of invertebrates and baitfish—down to the waiting trout. A seam line can be visualized in the following manner: Imagine an exposed cobblestone bar or island separating a back channel and the main channel. At the extreme downstream point of the bar or island, the two channels converge. One can draw an imaginary border from the point of the bar or island downstream along the line of convergence until the border eventually runs into another bank or dissipates into the full current of the main channel. This border is the seam line. The line itself is not necessarily fixed, and its width can vary from one to several feet. A band of foam running along its entire length can often identify a seam line. Many anglers will use the terms *seam line* and *foam line* interchangeably. Trout will hold and feed in this general vicinity.

There are important differences between the South Fork and the Upper Snake when it comes to seam lines. First of all, there are fewer on the South Fork, due to the fact that it is less heavily braided. The lower stretches of the South Fork, which do have more braided channels, are the one exception. However, what the South Fork does have is elongated seams. Some are so long that they can accommodate more than just one or two anglers. The other important difference is volume of water. Seam lines are almost always deeper on the South Fork. The depth and length of seam lines on this river allows for several trout to hold and feed. Unfortunately, this makes it difficult to fish from shore. The only possible position for a wading angler is the extreme upstream point of the seam line. Casting from this position makes it very difficult to get a good drift with a dry fly or nymph. Seam lines are much more effectively fished from a watercraft.

When I am guiding, I instruct my anglers to fish a seam in a similar manner to the way I fish confluence points. When approaching a seam from the main channel, with the seam line on the port side of the boat, I have my fly-fishers place their fly on the center of the line near its extreme upstream point. I then instruct them to throw a series of downstream mends and strip in slack until the current in the main channel has carried the boat to a point even with the flies. This keeps the flies from dragging in an unnatural manner. I then instruct them to either throw two more quick upstream mends or have them recast to a point farther down the seam line. Again, seams on the South Fork are long, and it is possible to have at least two or three casts on each.

Another tactic is to row across the seam line from the main channel and position the boat in the back channel. If the bow of the boat faces upstream and the seam is on the port side, then I instruct my clients to cast to their left. From this position, anglers can cast upstream and allow the fly to drift down with the current along the edge of the foam line. Because the boat is not struggling with the strong current the main channel, anglers will be able to make several unhurried casts. The pilot can navigate the boat up and down the length of the seam, allowing anglers to work the entire line many times.

Eddies are characteristically different from back channels. They exist primarily along the banks of the main channel. An eddy can be defined as a bight in a bank that allows a body of standing water to exist alongside a moving current. The standing water contained in the bight is the feature that the term *eddy* actually refers to. The water here is not necessarily motionless. In fact, most of the time the distinguishing feature of an eddy is a slow current moving back upstream. The line that runs from the upstream

Holding Water on a Seam Line

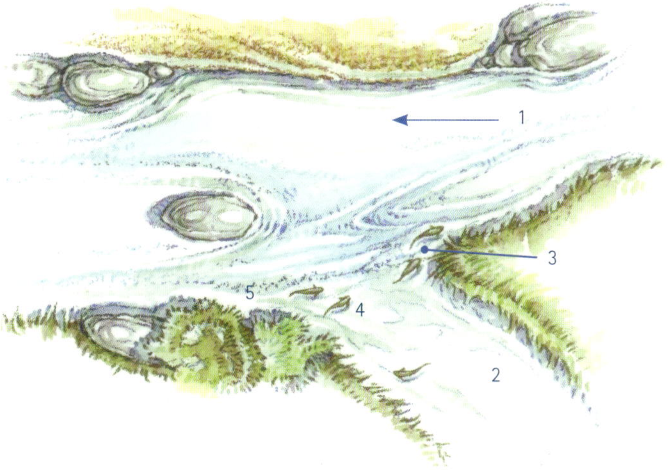

1. Main channel.
2. Back channel with no or minimal current.
3. Upstream portion of the seam line. Dominant trout will typically hold along this portion of the seam line, where they will have the first opportunity to feed on nutrients moving downstream in the main channel.
4. Downstream portion of the seam line. Typically, non-dominant trout along the seam line will hold in this position.
5. Partial current moving upstream into the back channel. Both dominant and non-dominant trout will hold and feed in this position.

point of the bight to the downstream point of the bight is the seam where trout will feed. Like seam lines formed along the border of a back channel and the main channel, a column of foam is a typical feature along an eddy's seam. This is the primary target of the eddy. But it is not uncommon to find fish feeding in the back current as well. Eddies occur infrequently on the Upper Snake River in Wyoming, except for in Snake River Canyon where they are created by a system of canyon ledges darting into the river. On the South Fork, eddies are everywhere. Like fishing backchannel seams, they are difficult to fish from shore. Often the banks bordering eddies are covered with vegetation. If the fly-fisher is able to take up a stable position, the only viable casts are roll casts or side-arm casts with the arm closest to the main current.

The formation of an eddy is strongly dictated by the speed of the current in the main channel. It is the fast-moving current that allows the standing water in the eddy to remain stationary. If the speed of the current, or the volume of the stream drops, the eddy will either dissolve or lose much of the features that make it prime feeding water for trout. This aspect can make fishing eddies somewhat difficult. If moving along in a boat in the main channel, anglers will only get off one good cast before their boat, and fly, are carried away by the fast current. A better strategy is to maneuver the boat into the eddy, face the bow upstream so that the pilot can work against any possible back current, and direct the casts toward the seam. This will allow for more water to be worked without rushing casts. However, such a maneuver will position the angler very close to the bank, so one must be careful of snagging into vegetation on back casts.

Subsurface Tactics: Streamers and Nymphs

The classic down-and-across and up-and-across presentations remain the most productive strategies when casting streamers and nymphs on the South Fork. It is important to incorporate into these presentations a set of upstream mends, similar to what I described in Part I of this book for fishing streamers on the Upper Snake River. This technique assists streamers and nymphs in reaching a depth where subsurface feeding occurs. It is a crucial element to streamer-fishing on the South Fork, where stream depths are 20 feet or more in some places even during low flows. While I have never used a full-sinking line, I have certainly used 10- to 15-foot sink tips to get down to the deeper holes that are prevalent in the Canyon and just below Palisades Reservoir. I cap my tip length at around 15 feet, as I find the 20- and 30-foot versions to be overkill for a stream like the South Fork. I would not recommend density-compensated lines, as they may get you a bit too deep. If the 15 feet of sinking tip isn't getting your fly deep enough, try dropping the tip of your rod below the surface. This is a trick I learned from Stacy Trimble, a Texas angler who uses the tactic to fish deep for bass. I have sunk the tip of my nine-foot rod at least six feet below the surface and have experienced some excellent strikes. This method takes some getting used to. Having a sunken rod tip does not allow you to set the hook by raising the rod. You must set the hook with a hard strip of the line, and then maintain tension until you can raise the rod from the water. Once the rod has left the water, you can begin stripping in the fish or you can take it to the reel.

If using a down-and-across presentation with streamers, it is important that you concentrate on the stripping technique you use. Stripping is more than just getting your fly and line in so you can prepare for another cast. Stripping gives your streamer motion. For flies like the J.J. Special or the Tequilley, stripping will give the rubber legs tied into the flanks a pulsating action. The same can be said for the Double Bunny or more traditional patterns like Woolly Buggers and Zonkers. The stripping motion gives a pulsating action to the rabbit fur and webbed hackle of which these flies are composed. The length of line one strips in is important. I bring in approximately one to one-and-a-half feet of line per strip in quick succession of each other. In some instances a dead-drift-and-swing technique should be used in place of a down-and-across presentation. With this method, you should cast downstream at approximately a 45-degree angle, and then let the streamer swing with the current. Your fly should eventually end up directly downstream from your position. From here, you lower your rod tip to the surface and then begin stripping in, again concentrating on the strip. This is an effective technique when fishing seam lines either from the shore or from a stationary boat. Trout often strike as the streamer completes its swing. But don't be surprised if a take occurs during the swing or while stripping in your line.

Using sink tips is an advantageous way to fish wet flies and streamers on the South Fork. I picked up on this several years ago following a season's worth of conversations with Scott Sanchez and Carter Andrews. I am now a big believer and use sinking tips most of the time when I am fishing big streamers on this river. Not only is the velocity of the river a concern (in that the speed of the current can force even heavy wet flies to the surface), so too is stream depth. Pools in the Canyon of the South Fork can reach depths well over 20 feet. Some of the biggest trout in the river live in the Canyon, and most of these feed very deep most of the time.

Over the past few years I have been relying on sink tips used for two-handed rods to reach the deepest parts of the South Fork. One of my favorite custom systems is a 15-foot, type 6 (six-inch-per-second sink rate) connected to a 24 foot, 400 grain tip. I picked up this sink tip combo from steelhead guides on the Bulkley and Kispiox rivers in British Columbia. It is a bear to cast with a one-handed rod, but it sinks like a rock and has produced some of the biggest browns and cutthroats I have ever caught on the South Fork over the past two seasons. For those who have experience fishing sinking lines and tips, I highly recommend using them with streamers on the South Fork of the Snake River. For those who have yet to fish sink tips, I would just say—start experimenting.

Jack Turner demonstrates the classic down-and-across streamer technique.

River Log: The South Fork & its Tributaries from Palisades Dam to Menan

River Flows, Safety, Seasons and Regulations

The South Fork of the Snake River may not have the same amount of rapids or steepness of grade as on the Snake River in Wyoming, but don't let this fool you. It is a big river that consistently carries a high volume of water. 20,000 cfs or greater is not uncommon in the spring. It can be dangerous. Wearing life vests is not required, but they certainly need to be in the boat. A Type V PDF is the minimum standard that should been used. When wading, remember that this is a cobblestone stream with unsure footing. One misstep and a wade fisherman can quickly be swept away by a deceivingly fast stream.

Stream-bound structure and the surprisingly strong current present their usual dangers to float-fishermen. But another concern, and one which does not exist on the Upper Snake River, is the use of motorized craft. The Bureau of Land Management (BLM) and the National Forest Service control recreational use on the South Fork and allow boats equipped with motors to navigate the stream. A significant portion of those who recreate on the South Fork are locals from East Idaho communities who prefer doing so with motorized boats. The South Fork is certainly large enough to accommodate motorized watercraft, and some of these are quite impressive, with high horsepower engines mounted on what can be classified as jet boats. The vast majority of these users are extremely responsible. The danger arises when a handful of motorboat users, making their way upstream, do not reduce speed at bends and fail to see other boaters coming downstream. Collisions rarely occur, but they can happen. Always keep your eyes and ears open. Whether you are in a boat or wade fishing, your best bet if you see or hear a motorized boat coming upstream or downstream is to hug the nearest bank or simply make your way onto shore. Boats with motors will generally stick to the center of the channel, where it is deeper.

The fishing season on the South Fork traditionally began on the last weekend in May above the Heise measuring cable and ended on November 30th. The river below remained open to fishing year round. These regulations were modified in 2003 to allow fishing year round from Palisades Reservoir downstream, mainly for the purpose of increasing the harvest of rainbow trout. The South Fork is less impacted by the spring runoff in comparison to the Upper Snake River, but water is still high throughout much of May and June because of increased releases at Palisades Reservoir. While fishing in late June—during the salmonfly hatch—can be excellent, it is also somewhat of a gamble because of the possibility of high water. The beginning of July is much more predictable as flows are generally lower and trout, coming off of the salmonfly hatch and starting in on the golden stone part of the season, have begun to feed in earnest. Fishing can slow significantly in late August and through the fall as Palisades Reservoir drops to levels that raise water temperatures on the river.

At the time of this writing, a non-resident daily fishing license costs $12.75 for the initial day and $6.00 for each additional consecutive day. Seasonal non-resident licenses cost $98.25. Seasonal resident licenses cost $25.75. Resident daily licenses cost $11.50 for the first day and $5.00 for each consecutive day. The licensing system in Idaho is computerized, making it quick and easy for anglers to obtain a permit. In addition, the information from the initial year of purchase is saved within the State's database so that it can be used and updated when one purchases a new license. (The system uses the applicant's social security number because that number, once assigned, never changes.)

Upper South Fork

Palisades Dam to Conant Valley
(Approximately 15 miles)
Most of the Upper South Fork is located in what is known as Most of the Upper South Fork is located in what is known as Swan Valley. It is a popular section because many fly shops and outfitters, such as the Lodge at Palisades Creek and the South Fork Lodge, are nearby. This reach is known for its large cutthroat and rainbow trout. The upper part of this stretch is, for the most part, a deep channel and is ideal for the use of large wet flies and streamers like Double Bunnies, Tequilleys, and dark Zonker patterns. If you are an experienced streamer fisherman, a standard 120- to 300-grain sink tip can help get your fly down to the depths where the bigger trout feed. But be careful of the wind, which is generally pretty heavy within a mile of the dam. It can wreck havoc with your cast.

Float-fishermen have very easy access on the Upper South Fork. Almost all the launch sites are developed, including the landings at Palisades, Husky, Spring Creek/ Highway 26 Bridge, and Conant Valley. There is a parking fee of $3.00, which can be paid at self-pay stations located at each site. Much of the surrounding land on the Upper

Fall Creek Falls, upper South Fork.

South Fork is private and wade fishermen will have a much more difficult time accessing the river. The best and easiest access is upstream of Spring Creek/Highway 26 Bridge on both sides of the river. You can park at one of a number of turnouts or campgrounds and walk the short distance down to the river. There are decent riffles and pools along two-sided channels that split away from, and then rejoin, the main channel near Fall Creek Falls. The confluence of these two channels with the main channel can fish especially well.

The river on this section of the South Fork is primarily one channel with the best fishing along banks with big dry flies, nymphs, and streamers. The lower half is characterized by a few braided channels and large riffles. Local guides and anglers have given very unique names to some of these features, which include monikers such as Power Line Riffle, God's Riffle, and The Playboy Channel. Large dries continue to work well here, but smaller patterns in the riffles—PMDs, Humpies, and Yellow Sallies—can produce, especially in the evening hours. A variety of nymphs will also work exceptionally well in the riffles. Large stonefly nymphs like a gold Crystal Creek Stone Nymph and Kaufmann's Golden Stone work best in July and August. In the fall, traditional patterns like Prince Nymphs, Hare's Ears, and bead-headed Flashback Pheasant Tails offer a greater chance for success.

The boat launches at Palisades and Husky (also called Timberwolf) are easily accessible from Highway 26 and are the most popular landings on this section of river. They are well developed and maintained by the Bureau of Land Management, as are the landings at Spring Creek Bridge and Conant Valley. Another boat access to the west of the town of Irwin is less developed and requires the watercraft to be slid down a dirt ramp and directly into the main current of the river. However, many choose to use this ramp because it's located only a short distance upstream from the beginning of the riffles, which usually provides better fishing in comparison to the channelized section of the river upstream. The riffles and islands below Irwin provide ample opportunity for float-fishermen to park their watercraft and wade fish. A float from Husky or Irwin down to Spring Creek Bridge or to the South Fork Lodge at Conant Valley can make for an excellent full day of fishing. When flow levels are low enough, the two-and-a-half-mile float from Spring Creek Bridge to Conant Valley is just right for those who have only a few hours of fishing available to them. I especially enjoy floating this section in the evening during the fall when caddis hatches can be at their fullest.

The original boat launch at Conant Valley was treacherous to both put in and land watercraft when river flows were high. In the early 1990s, it was moved downstream approximately 200 meters. The sight of the original landing is now a large eddy that is notorious for holding large trout. The new boat launch is much safer for those using watercraft. A much larger and softer eddy forms up at this new landing.

It has far more room for boats to hold while waiting to take out. However, those attempting to take out at this site still need to be cautious of heavy currents that can swing boats to the far northeast bank and away from the landing. Those approaching the Conant Valley boat launch should stay as close to the left bank as possible. Once your craft has moved past the exposed rock point, you can back row safely into the eddy that forms up at the landing, but be mindful of other boats that may be in the eddy waiting to take out.

Swan Valley offers beautiful scenery with clear views of the Big Hole Range and the distant Salt River Range. Highway 26 does not parallel the river like Highway 89 does in Snake River Canyon in Wyoming. Most of the land surrounding the South Fork is private. You will find a healthy population of ospreys and eagles on this section. They nest in the cottonwoods and firs directly along the stream. Quite possibly the most beautiful site on this section of the South Fork is Fall Creek Falls, just above Spring Creek Bridge on the west side of the river. The falls can be accessed via Snake River Road, a well-maintained gravel road that runs along the river's west bank. A National Forest campground is located roughly half-a-mile upstream of the falls. Access to the river and some very good fishing is fairly easy in this area.

The Canyon of the South Fork

Conant Valley to Cottonwood Flats

(Approximately 14 miles)

The Canyon of the South Fork is a deep gorge surrounded by high walls composed of volcanic and obsidian rock—primarily rhyolitic basalt. In some places, the cooled lava has shaped smooth, wave-like striations into the walls, giving the canyon a melting appearance. It is the most beautiful and scenic section of the South Fork of the Snake River, a characteristic that also makes it popular and crowded.

Access to the upper canyon section between Conant Valley and Cottonwood is difficult without some kind of watercraft. The majority of the riverbed between the canyon walls is public land maintained by the National Forest Service and the BLM. Those who wade along the banks of the river do not run the risk of trespassing onto private land for the most part. The problem, however, is that this public land is surrounded by private land, mainly large farms engaged in potato production. The one small piece of public access is Heise Road (also known as Forest Service Road 206) on the north and west side of the canyon. This road provides only limited access to the lower canyon. For the most part, the upper Canyon of the South Fork is very difficult to access unless one uses a boat.

Float-fishermen have easier access, but are faced with difficulties of their own. The landing at Conant Valley is well maintained and in excellent condition. To access the landing at Cottonwood, however, requires boaters to use the rutted, suspension jarring Forest Service road on the east bank. Vehicles must be shuttled from Conant Valley, down to Heise Bridge, and then up the northeast side of the river, a total of 45 miles.

If you have two consecutive days available, one of the best ways to experience the Canyon of the South Fork is to use one of the public campsites that are conveniently located streamside all along the upper half of the canyon. There are a total of 15 sites, all of which are maintained by the BLM and the National Forest Service. They are large and provide a lot of room and privacy for users. You can reserve a campsite at one of the free, self-issue permit stations located at Byington, Conant Valley, or Spring Creek Bridge boat launch. The most popular camping sites are located at Pine Creek, Dry Canyon, Gormer Canyon, and Lufkin Bottom. (Portable toilets are required! There is a dump station located at Byington for easy clean up.)

There is a wide variety of wildlife between Conant Valley and Cottonwood. Mega-fauna include mule and whitetail deer, elk, and moose. Over the last decade, there have been more sightings of black bear, particularly in the vicinity of Gormer and Dry canyons. The system of lush cottonwoods along the river here is recognized as one of the largest remaining in the American West. It is in peril because of human impacts such as unnatural flows in the river, motorized use, and increase habitation. This cottonwood system harbors one of the healthiest populations of eagles and ospreys found on any part of the Snake River. You will also find peregrine falcons that nest all along the canyon walls. To protect the nesting success of these birds of prey, there are frequent closures to bank occupancy and access. This typically occurs between February 1st and July 31st of each year. These areas are marked with bright orange Do-Not-Enter signs. You can contact the Idaho Department of Fish and Game or the BLM office in Idaho Falls to obtain information regarding closures prior to your trip on the river. This is easily accomplished through accessing their website.

Other birds present include great blue herons and waterfowl such as ducks and geese. The most noticeable birds in the canyon are the several species of sparrows that build their nests in the canyon walls close to the river using mud and sediment. Casting along these walls, you will see the heads of these little sparrows peaking in and out of the nest entrances or the mothers bringing food back to their chicks. The thoughtful fly-tying angler should consider presenting imitations of baby swallows as presenting such imitations beneath these nests could result in a trout of the season if not of a lifetime! Many kinds of insects act as food for birds, including those imitated with artificial flies. I have hooked birds on a couple of occasions as they dive for my bug while it's on the water or being cast through the air. So be careful and watch for sparrows that might be taking too much interest in your fly.

The Canyon of the South Fork.

The terrain in this part of the canyon is at its most dramatic between Dry Canyon and Cottonwood Flats. The volcanic walls are at their tallest and the angle of repose at its steepest. Here you will be fishing in the shadow of cliffs pocketed with deep caves and dotted with pillars of granite and obsidian rock. The names locals have give to particular parts of the canyon in this area—names like Hole in the Wall and Valley of Giants—give it a mythical aura that matches the landscape.

The fishing between Conant Valley and Cottonwood is exceptional and has a reputation for being the most consistent on South Fork. It is one of the most nutrient-rich sections of the entire Snake River. Intermittent tributaries flow into the river through feeder canyons on the north side of the stream. In addition, the cool waters coming from Palisades Dam remain such in the canyon. It is heavily riparian, with lush vegetation that helps contribute to the substantial supply of nutrients available to trout. I contend that the largest rainbows and hybrids on the river are found here.

This section of the canyon also offers very diverse fly-fishing. Exceptional riffles become exposed when flows from Palisades Reservoir drop to approximately 11,000 cfs. Some of the best are found upstream of Gormer Canyon. In 1999, during an overnight trip I was guiding in the canyon, clients Bryan Gentle and Rick Suman caught a total of eight trout on a riffle just below Dry Canyon that went between 15 and 19 inches! There are also extraordinarily deep holes found along the canyon walls on this stretch. These are some of my favorite places to throw big streamers and nymphs to some of the river's largest trout. Girdle Bugs, Double Bunnies, Tequillies, and J.J. Specials, if weighted properly, can get down to where trout hold before the current drags them away. This holds true for big nymphs like Kaufmann's Golden Stone and the Crystal Creek Stone Nymphs.

Adding to the diversity found in the canyon are the few small side channels that offer excellent wade fishing. Structure and riffles act as the primary target for a fly-fisher in these segments of the canyon. Large dry flies, especially attractors like Turck's Tarantulas, Tara Xs, Double Humpies, and Plan Bs can get trout to the surface in a hurry when fishing these spots. But I will often use a dropper rig with them to increase the chances of a hook-up. Prince Nymphs, Pheasant Tails, Copper Johns, Zug Bugs, Hare's Ears, and Flash Backs have always worked well. A Montana transplant known as the Lightning Bug has been among the most effective nymphs in side channel riffles that I have used over the past few years. This nymph has gained a strong following on the South Fork, and there is a lot of debate as to what it imitates. In my opinion, this pattern is taken by trout to be an emerging mayfly or midge. Its bright, almost opaque looking body gives the translucent appearance of gas building between the fly's body and its exoskeleton to assist its rise to the surface. I fish the Lightning Bug with a short dropper leader, not more than

Moose in the Canyon of the South Fork.

18 inches in length, to imitate an emerging nymph that is struggling its way to the surface. I fish them without any weight other than a small bead head.

During times of high water in June and the early half of July, it's possible to float from Conant Valley to another landing at Wolf Eddy, approximately seven miles downstream from Cottonwood. The total river distance of 22 miles seems excessive. However, with flows many times exceeding 16,000 cfs, this distance can easily be covered in a day of fishing.

Cottonwood Flats to Byington (Approximately 12 miles)
Anglers fishing this section of the Canyon of the South Fork will notice the subtle disappearance of the steep, volcanic walls that characterize the upper section. The canyon opens up into Idaho's vast parcels of agricultural land in the vicinity of Wolf Eddy. The walls become less abrupt, and slowly descend to nothing along the valley floor just upstream of Byington. Private holdings along the river increase. However, the river is far easier to access along this portion of the river because public land is not completely surrounded by private property. The best access points on this lower part of the canyon are on the northeast bank, where several undeveloped Forest Service campgrounds run alongside the river.

The diversity of trout species begins to change on this section of the South Fork. In the vicinity of Wolf Eddy, the abundance of rainbow trout declines and brown trout numbers rise dramatically. As one continues downstream, brown trout numbers continue to rise, cutthroat abundance drops, and rainbow trout become negligible. As I discussed earlier, some believe that a natural barrier hinders rainbow trout from populating the lower river. Fish biologists and anglers alike have theories, but there is little in the way of actual research that addresses this phenomenon. Whatever it is, rainbow trout and brown trout experience a literal 180 turnaround in total abundance from Wolf Eddy down.

I rate this section of the South Fork among the best for dry-fly fishing year around. In April and May, there can be heavy hatches of blue-winged olives. I have caught large cutthroat and browns in skinny water along banks and shallow riffles with standard blue-winged imitations. In October, the water immediately above and below Cottonwood hosts moderate hatches of October caddis that anglers can fish with Stimulators and lightly-weighted Chamois Caddis Nymphs. This section is also famous for its productivity during the salmonfly hatch in June and July. In my experience, the most prolific salmonfly hatches from year to year typically occur from Wolf Eddy down to Twin Bridges on the lower South Fork. The largest brown trout I have caught on a salmonfly imitation—21 inches—was on this section of the South Fork approximately one mile below Wolf Eddy.

Like the upper canyon, this section is relatively channelized and easy to navigate. However, boat users need to be cautious of an area at the lower part of the canyon, about two miles above the Byington Boat Launch. The river makes a hard horseshoe turn with strong currents and a series of standing waves. Powerboats have sometimes taken this turn at too high of speed and just barely miss hitting other boats coming downstream. River depth to the left on the first turn is significantly shallower than on the rest of the channel. Hugging this bank is the best way to avoid both waves and other boats.

The Lower South Fork

Byington to Twin Bridges (Approximately 7 miles)
The lower South Fork unofficially starts at Byington (also known as Poplar) and continues 24 miles downstream to Menan. This section has some of the easiest access on the entire South Fork. It is located close to eastern Idaho's urban centers like Idaho Falls, Blackfoot, Rexburg, and Pocatello. Most of the primary landings, including centrally located Lorenzo boat launch and Twin Bridges, are on major highway routes and are well developed. Yet despite these proximal advantages, the lower South Fork is consistently the least fished part of river. Most anglers concentrate their activities on the more scenic sections upstream. This is unfortunate, because what the lower South Fork lacks in scenery, it more than makes up for in fishing. It can, at times, offer not only the best fishing on the South Fork, but probably the entire region.

One will notice a considerable change in the physical character of the river between Byington and Twin Bridges. The upper half remains fairly channelized with a smattering of islands and side channels. Approximately four miles above Twin Bridges, significant braiding begins to take

One of many diversion canals on the lower South Fork.

place in the riverbed. Side channels split away from the main river channel, creating diverse forms of holding water. Those floating the river must be mindful of logjams, brush piles, and other types of stream-bound structure. For waders, these side channels, logjams, and brush piles present excellent opportunities to catch some of the largest trout on the lower South Fork. In this way, it is somewhat similar to the Upper Snake River in Wyoming.

This stretch of the South Fork does have some rather unique dangers and annoyances that float-fishermen must be ready for. One of these is in the vicinity of the major stream crossing at Twin Bridges. The river is heavily braided here and a major channel flows away from the actual boat launch. If planning to take out at Twin Bridges, you must make sure that you take the correct channel to the landing. This channel splits to the left away from the main channel, and then flows under the Twin Bridges. The landing is on the right side of the river. If you do not take this channel, you will end up floating all the way to the next landing at Lorenzo, another eight miles downstream.

The biggest danger, however, are the several diversion channels—used for irrigation purposes by local farmers—that exist throughout this section. The most prominent exists three miles downstream from Byington. This is where the Great Idaho Feeder Canal diverts upwards of 15,000 cfs of the Snake River through its gates to irrigate thousands of acres of dry farms. You should exercise extreme caution in this area. There are warning signs above the spillway. Hugging the right bank will keep you away from danger. Two other diversions to be aware of are the Reid and Sunnydell canals, which divert water from the right bank of the river, but these are also well marked. Staying left will keep you safe. To avoid potential problems with these diversion channels, a good plan of action is to make friends with someone who has experience floating these stretches. Go with them and familiarize yourself with the channels that should be avoided and those that are necessary for a successful float. Over the years, several anglers and boaters have been swept into the gates at the head of these canals, never to return again.

For those who know how good the fishing is, a favorite time to be on this section of the South Fork is mid- to late June, just as the salmonfly hatch is getting started. The hatch generally originates above Menan Buttes and works its way upstream and into the canyon. By the time it reaches Twin Bridges, the hatch is in full swing and a feeding frenzy begins amongst all trout large enough to engulf these monster bugs. The same stonefly imitations and attractors that work for salmonflies upstream—Double Humpies, Tarantulas, Tara Xs, Burkholder's Bareback Rider, Chernobyl Ants—will work on this section as well. I rate the section of river running from Wolf Eddy down to Twin Bridges among the best and most consistent for fishing during the salmonfly hatch. The hatch tends to be at its most prolific in this area, and the trout are among the largest in the entire system.

The majority of land surrounding the South Fork between Byington and Twin Bridges is privately owned. Public access to the river is possible at Railroad Bridge, Twin Bridges, Heise Bridge, and the Kelly Island Campground (maintained by the BLM) just above Heise Hot Springs. All these access points are in areas where significant braiding occurs and stream-bound structure is plentiful. Wading in the vicinity of these access points is relatively safe and easy and can be productive throughout the year.

One convenient feature of this section of the South Fork for float-fishermen is the number of alternative launches. During times of high water, typically in June and the early part of July, I prefer to float from Wolf Eddy to Twin Bridges, a total of 11 miles. Brown trout will begin to stage in preparation for their run upstream to spawn in late September and early October. However, they typically do not migrate very far upstream. My experience suggests that a run will only be a total distance of a few miles. In fact, I believe that many will just spawn where they stage. More research by fishery biologists is needed to determine if this is the case.

Later in the season, when the river is likely to experience moderate to low flows, I will float the seven-mile stretch from Byington to Twin Bridges. For those interested in only a half-day or evening float, a good choice is to launch at Heise Bridge and take out at Twin Bridges, a stretch that is approximately four miles long.

One of numerous side channels found between Twin Bridges and Menan.

Twin Bridges to Lorenzo (Approximately 8 miles)
Twin Bridges and Lorenzo boat launchs are easily accessible from the Ririe-Archer Highway. (running north from the town of Ririe) and Highway 20 respectively. The launch at Lorenzo underwent major renovations in 2004-2005 and is now as well developed as the launches at Conant Valley and Byington. Despite the level of development and its easy access, this stretch, like much of the lower South Fork, remains underutilized by local and visiting river enthusiasts. This is good news for those anglers wishing to get away from the crowds while still enjoying some fabulous fishing.

The braided channels that begin to take shape above Twin Bridges become even more pronounced on this stretch. There are several logjams and brush piles that create obstacles for those using boats. But these same obstacles also create prime holding water for trout. In many ways, the physical character of the river here is much more similar to the Snake River in Wyoming than the South Fork above Byington. The major difference, however, is in the trout that call this piece of river home. The South Fork between Twin Bridges and Lorenzo does not have a more plentiful trout population than the rest of the system, but in my experience it does have larger trout on average. Twenty-plus-inch hook-jawed browns are not uncommon and some clearing 24 inches are caught every season. Browns are also the most abundant trout species on this stretch of river. The most recent electroshock data suggests that brown trout make up over 80% of total trout abundance in the vicinity of the Lorenzo boat launch.

Twin Bridges to Lorenzo experiences as strong of a salmonfly hatch as any other stretch on the South Fork. The golden stoneflies that follow on the heels of the salmonflies generally emerge earlier here than on other stretches. In fact, it is common to see thick golden stones intermixed with the thick hatches of salmonflies during the last week of June. But one of my favorite times for being on this section of river is in autumn when air temperatures have cooled significantly. The Lower Snake River can be uncomfortably warm in July and August. This part of Eastern Idaho is a desert for the most part and temperatures can regularly approach 100 degrees Fahrenheit. This has a significant influence on water temperatures. In July, midday water temperatures at Lorenzo can be close to 70 degrees Fahrenheit. From the first of October on, both air and water temperatures continually drop. The fishing on the Lower South Fork at this time is more comfortable and generally better. The big bugs used earlier in the season will continue to work, but I really enjoy using small mayfly patterns such as PMDs,

Rusty Spinners, Elk Hair Caddis and small attractors like Humpies and Royal Wulffs. These imitate the much more apparent hatches of caddis, PMDs, and blue-winged olives that occur at this time.

One saving grace for this section during the heat of the summer—the middle of July to the first part of September—is the healthy population of terrestrials that make their home along the banks, particularly grasshoppers and beetles. Rich farmland borders the river here, and although pesticides keep much of the insect population down, it by no means kills them all. Large hoppers, Mormon crickets, and various species of beetles can find themselves in the river and these bugs are typically the only thing that can bring trout to the surface during the hot summer months. I use Whitlock Hoppers, Jay-Dave's Hoppers, and Ken Burkholder's Club Sandwich. I use these flies with a deep-running nymph as a dropper—approximately seven feet from the surface fly. I fish these droppers close to bottom, which is often the only place bigger trout will sub-surface feed when water and air temperatures are high.

When flows are high in June and July, boat users have the luxury of putting in at Heise Bridge, approximately three miles upstream of Twin Bridges, and taking out at Lorenzo, a float of approximately 11 miles. Wading anglers can access the river from all these sites and walk upstream or downstream to fish the numerous riffles, side channels, or pieces of individual structure that are found all along the lower South Fork. Heise Bridge and Twin Bridges are particularly good access points because of the availability of nearby holding water for trout. All these sites, except for Heise, are maintained by the BLM and require the same $3.00 parking fee that is required upstream.

Despite its close proximity to urban centers and major highway arteries, there is a surprisingly robust wildlife on this section of the South Fork. A population of eagles and ospreys reside here. At times their numbers seem to rival the population found upstream in the canyon and on the upper stretch. There is also a very healthy population of moose, including what appears to be a pair of resident cows on the islands immediately below Twin Bridges. These two often have a calf in-tow throughout the summer season. It is no surprise that a number of bulls make an appearance here in autumn too, but only a lucky few who I have spoken to have actually seen bulls square off on the islands. I am still waiting for my chance to see such a spectacle.

Lorenzo to Menan (Approximately 9 miles)

The stretch of river running from Lorenzo to Menan is the last official section of the South Fork. The only access points for wading anglers are the boat launches at the extreme upstream and downstream portions. This stretch is far friendlier to those using a boat. There are plenty of islands, riffles, and structure, similar to what is found on most of the lower South Fork. Anglers who are float-fishing can anchor down almost anywhere in the riverbed and experience some incredible fishing.

I particularly enjoy fishing this stretch in the fall, after air and water temperatures begin to drop. Brown trout completely dominate the river here. In late September and early October, they begin to stage in preparation for their annual spawning run up the South Fork. It is a terrific time to fish with big streamers and wet flies. I will go with lightly weighted J.J. Specials, Tequilleys, and Girdle Bugs. An old South Fork stand-by—the Super X—is one of my favorite wet flies to use when fishing for brown trout in autumn. Most feel that it imitates a feeding egg-sucking leech. Some local anglers fish standard egg patterns with success in the skinny water close to island banks as brown trout prepare to form their beds.

Wildlife is still quite plentiful on this part of the South Fork; it's one of the best stretches to view upland sage birds and waterfowl. Late September through October and November, greater Canadian geese, mallards, wood ducks, and teals congregate in the vicinity of Menan Buttes before migrating south.

The South Fork and the Henry's Fork come together just upstream from the Menan Buttes to form the main stem of the Snake River. Continuing downstream, the size of the river fluctuates dramatically as it takes on more tributaries, and then drains to feed the demands of irrigators. It flows through impressive canyons and massive man-made reservoirs, and parches the thirst of deserts that, for better or for worse, have been turned into fertile farmland. The fishing on the main stem is good. In fact, below Idaho Falls, there are cutthroat and brown trout that clear 25 and 30 inches respectively. But this part of the stream does not have the appeal of the Snake River upstream. Much of this comes from the severe and clearly visible impact man has made. The main stem should serve as a reminder to fly-fishers and sportsmen of the dangers that the Snake River, as I have presented it here, faces. The Snake has its share of problems, some of which are reaching a critical plateau. But unless we protect it, there will be worse to come.

Tributaries of the South Fork

I have spoken already of the lack of tributaries to the South Fork of the Snake River. Most of those that do exist are too small to fish, only run intermittently, or are not accessible to trout from the main river. Still, there are a few that can be fished. They provide excellent opportunities to get away from the crowds found on the main stream and get fish in a more solitary setting. Such fishing allows anglers to come in touch with the lifeblood of the river. These tributaries are absolutely critical to South Fork trout as spawning streams and as suppliers of fresh, nutrient-rich water.

Palisades Reservoir and its Tributaries (Big Elk Creek, Little Elk Creek, Indian Creek)

Despite the fact that the South Fork officially starts below the dam, I talk about Palisades Reservoir in this part of the journal for the following reasons: (1) the vast majority of this man-made lake is on the Idaho side of the border, (2) the waters of the Grand Valley were considered a part of the South Fork before the construction of the dam in 1957, and (3) as the principle source of water, it is an essential piece of the South Fork.

Palisades Reservoir is known more as a trolling lake but offers excellent fly-fishing for those willing to do some work. As a lake completely at the mercy of Idaho agriculture, its depth changes dramatically throughout any given season. It can go from 100% capacity in the middle of June to less than 15% capacity by the first of September. Like the lakes in Jackson Hole, evening on Palisades is the best time to fish on the surface. The reservoir is much warmer than the lakes farther north, which makes it a better lake to fish dry flies. It is predominantly a cutthroat lake, but its proximity to the Salt River makes it a wonderful body of water to catch brown trout. Fishing deep can bring up an occasional lake trout. Perhaps the most unique feature of fishing on Palisades Reservoir is its small population of kokanee salmon—a lake-resident form of sockeye salmon (*Ocorhynchus nerka*)—that were stocked in these waters after the establishment of the reservoir. Kokanee are stunted and never reach the size of their ocean-going brethren. They typically reach sexual maturity around seven to nine inches and max out at approximately 16 to 17 inches. Many fly-fishers, however, report catching kokanee in excess of 20 inches. These can be difficult to catch on flies. Most anglers have luck fishing deep with streamers on a full-sinking or sink-tip line.

Some of the best fishing on the entire reservoir occurs at the outlets of its several tributaries. This includes the Salt River, McCoy Creek, Indian Creek, Bear Creek, Big Elk Creek, and Little Elk Creek. Indian Creek and Big and Little Elk creeks flow into the lake via elongated bays alongside Highway 26. Bear Creek flows into an elongated bay and is accessed by the Forest Service road going southwest from the south side of Palisades Dam. When the water level is high enough, these bays can accommodate watercraft, but they can be just as easily fished from shore which is most popular early in the season. Fishing at the mouth of these streams is good with both dry flies and streamers. These three tributaries are popular to fish due to their easy access and because, when conditions are right, some members of the reservoir's kokanee population will make a run up these streams in the fall of the year. Big Elk Creek and McCoy Creek are perhaps the best tributaries for cutthroats in terms of size. McCoy Creek inparticular holds big cutthroat in the early part of the season, which spawn within, then head back to the reservoir.

Fishing Palisades Reservoir and its tributaries begins Memorial Day weekend and end on November 30th.

Palisades Creek

This stream offers some of the best fly-fishing among the tributaries on the Upper South Fork. It is within the boundaries of Targhee National Forest and can be fished by the public from its mouth to its headwaters. Palisades Creek is a small stream and does not necessarily produce large fish, but the fishing can still be fun, especially when flows on the river are too high. A large trout on this stream can be between 15 and 18 inches, but expect a catch to be more in the range of 10 to 13 inches. I prefer using smaller, more imitative patterns of resident aquatic insects. Standard caddis and mayfly patterns do fine. Palisades is one of the major spawning streams for native cutthroat. To control hybridization, the Idaho Department of Fish and Game has installed weirs on the creek to keep rainbows from following cutthroat upstream to spawn in the spring of the year.

Palisades Creek can be accessed via Palisades Creek Road off Highway 26. The turnoff is adjacent to the Lodge at Palisades Creek approximately two miles northwest of Palisades Dam. This is a dirt road but is generally well maintained by the Forest Service. The end of this road goes into a USFS campground that has a trailhead for Forest Service Trail 084 which accesses the creek. The trailhead is a perfect place to gear up. Fishing upstream or downstream from this point will offer equally good opportunities. Because it is a major spawning stream for cutthroat trout, fishing season does not open on Palisades Creek until July 1st, after the primary spawning period has ended.

Fly-fishers can also access Lower Palisades Lake and Upper Palisades Lake via Forest Service Trail 084. The lower lake is approximately four miles from the trailhead and the upper lake is two miles up the trail. Upper Palisades Lake offers the best fishing in my opinion, but the fish are smaller than those in the lower lake. A few anglers chose to access these waters on horseback and camp along the shore, often spending two or three days fishing both the lakes and the creeks.

Rainey Creek and Pine Creek

I talk about these two tributaries together because they are very similar in their importance to the South Fork and the communities within and surrounding Swan Valley. Both are critical spawning waters for native Yellowstone cutthroat and the Idaho Department of Fish and Game has established weirs on each in an attempt to prevent hybridization. Cutthroat will run up these creeks during the months of May and June. This overlaps the tail end of the spawning periods for rainbows and hybrids, which is generally from the middle of April to the middle of June. The demand for irrigation water during our most recent drought years has made it difficult for cutthroat to run up Rainey Creek and successfully spawn; 2001 was one of the worst years on record. Idaho Fish and Game biologists believe that low flows and irrigation eliminated most of the spawning for fluvial trout during that season.

Rainey Creek's headwaters can be found deep in the mountains to the northeast of Swan Valley. As it flows to the west and south, it picks up water from several smaller creeks coming from a series of heavily wooded canyons before reaching the valley floor. Here it begins to flow to the north and west and takes on water from spring creeks bubbling to the surface throughout the valley. Rainey Creek flows through the town of Swan Valley—were it crosses Highways 31 and 26—before entering the South Fork. Almost all of the land in the valley through which Rainey Creek flows is private ranch and farmland. The best public access is found in the Big Hole Range, where it flows through Targhee National Forest. Rainey Creek Road is one-and-a-half-miles south of the town of Swan Valley. The water in this area is small and the fishing opportunities are not necessarily plentiful. However, armed with a light-weight rod and small flies, Rainey Creek can be a fun experience.

Pine Creek is commonly called Piney Creek by local residents. It is important for irrigation in the Swan Valley area, but noticeably less so than Rainey Creek. It also drains a larger area than Rainey Creek. These two factors make it less susceptible to low flows that can render spawning runs impossible. The weir protecting cutthroat spawning runs on this stream is located in Pine Basin on Pine Creek Pass, just off the highway. The Idaho Department of Fish and Game mans the station during spawning runs in the spring and welcomes visitors wishing to observe the process of physically removing rainbow and hybrids from the stream. I have witnessed the activities at the weir and I am very impressed at the size of cutthroat that make their way up Pine Creek. It's actually kind of humbling, considering that the trout I have caught on the stream are quite a bit smaller than the ones I have seen at the weir.

The upper reaches of Rainy Creek.

The IDF&G fish weir has been a successful deterrent to hybridization on Piney Creek.

The vast majority of lower Pine Creek flows through private ranch and farmland and is inaccessible to the public. But above Pine Creek Canyon, the stream flows almost entirely through Targhee National Forest in the Big Hole Mountains. Highway 31 runs alongside the creek in many places. Anglers can park at a variety of turnoffs to access the river. Here, the stream flows through the basin of Pine Creek Pass, winding its way through a heavy thicket of willows. Casting on this portion of the creek can be frustrating with all of the cover, but using a light rod (six- to seven-and-a-half-foot, three-weight) with short leader can help make the fishing here more enjoyable. The fish I have caught on Pine Creek are larger than what I have caught on other tributaries of the South Fork. It is best fished in July, after the stream clears and there is still enough water to support larger fish. Fishing is good within Pine Creek Basin upstream to the confluence of West Pine Creek. The water upstream of the confluence is typically too low to hold an abundant number of trout. Like Palisades Creek, fishing on Pine Creek begins on July 1st to protect spawning cutthroat.

Burns Creek

The Canyon of the South Fork has several tributaries but most of these are intermittent. Most simply drain feeder canyons and dry up after the last of the snow has melted in the spring and early summer. Only a handful run throughout the season. The most notable of these is Burns Creek. Like Palisades, Rainey and Pine creeks, Burns Creek is an essential spawning stream for cutthroat. It is a small stream that doesn't hold much by way of large fish. Anglers can reach it via Forest Service Road 206, about a mile-and-a-half east of Cottonwood Boat Launch. There is a road going a half-mile up it from the river road, then a trail going up to the creek. I prefer to access Burns Creek by floating the South Fork down to the confluence with the stream, mixing it in with a day of fishing on the river. The best fishing can be found at the mouth of the creek. Here the stream feeds into a large back channel that offers consistently clear water and excellent fishing with PMDs and Rusty Spinners during cold, wet, and cloudy weather. There are times when this channel is completely carpeted with PMDs or mahogany duns, only broken by the several ripples of rising trout sipping them down with abandon.

As a recognized spawning stream of much importance, Burns Creek does not open to fishing until after July 1st.

The Snake River fine-spotted cutthroat is one of only two cutthroat sub-species that are native to the drainage.

Part III: Snake River Flies

The angling culture developed on the Snake River over the past three quarters of a century is responsible for some of the most popular and effective artificial flies found in the sport today. In the 1930s and 1940s, only a handful of individuals in Jackson Hole and along the South Fork were involved in tying. Principally these were Bob Carmichael, Leonard "Boots" Allen, Don Martinez, Etsel Radford, and Marcella Oswald. The post-war development of fly-fishing in the region demanded more flies and, consequently, more tiers. This was the era of Jack Dennis, Ardell Jeppsen, Jay Buchner, and Joe Allen. The number of tiers honing their skills on the Snake River today is probably as great as on any other stream in North America. The result has been a literal explosion of patterns. Since roughly 1990, shops catering to Snake River fishermen have tripled their fly-carrying capacity. Many traditional patterns have been phased out for new flies constructed from synthetic materials like foam and rubber. Still, a number of pioneering flies remain popular even today.

What I present here is far from being representative of all the flies ever designed by Snake River tiers. Instead, I have selected those that best represent the innovative heritage of pattern creation in the area. Some are fantastically effective year round while others are designed for use during a specific hatch or lifecycle stage. I have had a chance to fish a version of all of these and can attest to the effectiveness of each.

Two predominant features of this selection should be immediately noticeable to the reader. First is the number of attractors. They comprise a majority of the flies presented here. Early on, tiers like Carmichael, Allen, and Dennis noticed the broadness of hatches on the Snake River. They also recognized the opportunistic feeding behavior of the river's primary trout species, the cutthroat. These tiers needed to create flies that could successfully represent a number of different trout foods at once. This trend continues with more recent creations by the likes of Guy Turck, Will Dornan, and Brenda Swinney.

The second most noticeable feature is the large size of many of these patterns. Many are tied on hook #2 to 8. Classic patterns like the Humpy and Variant series, while more likely to be offered in #12 to 18 today, were commonly tied in #8 in the pre and immediate post-war era. There are several reasons for this fascination with large flies. One is that many early Snake River patterns originated from flies tied for softer, suppler streams. Tiers had to construct flies that could withstand the swift, raging currents of the Snake and its tributaries. This meant more material—hackle, dubbing, and hair—on larger hooks. In some cases, Carmichael and Donnelly's Variant series for example, material requirements for previously existing flies were manipulated in various ways to allow for better flotation and presentation. Once again, this is a trend that continues today.

Another reason local fly-fishers prefer large patterns is that large insects are common on the Snake River. October caddis, *hecubas*, and a whole range of giant stoneflies and grasshoppers call the Snake River home. Imitations of these kinds of trout food make sense. But there is also the belief among many fly-fishermen that larger bugs will catch larger fish. Paul Bruun and Guy Turck have written about this several times when introducing readers to fly-fishing in the Snake River region. It is something that my father believed in faithfully. I am yet to be completely convinced of this myself. I must admit, however, that much of the evidence I have collected over the years suggests that this might be the case.

Still, there are several smaller and stage-specific patterns presented here. Many of these come from the Snake's most renowned contemporary tiers—individuals like Jay Buchner, Howard Cole, and Scott Sanchez. I consider these individuals to be among the best and most innovative tiers in the country today. This is in large measure due to the amount of work they put into creating their patterns. Buchner and Cole perform considerable entomological and habitat research before designing their flies.

What I admire most about Snake River flies is their effectiveness throughout a variety of trout water. Reports of success are not just found in North America. There are many tales of these flies producing good catches in New Zealand, Europe, Mongolia, Russia, Chile, and Argentina. So don't consider this section to be just about flies fished on the Snake River. Instead, consider this to be a compilation of effective Snake River patterns that can be used on waters throughout the world.

The flies presented here are in chronological order, starting with the earliest patterns and ending with the most recent. Space does not permit tying steps to be presented along with these patterns. What I try and give instead is a description of when, where, and how to fish each of them. I find this to be much more significant advice. There is an abundance of books on the market that give excellent tying instructions for many of these patterns. I suggest Jack Dennis' *Western Trout Fly Tying Manual* (Volumes I and II). These are two of the best-selling tying books of all time and many tiers learned the art from these manuals. Another excellent source is *The Fly Tier's Benchside Reference* by Ted Leeson and Jim Schollmeyer. With full-color steps for hundreds of techniques, it is probably the best tying manual available today.

In the same tradition as Bruce Staples (*Snake River Country Flies and Waters*; *Trout Country Flies*), one of my goals here is to preserve a bit of history on Snake River fly-fishing—before it's lost forever. Staples himself has done a tremendous job in this regard, but even in his grand works there are missing patterns, something he himself would point out. New patterns are being developed continually. Some of the newest that are missing in Staples' work are included here. Ideally, I would like to present as many Snake River patterns as possible, but a future volume on this topic might be in order.

Carmichael Indispensable

Fly type: Attractor
Created by Bob Carmichael, mid-1930s

Hook: Dai-Riki 300 or equivalent, size 8 to 14
Thread: Black 6/0
Tail: Red or brown hackle fibers or moose mane hair
Abdomen: Yellow floss or flat wax nylon thread
Thorax: Pink dubbing
Wing: Grizzly hackle tips
Hackle: Brown and grizzly

The Carmichael Indispensable is among the first patterns created by a Snake River tier. It is often referred to as either an Indispensable or a Carmichael. Like so many of the patterns developed by its namesake, this one uses hackle tips for wing material and hackle fibers as the tail. The Indispensable very closely follows the design of the classic Adams. In *The Western Trout Fly Tying Manual: Volume I*, Jack Dennis suggests using an Indispensable in place of an Adams when casting to selective trout.

The material requirements given above follow those in Dennis' first tying manual. Bruce Staples relates that the original pattern had Rhode Island red hackle fibers for the tail. Dennis substituted moose body hair, no doubt because of the superior durability of this material and its abundance in the Yellowstone area. The Indispensable pictured here uses hackle fibers as the tail. The oversized hackle, dressed sparse, is a signature component of many flies designed by Bob Carmichael.

Light Variant

Fly type: Attractor
Created by Bob Carmichael and Roy Donnelly, early 1940s

Hook: Mustad 94840, Size 8 to16
Thread: Cream 3/0 to 6/0 UNI-Thread, depending on hook size
Wing: Honey dun or Cahill hackle tips
Tail: Brown hackle
Body: Badger underfur, gray squirrel, or cream dubbing
Hackle: Brown and honey dun or brown and Cahill hackle

This version of the Light Variant is one of the first ever flies created for the Snake River by Snake River tiers. Only a few other patterns—the Whitcraft, and the Indispensable—predate Carmichael and Donnelly's Variant series, of which the Light Variant is an important part. Over roughly a 20-year period, the combined efforts of this talented tying duo created a vast assortment of effective trout flies, including the Spruce Fly and the Carey Spider. The Variant series—the Light Variant, Dark Variant, and the H and L Variant—was debatably their most successful group of flies. They have withstood the test of time, too. Here in the twenty-first century, you can still find Variants at fly shops throughout the American West.

The Light Variant is my favorite because it does an excellent job of imitating a variety of mayfly duns, particularly PMDs (#12 to 16), gray drakes (#10 to 14), and blue-winged olives (#14 to 18). These versions work tremendously well during the carpeting hatches that can occur on the South Fork. Moderate hatches of these mayflies also occur along the Upper Snake River as well, especially between Pacific Creek and Moose. Tom Carmichael relates that larger versions of the light variant are effective as imitations of golden stoneflies. The Light Variant pictured here features long, oversized hackle, a trait common among many patterns designed by Carmichael, Donnelly, and Don Martinez. Carmichael spoke highly of this pattern in J. Edson Leonard's *Flies*.

The Humpy

Fly type: Attractor
Popularized by Leonard "Boots" Allen, late 1940s

Hook: Standard dry-fly hook, size 8 to 16
Thread: Yellow, orange, or red 3/0 flat wax nylon or UNI-Thread
Tail: Mule deer hair from the neck and facial area
Wing and shellback: Mule deer hair from the neck and facial area, wing tied clump-style
Hackle: Grizzly

The true origins of the Humpy are sketchy at best. Claims of creation abound throughout North America, as do the variety of names it might go by. In Montana, it's known as the Goofus Bug. In Northern California, it's called Horner's Deer Hair. It is commonly believed that the name "Humpy" originated in the Snake River region of Wyoming. Leonard "Boots" Allen was tying a version of the Humpy in the immediate post-war period, probably as early as 1947. Anglers throughout Wyoming and Idaho credit Allen with the fly's creation. While this is debatable, there is no question that he was significant in its popularization.

The fly shown here is similar to how Allen would have tied it in the 1940s and 1950s. Since then, there have been major changes to the Humpy. The improvements to the Humpy made by Jack Dennis and Jay and Kathy Buchner have been among the most significant. These include an upright and divided hair wing to replace the clump wing and a more sparse and imitative tail. Different hair materials have replaced the original light mule deer hair taken from the face and neck. This decreases the fly's buoyancy, but also makes it more durable.

Gros Ventre Nymph

Fly type: General Nymph
Created by Leonard "Boots" Allen, late 1940s

Hook: Mustad 94840 or equivalent, size 10 to 16
Thread: Brown or yellow 3/0 flat wax nylon
Weight: Lead wire
Tail and antennae: 20-pound, .017-inch monofilament
Hackle: Brown
Shellback: Flat brown cattail trimming material
Head: Peacock herl

This general nymph pattern seems unique today because of its unorthodox material requirements and appearance. However, it is a fair representation of many early Snake River patterns. Most tiers in the first half of the twentieth century made use of what materials were available. Allen created this fly by using monofilament for legs and antennae. As an early guide on Jackson and Jenny lakes, heavy-gauge monofilament line was always around for Allen. It was essential gear when trolling for large mackinaw lake trout. The flat brown cattail trimming used for the shellback is a common craft material for designing various fabrics too. Boots' wife, Gail, was a knitter who created blankets, rugs, and dresses for friends and family. I have found cattail in dark and light brown colors at craft stores throughout Wyoming and Idaho.

The name for this nymph obviously comes from the Gros Ventre River, a major tributary of the Upper Snake River. It is known that Allen used to guide clients on this stream. He told stories of the days when it was possible to drive clients to Darwin Ranch near the river's headwaters and fish below Ouzel Falls. That road cannot be used today and reaching the falls requires a nine-mile hike. The version pictured here is tied like the original, and is not available on the market. The few who do use it fish it as either a little yellow stonefly (Perlodidae *Isoperla* sp.) or clip off the hind legs and fish it as a loose tube-case caddis (Brachycentridae). Many replace the monofilament with rubber legs.

Marcella's Trout Fly

Fly type: Stonefly Adult
Created by Marcella Oswald, early 1950s

Hook: Mustad 9672 or equivalent, size 6 to 10
Thread: Black 3/0 flat wax nylon
Tail: Light elk rump hair
Ribbing: Black hackle
Body: Orange or red yarn; alternatively orange Angora goat dubbing
Wing: Whitetail deer hair
Hackle: Furnace saddle hackle or blended dark cahill and brown hackle

Probably no other pattern is more synonymous with the South Fork of the Snake River than Marcella Oswald's original Trout Fly. It is virtually impossible to find commercially these days, but enough tiers in East Idaho have learned the recipe for Marcella's Trout Fly, and have added their own variations, that it remains an ever-present pattern in the Snake River drainage. I consider this to be a true testament to Oswald's influence. Through the Idaho Falls City Recreation Department, she taught tying seminars for several years in Idaho Falls, Idaho. Those she instructed have passed down the art of tying this fly to succeeding generations. The versions found on the Snake River today can in many ways be traced directly back to her.

The pattern above is a version of Marcella's Trout Fly that I often tie. The recipe, for the most part, follows that of the original. The one exception is that I substitute dark cahill and brown hackle for Marcella's original furnace saddle hackle. I also use Angora goat dubbing in place of yarn. I find this coarse material to be far more water resistant than yarn. It also dries quickly while being cast through the air. Other tiers have incorporated assorted materials for the wing, or have added rubber legs to their versions.

Super Renegade

Fly type: Wet Fly/Attractor
Created by Etsel Radford and Ardell Jeppsen, circa 1959

Hook: Mustad 9672 or equivalent, size 4 to 8
Thread: Black 6/0
Rear hackle: Soft grizzly
Rear body: White, brown, or yellow chenille
Middle hackle: Soft brown
Front body: Peacock herl
Front hackle: Soft white, dun, or grizzly

The Super Renegade is a creation of East Idaho locals Etsel Radford and Ardell Jeppsen, unofficial tying instructors whose skills have been passed down to current generations. (Radford is the creator of another popular South Fork pattern—the Fizzler.) The Super Renegade builds upon the classic Renegade, a fly that also has an intimate connection to Idaho waters. The primary variation here is the added body segment and hackle. Different materials are used for the body as well. Where the original Renegade used peacock herl for the body, the Super has assorted colors of chenille. Various colors of hackle can be incorporated into this pattern as well.

Kevin Radford, Etsel Radford's son, suggests fishing the Super Renegade in tandem with a Fizzler dropping off the rear with two feet of monofilament. He does not recommend fishing it with weight. Casts should be directed toward structure and undercut banks. Another option is to apply floatant to the Super and fish it on the surface. I have known some to fish it in this manner on the South Fork during stonefly hatches and when grasshoppers are plentiful in late July and August. Whether it is fished wet or dry, #4 to 6 are generally the most productive versions of the Super Renegade.

Black Humpy

Fly type: Attractor
Created by Ramona Bressler, early 1960s

Hook: Standard dry-fly hook, size 12 to 24
Thread: 6/0 to 8/0 black UNI-Thread, dependent on size
Tail: Mule deer hair dyed black
Shellback: Mule deer hair dyed black
Hackle: Black

There are several Humpy variations, but I mention Ramona Bressler's because it was one of the first, pre-dating the Buchner's Humpies and occurring no later than those being designed by Jack Dennis. Ramona's inspiration was a dry fly that would be easier to see through the surface glare created on riffles during overcast days. Tiers today accomplish this by tying black parachute posts, commonly called Glarachutes, onto small mayfly patterns. Bressler later found this fly to be an excellent match for slate wings and mahogany duns when tied in #12 to 16.

Ramona tied this bug with black hackle and dyed deer hair. She clipped the front excess after creating the shellback, rendering it a wingless version of a Humpy. I do not know of this version of the Humpy being sold commercially in North America today.

It remains a highly productive fly for those lucky enough to find one or tie their own. I rarely fish patterns smaller than a #18 on the Snake and its tributaries, but if I do, and I want to use an attractor, this is one of the flies I go with. A #20 to 22 can offer an excellent imitation of an adult midge. I use such a fly when guiding experienced anglers between Jackson Lake Dam and Pacific Creek on the Upper Snake River.

Bob's Hopper

Fly type: Terrestrial
Created by Bob Bean, late 1960s

Hook: Mustad 9672 or equivalent, size 6 to 10
Thread: Cream, tan, orange, olive, or yellow 3/0
Body: Cream, tan, orange, olive, or yellow open-cell foam
Underwing: Orange doll hair
Legs: Teal duck flank fibers
Overwing and head: Texas whitetail hair

Innovative tier Bob Bean was one of the first in the Snake River region to incorporate foam into his surface patterns. With this hopper imitation, he used tight wraps of foam to create a ribbed appearance for the body. Bean also used different colors of foam throughout the season to imitate the color change of natural hoppers, which typically move from a light green color to a yellow, and then to a tan. He also stressed size, relying primarily on #6 to 8 versions, and only moving to #10 when small naturals were present or trout were feeding more selectively than usual. This terrestrial is as deadly as any other on the South Fork during the stifling heat that can hit the lower sections of the river in August.

Like Marcella's Trout Fly, versions of Bob's Hopper are hard to find commercially these days, but the rich heritage of tying and angling in the region has allowed this pattern to persevere. Many learned to tie Bob's Hopper through the courses he offered at Blackfoot, Idaho high schools and the city's Community Education Program. These tiers have passed down this valuable knowledge to a new generation of tiers, who now produce their own personal variations of Bean's original. These newer versions typically incorporate either more visible legs, different wing materials, or a tail. The fly above is one that I tied with Texas whitetail deer hair for the wing. I find the color of this material to be more imitative. In addition, Texas whitetail hair lays down in a way that resembles a natural grasshopper wing. It does not flare in a dramatic fashion as more commonly used mule deer and coastal blacktail hair do.

Jay-Dave's Hopper

Fly type: Terrestrial
Created by Jay Buchner, mid-1970s

Hook: Mustad 9671 or equivalent, size 6 to 12
Thread: Yellow or white 3/0 monocord
Tail: Dyed red deer hair or brown hackle fibers
Ribbing: Clipped brown or ginger hackle
Body: Yellow poly yarn
Underwing: Deer body hair
Overwing: Turkey wing
Legs: Golden pheasant tail feather fibers, knotted to form joints
Head: Flared and spun deer hair, trimmed to shape

Terrestrial patterns are among the most popular dry flies in use on the Snake River and its tributaries. Jay Buchner's version of Dave Whitlock's classic has a 30-year history of effectiveness; it's a must-have for Flat Creek. The section of this stream flowing through the National Elk Refuge has intense hopper populations that typically peak when the creek opens on August 1st. In addition, many of the smaller feeder streams coming off the southern Teton and the Snake River ranges, in particular Fish and Fall creeks, have substantial grasshopper populations where the Jay-Dave's can have a high degree of success. In the heat of August, when midday surface activity on some stretches of the Snake River slows to a crawl, this terrestrial pattern can be just the ticket. I use terrestrials throughout much of August when fishing the Snake River between Pacific Creek and Moose Landing, and the Jay-Dave's is one of the patterns I rely on most.

When I tie versions of the Jay-Dave's Hopper, I often substitute the dyed-red deer hair called for in the original with dyed-red hackle fibers or brown hackle fibers. This is best done with smaller patterns in #10 or 12, where the naturally short length of hackle fibers will be less of an issue. I also find the original legless versions of the Jay-Dave's to be as effective as those tied with legs.

Double Humpy

Fly type: Attractor
Created by Joe Allen, circa 1981

Hook: Dai Riki 700 or equivalent, size 6 to 10
Thread: Yellow, red, orange, or green 3/0 flat wax nylon or monochord
Tail: Mule deer hair taken from the facial and neck region
Shellbacks and wings: Mule deer hair taken from the facial and neck region
Hackle: Grizzly

A mistake at the tying vise led to the creation of this fly by Joe Allen in the winter of 1980-1981. It was a major Humpy variation, an immediate success, and remains one of the most popular dry attractors on the Snake River to this day. Joe always stressed that the most important feature of this fly is not the heavy wraps of hackle (up to 18 per segment), but the type of deer hair. Mule deer hair from the mask, neck, and lower flank, offer some of the lightest type of hair material available. One downside of this type of material though is that it is less durable than elk or caribou hair. Joe often compensated for this by criss-crossing the thread over each shellback.

The Double Humpy is as true an attractor as a fly can get. Trout often strike while it's dragged wet along structure and banks, where it is possibly taken for a baitfish or an emerging or swimming stonefly. On the surface, many anglers fish it as a hopper, but this might be a misrepresentation. Writer and angler Paul Bruun pointed out to me that the Double Humpy, when dragged (not skittered!) along the surface, imitates the wake of a moving stonefly. I get many requests to tie Double Humpies with rubber legs. These versions are certainly productive, but I have noticed that the rubber legs get in the way of the imitative wake created by an original Double Humpy.

Kiwi Muddler

Fly type: Streamer
Created by Jack Dennis, early 1980s

Hook: Mustad 9672 or equivalent, size 2 to 8
Thread: Black or olive 3/0
Body: Black or olive sparkle dubbing
Ribbing: Medium flat tinsel
Wing: Strip of Zonker rabbit fur, color to match body
Interior collar: Fine red tinsel or Flashabou accent
Head and exterior collar: Deer hair

The Kiwi Muddler is a favorite among both stream and lake fly-fishermen across the Rocky Mountain West. In the Snake River drainage, a variety of color combinations are used to imitate local baitfish. Black with olive, olive with natural, and gray with natural will match fingerling trout, Utah chubs, shiners, and sculpins. Color combinations that incorporate yellow, silver, brown and white will simulate whitefish and sucker minnows. Originally tied with spun deer hair for the head, coneheads have recently been added and help submerge the Kiwi Muddler to depths that could previously only be reached with full-sinking lines. Still, many anglers use sink tips and full-sinking lines when using a Kiwi Muddler on lakes. The pattern has taken lake trout at depths estimated to be close to 50 feet on Jackson Lake.

Super X

Fly type: Wet Fly/Attractor
Created by Wes Newman, mid-1980s

Hook: Mustad 9672 or equivalent, size 4 to 8
Thread: Black 6/0
Rear hackle: Soft grizzly
Rear body: Black chenille
Legs: Large white rubber or two strands of medium white rubber
Front body: Pink or orange chenille
Front hackle: Soft white or brown hackle

Wes Newman developed this pattern as an improvement on the Super Renegade, a highly popular South Fork fly created by Etsel Radford and Ardell Jeppsen. Throughout the 1980s and early 1990s, the Super-X became a popular South Fork pattern in its own right. Still available commercially, many local tiers continue to produce their own versions. Newman, now living in Kansas, relates that he never weighted the Super-X. Instead, he relied on saturation to take the fly just under the surface. Fished in this manner, the Super-X produces as a just-below-the-film subsurface pattern. Many times trout are completely visible when they strike. Most versions today come weighted though with lead-free wire wrap, allowing it to sink well below the surface.

Like its forerunner, the Super-X comes in a variety of color combinations. Tiers also use an assortment of hackles, including ginger and dun. This pattern is a true wet attractor in that it does not imitate anything specific. In fact, a case can be made that it's not really even suggestive of any kind of trout food. Still, it attracts the attention of trout and continually produces on the water.

Silistreamer

Fly type: Streamer
Created by Bruce James, mid-1980s

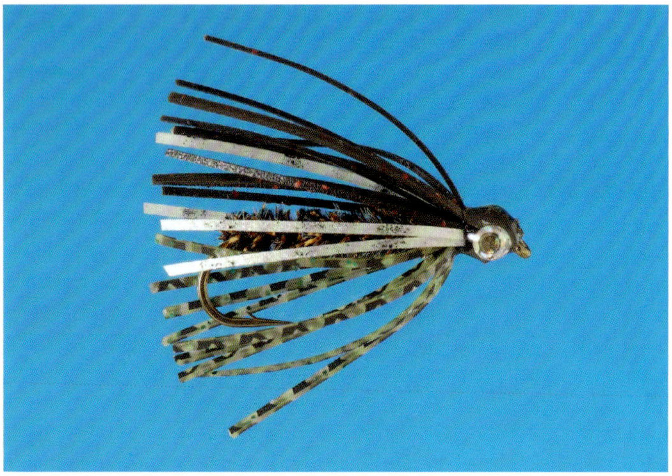

Hook: Tiemco 9395 or equivalent, size 2 to 6
Thread: Black 3/0 monocord or 6/0 Gudebrod
Body: Ice dubbing or ice chenille
Legs: Sili Legs, color to match body
Head: Small dumbbell eyes with epoxy or stick-on eyes with epoxy

Bruce James has been a fixture at the Jack Dennis Outdoor Shop for over 30 years. He developed this pattern for use on a variety of waters, with Sili Legs acting as the key component to this streamer. The material comes in a multitude of colors, which allows anglers to imitate a number of different baitfish. Like the Double Bunny, a dark-over-light color configuration enhances the Silistreamer's imitative ability. Sili Legs, no matter what the color, have a slight transparency that reacts well to light. They also have a pulsating affect when stripped through a current. Like the J.J. Special, this can act as a key attractant to trout.

The Silistreamer is recognized as one of the best subsurface patterns for lakes in Jackson Hole and the headwater lakes in Yellowstone. I have used it on Jackson, Jenny, and Lewis lakes several times with a high degree of success. My all-around favorite is black over dark olive in a #4 to 6. I use two strips of white Sili Legs along each side as the lateral line. This pattern often produces when other reliable stand-bys fail.

Parachute Midge Emerger

Fly type: Midge
Created by Scott Sanchez, mid-1980s

Hook: Dai-Riki 305 or equivalent, size 18 to 24
Thread: Black 8/0 UNI-Thread
Parachute: White Antron or poly yarn
Tail: Two strips of pearl Krystal Flash
Abdomen: Peacock dubbing
Ribbing: Krystal Flash
Hackle: Grizzly hackle

This rather simple midge pattern developed by Scott Sanchez has produced some very impressive results for fly-fishers on the stretch of the Snake River immediately below Jackson Lake. I recall one day in late May several years ago when a group of anglers was fishing in the vicinity of the first bend below the dam. After successive strikes on multiple rods, the fishermen began to yell back and forth to each other, inquiring as to what they were having their luck on. Each replied with either, "a Parachute Midge," or, "a Parachute Midge Emerger," or, " yep, I'm getting mine on a Parachute Midge, too." This pattern has earned a special spot on one section of river for one specific emergence, and it works masterfully.

I believe that the luminescent combination of the Krystal Flash ribbing and peacock dubbing makes this midge more effective than others. The material creates a significant amount of translucence with even minimal sunlight. The Parachute Midge also floats at a vertical angle in the surface film that closely imitates a natural as it attempts to break from its shuck. These struggling insects are easy meals for hungry trout. When you add these two factors together—the luminescent body and the imitative suspension at which it floats in the surface film—what you get is one of the most effective midge emergers a fly-fisher can use today.

LBS

Fly type: Stonefly Nymph
Created by Dave Brackett, late 1980s

Hook: Mustad 3906B or equivalent, size 12 to 20
Thread: Black 8/0
Tail: Grizzly hackle fibers
Body: Black dubbing
Wing case: White box sheeting
Legs: Grizzly hackle fibers

Little black stoneflies (*Capnia*), also known as tiny winter black stones, generally emerge on the Snake River from late February through May. Dave Brackett produced the LBS (short for Little Black Stone) to imitate this early-season emerger. I use this pattern throughout much of April, when little black stone emergences are at their heaviest. When the skies are clear and temperatures begin to push toward 50 degrees Fahrenheit, something that can occur in the Snake River drainage in early spring, the LBS can be one of the most productive flies in an angler's box.

A float trip in April 2001 from Wilson to South Park Bridge made me a big believer in fishing this pattern unweighted and close to the surface. While I kept my LBS as deep as I could get it, my guide friend Jason Wright fished his just below the surface film and caught four trout for every one that I landed. Since that day, I only use the saturated dubbing material as weight.

Increasingly, #12 to 14 versions are replacing the #16 to 20 originals that Brackett first designed. A number of variations of the LBS also incorporate super-thin 1mm foam as a substitute for the box sheeting specified in the original pattern. Brackett, however, suggests that box sheeting provides more than just floatation. "It creates a degree of translucence that you just don't get from foam," Dave states. I have noticed a significant difference between the two versions, with the original version far outperforming those now tied with foam.

U-Con Emerger

Fly type: Caddis Emerger
Created by Howard Cole, late 1980s

Hook: TMC 900 BL or equivalent, size 12 to 16
Thread: Brown 6/0 or 8/0, dependent on size
Trailing shuck: Amber Z-lon
Body: Olive, brown, rust orange, tan, or *Hexagenia* natural dubbing
Shellback: Olive, brown, rust orange, tan Antron
Thorax: Clear glass-bead
Wing: Deer hair

Also known as the U-Con 2, this pattern incorporates innovative yet practical tying techniques to create one of the most effective caddis emergers on the market today. Most patterns of this type float exceptionally well, but tend to roll onto their sides while drifting on the surface film. Howard Cole solved this problem by widening the overbody with a bobbin, allowing both sides of the fly to lay even with the hook shank. For added stability, Cole ties-in a wide deer-hair wing that forces the fly to roll upright even if it lands awkwardly on its side. The glass bead is not used for weight, but rather to imitate an air bubble trapped between the body and the shuck.

The U-Con is an exceptional emerger to use when fishing the several caddis hatches that occur all along the Snake River. Like many other patterns created by Howard Cole, simple alterations to material colors allow the U-Con to be fished during a variety of hatches. Howard himself suggests olive and gray for *Rhyacophila* and *Brachycentrus*.

J.J. Special

Fly type: Streamer/Wet Attractor
Created by Jim Jones, late 1980s

Hook: Dai-Riki 710 or equivalent, size 2 to 8
Thread: Black, brown, or yellow 3/0 monocord
Tail: Blended yellow and brown marabou, typically with either (a) yellow on sides and brown in the center, or (b) yellow on bottom and brown on top, Flashabou accent inter-mixed
Body: Brown chenille
Legs: Medium yellow rubber
Hackle: Grizzly or brown
Ribbing: Copper or brass wire
Weight: Lead-free wire; alternatively a conehead, bead head, or both

Jim Jones is co-owner of High Country Flies in Jackson, Wyoming. The story behind the development of this pattern has become a part of Snake River lore. He and a group of fellow anglers, while fishing the Bighorn River, decided to have a personal competition on the final day of their expedition where they would each fish a fly that they personally tied. As the last one at the tying bench, Jim decided on a creation using only scraps of material left by the previous tiers. The result was the J.J. Special, and the rest is history. The J.J. is one of the most popular subsurface patterns on the Snake River. In fact, I would suggest that Jim Jones' fly is probably *the* "go-to" wet fly for most anglers in the area.

The pattern pictured here is a version of the J.J. Special that I tie. It varies slightly from Jones' original. I do not add accenting Flashabou along the sides like the original. I also spackle the yellow legs with black ink, similar to how Zebra Legs would look. I feel this gives the legs more of a shadowy effect as they pulsate through the water when being stripped in. Lastly, I use both a conehead- and a bead head to help get the fly down near the bottom, where I have the majority of my luck with the pattern. Jones' original used weighted wire wrapped to the shank of the hook. He suggests that this not only gives balance to the pattern when it's stripped and jigged through a current, but it actually provides more weight than a *visually* heavy conehead- or beadhead version.

Paul Bruun has theorized that the J.J. Special's color scheme imitates the sucker minnow, which are abundant on the Snake. These baitfish congregate near the stream bottom. Others suggest that it could represent a bottom-dwelling crayfish.

Turck's Tarantula

Fly type: Attractor
Created by Guy Turck, circa 1990

Hook: Dai-Riki 700 or 710 or equivalent, size 4 to 10
Thread: Tan or black 3/0 monocord
Tail: Amhurst or golden pheasant neck-wing fibers
Body: Red, green, gold or gray rabbit-fur dubbing
Interior wing: Calf tail
Exterior wing and head: Spun and trimmed deer hair
Legs: Medium brown or white rubber

Guy Turck used the Madam X as inspiration for this fly. He developed it in 1990 and it quickly gained a large and loyal following. It might be one of the best-selling attractors on the market today. (George Anderson used it to win the One-Fly Competition in 1990.) The Tarantula has been one of my favorite trout flies for over a decade, but I prefer to use golden pheasant neck-wing fibers for the tail as a substitute for the Amherst wing used in the original. I tend to also get better results from white rubber legs over brown. Color is another concern. Most anglers I know who are Tarantula fans choose red over any other color. I tend to lean to more earth-tone colors like gold or gray.

The beauty of the Tarantula is its ability to resemble many different types of trout food at once. Depending on the size one uses, it can imitate a grasshopper or a variety of stoneflies. Probably its best quality is its subsurface effectiveness. When I guide clients and trout are continually hitting the Tarantula on the surface, it obviously becomes saturated and begins to submerge. I often instruct these anglers to let it go wet and fish it either with a dead-drift or with a stripping motion like a streamer. Trout typically continue to strike when it's fished in this manner. One of my clients landed his largest trout ever—a 19-and-1/2-inch cutthroat—fishing a #6 gold-bodied Tarantula wet just above the Cottonwood Creek confluence on the Snake River in Grand Teton National Park.

Fore and Aft Nymph

Fly type: Stonefly Nymph
Created by Dave Brackett, early 1990s

Hook: Mustad 9671 or equivalent, size 8 to 14
Thread: Brown 6/0
Beads: Front: 5/32-inch-diameter gold or tungsten; rear: 3/32-inch-diameter gold (bead diameters given for a size-8 pattern)
Tail: Pheasant-tail feather fibers or light elk hair
Body: Dubbed blend of orange and brown yarn or dubbing to obtain golden brown color
Wingcase: Pheasant-tail fibers or light elk hair

Dave Brackett of Jackson Hole, Wyoming, developed this pattern to imitate a variety of stonefly nymphs, especially the brown stonefly (*Brachyptera*) that produces light to moderate hatches throughout the Upper Snake River drainage in April and May. These insects are generally 9 to 12 millimeters in length on the Snake River, equating to a #12 to 14 imitation. However, I have found larger versions, #8 to 10, to be just as productive, if not more so.

The creativity of this pattern is found in the unusual double-bead design. A bead is placed at the eye of the hook and then hidden by the body and wingcase material. Another is tied in where the shank begins to make its bend. This not only creates a deep-sinking nymph, it also produces a more even ride on a dead-drift, instead of the typical nose-down ride that occurs with single-beaded nymphs. I fish the Fore and Aft almost exclusively in riffles and riffle pools. I rarely use an indicator with this pattern, as this can interfere with the drift and many times doesn't allow the fly to fully reach the bottom.

Double Bunny

Fly type: Streamer
Created by Scott Sanchez, early 1990s

Hook: Dai-Riki 700 or equivalent, size 2 to 4
Thread: Gray or black 3/0 monocord
Weight: lead wire or alternatively a tungsten or brass-conehead
Underbody: Light-colored strip of rabbit fur
Overbody: Dark-colored strip of rabbit fur
Lateral line: Long Krystal Flash, Ice Chenille or Flashabou tied at mid-body point
Eyes: Stick-on pairs (with epoxy as an adhesive), or dumbbell eyes

Scott Sanchez is a master tier who created this large, saltwater-inspired streamer in the early 1990s. Sanchez is a firm believer in the *large flies=large trout theory*. This is among the largest of all the patterns to originate from Snake River tiers. It can be intimidating for many, but it's certainly one of the best streamers available for those stalking large trout. The Double Bunny became the most infamous of all One-Fly patterns when it won the competition three years running from 1992 to 1994. Tournament rule changes in 1995 limited hooks to nothing larger than a #8, thus taking large streamers like the Double Bunny out of the competition (rules were changed again in 2005 to allow #6 hooks).

There are certain secrets to both tying and fishing this fly. One is the color combination of the rabbit-fur strips. Scott stresses the importance of using dark over light. He suggests gray or natural over white, black over olive, or olive over gray. He marries the tail end of the strips with a fabric adhesive like VAL-A Tear Mender. This allows the tail to move naturally without the stiffness caused by a hard-binding adhesive. Second is the use of weight. Sanchez tends to stay away from cones, beads, and dumbbells and instead simply relies on saturated rabbit fur as weight.

I have found all of these weights to be effective, but I tend to lean toward a tungsten conehead. The success of the Double Bunny is not limited to the Snake either. I have had success with them fishing for taimen, pike, and lenok in Mongolia, Kazakhstan, and Russia.

LOF Pheasant Tail Nymph

Fly type: General Nymph
Created by Howard Cole, early 1990s

Hook: Tiemco 3769 or equivalent, size 14 to 18
Thread: Rust brown 8/0 UNI-Thread
Tail: Ring-necked pheasant-tail fibers
Abdomen: Twisted Krystal Flash, red, orange, root beer, yellow, green, or pearlescent
Thorax: Pheasant tail pulled over silver bead
Hackle: Pheasant breast feather

LOF is an acronym for "Lots of Flash" something that this nymph definitely has. It builds upon the success of Flashback Nymphs that feature bright synthetics for wing casings, particularly on Copper Johns and Hare's Ears. The abdomen is constructed of a variety of Krystal Flash that is twisted together and then wrapped forward in the same fashion as dubbing. This material, along with the bead head, provides significant weight, allowing the LOF to be fished in deep runs, canyon walls, and banks. It is a terrific all-around pattern that works on many streams throughout the West. The LOF is a favorite for anglers on the upper Snake River just after the runoff ends, when the river is still high and trout sometimes need added incentive to take interest in a small aquatic insect.

Gray Parawulff

Fly type: Attractor
Created by Jack Dennis, early 1990s

Hook: DaiRiki 300 or equivalent, size 8 to 16
Thread: Gray 6/0 Gudebrod
Tail: Gray or olive microfibbets or gray hackle fibers
Body: Gray dubbing
Ribbing (optional): Pearl rainbow thread or fine tinsel
Wing: White calf tail
Hackle: Grizzly and brown

The Parawulff combines the best attributes of the parachute and Wulff-wing construction on standard attractor and mayfly patterns. The idea is to create a parachute post that allows the hackle to be wrapped parallel to the body, while at the same time allowing the post to be divided to create a Wulff-style wing that is more visible to trout below. The Royal Parawulff and Adams Parawulff can be found throughout the West today, but this innovation partially began with Jack Dennis' Gray Parawulff in the 1990s.

Many anglers I have talked with agree that Parawulffs in #12 to 16 are the most realistic and work the best. It's an excellent match for blue-winged olives and PMDs on the South Fork and the Upper Snake. During the thick carpets of PMDs that can afflict the South Fork on damp, overcast days, the Gray Parawulff can be a highly effective imitation. On just such a day in June 2000, resident fly-fisher Brad Sutton and I floated through the Canyon of the South Fork during an impressive PMD hatch. We used Gray Parawulffs exclusively in the vicinity of Lufkin Bottom and landed over 20 fish between us in just over 40 minutes.

Jay's Humpback Emerger

Fly type: Mayfly Emerger
Created by Jay Buchner, early 1990s

Hook: Mustad 94845 or equivalent, size 14 to 22
Thread: Black, brown, olive, or dun 8/0 UNI-Thread
Tail: Brown hackle fibers or pheasant-tail fibers
Body: Thread suggested above or dubbing to match thread color
Hackle: Dun or grizzly
Shellback: Deer hair

Jay Buchner's Humpback Emerger is a fantastic all-around pattern for a variety of mayflies. It's most often used to imitate blue-winged olives, but it can also represent emerging PMDs, flavs, and Tricos. This is done with slight changes to size and color. Size 16 to 18 in an olive or dark brown body is what many will use for blue-winged olives. Size 12 to 14 in an olive or light brown body will work for a PMD. For Tricos, I use a #18 to 22 with a light olive or light brown body. These changes are considered insignificant by some anglers and there is debate as to whether one light brown Humpback Emerger in #16 will work for just about any mayfly emergence. My opinion is that this is probably true, especially when the opportunistic feeding behavior of Snake River trout is taken into account. Still, there are many times when an angler will happen upon a selectively feeding cutthroat during a PMD or blue-winged olive emergence. When this occurs, a Humpback Emerger, in the right size and color, comes in handy.

Convertible

Fly type: Attractor
Created by Scott Sanchez, early 1990s

Hook: Dai-Riki 300 or equivalent, size 8 to 14
Thread: Tan, black, or brown 6/0
Undertail: Moose or elk hair
Overtail: Brown marabou or root beer Krystal Flash
Body: Tan or *Hexagenia* dubbing
Legs: Medium brown rubber
Back wing: White calf tail
Front wings: White calf tail
Hackle: Grizzly and brown

The demands of the Jackson Hole One-Fly Competition were Scott Sanchez's inspiration for this unique attractor pattern. It had a high degree of success in the contest in 1993. As is, it can imitate a cranefly or a variety of stoneflies and hoppers. Weight can be added to the leader and, with the correct subsurface movement of the fly, it will imitate an emergent stonefly. An angler can remove the legs, the trude wing, and the overtail to produce a mayfly imitation. If one is in the midst of a caddis hatch, the Trude wing can be retained and the front upright and divided wings removed along with the two tails to produce a caddis imitation. Still another possibility is to remove the legs and the marabou overtail of #12 to 14 patterns to create a yellow sally adult or emerger.

Scott has recently produced a Stimulator version of the Convertible that features a hackled body and very noticeable cottontail hair for the tail. It has proved to be quite effective as well. Anglers tempted to give the Convertible a try should not restrict themselves to the Snake River proper. I have had an enormous amount of success with Convertible variations on the Greys River, Flat Creek, and the upper reaches of the Gros Ventre and its tributaries. This is one of the most versatile patterns out there today and can be used for a variety of hatches and conditions.

Cole's CDC Split Wing Cripple

Fly type: Mayfly Adult/Emerger
Created by Howard Cole, early 1990s

Hook: Tiemco 100, sizes 14 to 22
Thread: 8/0 UNI-Thread, olive dun
Tail: Cream or amber Z-lon topped with woodduck breast feather
Abdomen: Stripped peacock herl, stripped hackle tip, or light olive dubbing
Loop: Olive CDC feather
Thorax: Olive dubbing
Wing: Black Z-lon or calf tail

The development of crippled or challenged emerger patterns has grown significantly over the past 15 years. These patterns are best chronicled in Schollmeyer and Leeson's *Tying Emergers*. Defining characteristics of these lifestyle-specific flies are: a trailing shuck and, more importantly, a protruding wing. Howard Cole added a twist to this concept though by splitting the wing of his blue-winged olive cripple. This gives the fly the appearance of two wings protruding from the sides of a wing case while the rest of the fly remains trapped within the shuck.

The magic of Cole's Split Wing Cripple is the near perfect balance of the pattern. The CDC wingcase, dubbed thorax, and wings create sufficient floatation above the surface while the tail and abdomen remain submerged in true emerger fashion. While the blue-winged olive Split Wing Cripple is the most popular version in the Snake River drainage, simple color alterations allow this pattern to be used for many other mayfly hatches.

Amy's Ant

Fly type: Attractor
Created by Jack Dennis, circa 1994

Hook: Mustad 9672 or equivalent, size 4 to10
Thread: Brown 3/0
Underbody: Tan foam
Overbody: Brown foam, strip slightly wider than the underbody
Legs: Medium brown rubber
Body: Gold or light olive ice chenille
Hackle: Fine brown
Wing: Light elk hair over small clump of pearl Krystal Flash
Thorax: Peacock herl
Wingcase: Overbody foam pulled back and tied down

This is Jack Dennis' answer to the explosive popularity of foam-bodied ant patterns. It is one of the first Chernobyl Ant variations to incorporate natural hair as wing material. Early in his career, Dennis recognized the superior durability of elk and moose hair over more commonly used deer hair. No doubt this quality played a role in his decision to use elk hair as the wing for his ant pattern. In 1999, Joe Bressler scored over 700 points on the first day of competition with this fly and swept his way to the top score in the professional division.

I prefer to fish Amy's Ant as a mid-season hopper and a golden stonefly adult. Gold or light-olive ice chenille imitates the color of a natural hopper that is making its color transition from green to gold or tan. These colors also sufficiently imitate the color of a natural golden stonefly. Like most terrestrial, stonefly, and attractor patterns, size and motion are the more important factors when fishing this fly. Taking into account the extended body of the Amy's Ant, a #6 to 8 most closely mimics the size of Snake River hoppers and stoneflies. It is best to fish this pattern with deliberate movement: sporadic twitches if imitating a grasshopper, consistent skittering motions if imitating a golden stone.

LiteBright Serendipity

Fly type: Caddis Pupa/Larva
Created by Howard Cole, mid-1990s

Hook: Tiemco 2457 or equivalent, size 12 to 18
Thread: Tan 8/0 UNI-Thread
Abdomen: Olive Z-Lon, twisted
Thorax: Dubbed Pearlescent LiteBright and Sparkle Hare's Mask
Head: Silver bead

Serendipity-style flies are popular throughout the West. Howard Cole's LiteBright is among the more detailed versions available. It is one of the most effective caddis nymph imitations used on the Snake River today, but area anglers debate over the actual type of caddis it simulates. The olive Z-Lon abdomen leads many to believe the LiteBright is an imitation of the *Rhyacophila*, *Hydropsyche*, or *Glossossoma* genera, all of which exist throughout the drainage. These will hatch all season long. Their populations are particularly strong on the South Fork, where early evening hatches are something to note. The massive hatch of multiple caddis species in June on the Upper Snake creates an excellent opportunity to fish this pattern. That is, if the runoff has subsided.

Foam Wing Hopper

Fly type: Terrestrial
Created by Scott Sanchez, mid-1990s

Thread: Tan 6/0
Hook: Dai-Riki 730 or equivalent, size 8 to 12
Body: Brown-dyed elk body hair
Legs: Medium brown rubber
Wing: Brown foam
Head: Brown-dyed elk body hair
Indicator: Green, yellow, orange, or white foam

The Foam Wing Hopper is just one in a series of top-water foam-wing flies designed by Scott Sanchez. His hopper tends to be among my favorites because different colored foam and dyed elk hair can be substituted for the standard brown to more accurately simulate natural hoppers at different times during the season. This is less of a concern on the main freestone streams like the Upper Snake, the South Fork, the Gros Ventre, and the Grays River, where trout-feeding behavior is opportunistic. However, on streams where feeding is performed in a much more selective manner, such as Flat Creek and certain portions of Fish Creek, such changes can almost be considered an imperative. I do not regard this hopper to be my favorite terrestrial pattern, but I am taken in by the realistic look of this fly and its ability to fool even the pickiest of Snake River trout.

Scott suggests using a bullet-head tool for tying the Foam Wing Hopper. This device allows the tier to more evenly distribute the elk hair in a rounded style, similar to what is found on a Madam X. I typically leave the elk hair a little longer on the top of the fly, creating a sparse exterior wing over the more visible foam wing.

I have had tremendous success with this fly on Flat Creek in August. When midday temperatures begin to warm the valley floor, around 11 a.m., grasshoppers become more active. Sanchez's Foam Wing Hopper, along with Jay-Dave's, Schroeder's Hopper, and the Joe's Hopper are among the most used terrestrial patterns on Flat Creek during this time.

Spandex Stone Nymph

Fly type: Stonefly Nymph
Created by Scott Sanchez, mid-1990s

Hook: Dai-Riki 270 or equivalent, size 4 to 8
Thread: Yellow 3/0
Tail: Brown goose biots
Ribbing: Doubled yellow tying thread
Abdomen: Gold, brown, tan, or *Hexagenia* dubbing
Shellback and wingcase: Six to eight strands of spandex
Thorax and head: Brass or tungsten beads
Legs: Six strands of Spandex
Antennae: Brown goose biots

Scott Sanchez's Spandex Stonefly Nymph has developed a rather strong following since its creation roughly one decade ago. It has proven successful on the South Fork, the upper Snake River, and the Hoback River on several occasions when trout focus on stonefly nymphs just prior to hatches. In my opinion, the Spandex Stone Nymph is most effective as a golden stonefly nymph when tied with tan or *Hexagenia* dubbing on a #8 hook. It is a killer on the South Fork following the salmonfly hatch and works consistently throughout the season on Jackson Hole streams.

While the Spandex Stonefly Nymph looks somewhat complex, it's actually rather simple to tie, specifically because of the material requirements. The Spandex strands used for the shellback and wing casing are used for the legs. This reduces thread bulk near the head and the Spandex itself is very animated in currents or when the fly is stripped. Sanchez ties this fly with a tandem set of beads at the eye of the hook to add sufficient weight to the pattern. I recommend fishing it as close to the stream floor as possible and concentrating on water close to banks during emergences.

Will's Crane Fly

Fly type: Cranefly
Created by Will Dornan, mid-1990s

Hook: Dai-Riki 300 or equivalent, size 8 to 12
Thread: Tan 8/0
Body: Ultra Chenille, tail tip burnt to prevent unraveling
Wingcase: Tan, ginger, or gray closed-cell foam
Hackle: Light ginger
Wings: Light ginger hackle tips
Legs: Tan Silly Legs, knotted to form joints and spackled with brown or black ink

Will Dornan grew up on his family's Teton Valley Ranch near Kelly, Wyoming, in Jackson Hole. This location gave him easy access to excellent trout water, including the lower Gros Ventre River and Flat Creek. This is dry, upland sage country, but the cool, damp corridors through which these streams flow provide ideal habitat for craneflies (family Tipulidae). There are only a few species of truly aquatic craneflies, but the larvae of terrestrial versions tend to prefer moist soil, including that near streams. Dornan discovered the importance of craneflies to trout in this part of Jackson Hole early on, and in the 1990s he developed this very realistic imitation.

Will designed his cranefly to be ultra-light so that it would rest high on the water. This is further enhanced by the light ginger hackle wrapped between the abdomen and thorax. The result is a pattern that imitates the hovering ability of a natural cranefly. Generally, only the hook and tips of the legs, hackle, and Ultra Chenille body touch the water. The lack of bulk on any part of this fly facilitates its drying while being cast. I tend to fish Will's pattern with some motion, which creates the skirting effect. This imitates a natural as it hovers close to the surface, touching the film ever so slightly.

Power Ant

Fly type: Terrestrial
Created by Guy Turck, mid-1990s

Hook: Tiemco 103BL or equivalent, size 8 to 16
Thread: Rust brown or black 8/0 UNI-Thread
Abdomen: Black, brown or cinnamon rabbit fur dubbing
Wing: White calf tail
Hackle: Oversized brown
Legs: Medium brown rubber
Head: Same as abdomen

Guy Turck describes his Power Ant as not so much a terrestrial as an attractor ant pattern. Movement, in the form of short twitches, is a key tactic when fishing Power Ants. Most traditional ants are tied with dark foam and other materials, making them very difficult to see on the water. Guy's ant bucks this trend by incorporating lots of hackle and a white calf-tail wing. It's the most visible and high-riding ant pattern available. Many anglers claim it to be the most productive fast-water ant they use, precisely because of its visibility in conditions that make other patterns hard to see. I have used it with success during those times when winged carpenter ants make their appearance on area streams. Turck suggests fishing the Power Ant on lakes when carpenter ants are about.

Tequilley

Fly type: Streamer/Wet Attractor
Created by Kim Keeley, circa 1996

Hook: Dai-Riki 710 or equivalent, size 2 to 8
Thread: Black or gold 3/0 monocord
Tail: Yellow and black marabou
Body: Long flash chenille, root beer or red color
Legs: Medium yellow rubber
Weight: Brass or tungsten bead to match hook

Kim Keeley, a former head guide for Reel Women Outfitters and now proprietor of the Victor Emporium in Victor, Idaho, is recognized as one of the best streamer-fishermen in the region. The Tequilley is her answer for deep-feeding trout that are unresponsive to traditional baitfish imitations. (The pattern is very similar to the J.J. Special.) Trout may mistake the fly for a bottom-dwelling baitfish—such as a sucker or chub. Others theorize that the Tequilley's intense coloring scheme simply triggers aggressive responses by territorial trout. This would make it a quintessential wet attractor. Most anglers admit to fishing this pattern either heavily weighted or with sinking or sink-tip line, meaning that it could imitate one of three types of trout food, depending on size, color and movement: a baitfish (in #2 to 4 and stripped in or trolled), a crayfish (in #2 to 8 and jigged along the bottom with the rod tip), or a stonefly nymph (in #4 to 8) with darker earth-tone colors and fished either with a dead-drift or jigged). I have had success with all three techniques when matched with the correct size/color specifications.

Donna's Pink Lady

Fly type: Attractor/Terrestrial
Created by Donna Allen, mid-1990s

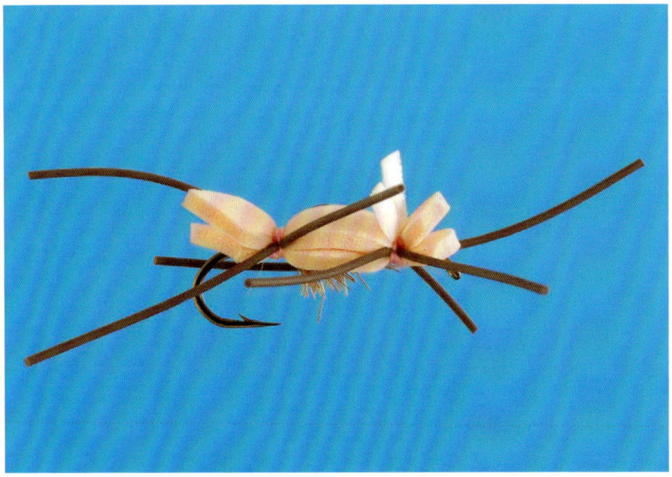

Hook: Dai-Riki 1720 or equivalent, size 6 to 10
Thread: Pink 3/0
Body: Double layer of pink open-cell foam
Hackle: Dun or ginger
Legs: Medium round white or brown rubber
Indicator: Red or white open-cell foam

Donna Allen has a long history of fly-tying in East Idaho. For years she has produced patterns for shops and outfitters along the South Fork of the Snake River. The Pink Ant is one of her more popular creations. It is commonly used as a terrestrial imitation. Foam color can be changed to simulate a variety of stoneflies, but most who use this pattern on a regular basis rely on the highly effective pink foam. Historically, pink has been recognized as a very attractive body color for Snake River trout. The original Carmichael Indispensable, one of the earliest of all Snake River flies, incorporated pink dubbing as the thorax.

Agnel Eye Sculpin

Fly type: Streamer
Created by Will Dornan, circa 1997

Hook: Dai-Riki 710 or equivalent, sizes 4 to 8
Thread: Tan, black, or olive 3/0
Tail and rear body: Magnum rabbit-fur strip in natural, gray, black, or olive
Centered collar: Grizzly marabou
Eye: Blend of Krystal Flash Accent and salmon egg fur as the pupil, surrounded by rolled white wool fur
Head: Olive or black wool fur
Weight: Tungsten bead (lead-free wire optional)

Like many recent sculpin patterns, the Angel Eye Sculpin builds upon the original design by Mike Lawson. Will Dornan rolls several layers of material into his—specifically Krystal Flash Accent, salmon egg fur, and white wool—to create a realistic set of eyes. This is the major departure the pattern offers from Lawson's original wool-head sculpin. A single tungsten bead provides the weight. However, because of the significant buoyancy provided by the wool, Dornan advises supplementing this with lead-free wire wrapped around the hook shank. It's hidden by the tail material, which is wrapped forward and trimmed to form the rear body.

Although it's a proven lake pattern, in particular on Jenny, Lewis, and Jackson lakes, the Angel Eye Sculpin is most effective on area streams. During the October brown runs that occur on the Snake above Jackson Lake and in the Lewis River channel above Lewis Lake, the Angel Eye is a favorite among local guides and fly-fishers. Guide Jason Sutton used a version of the Angel Eye Sculpin to land a pair of 24-inch browns in the Lewis Lake channel in 2002.

Tara X

Fly type: Attractor
Creator unknown, late 1990s

Hook: Dai-Riki 700 or 300 or equivalent, size 4 to 10
Thread: Gray, rust orange, olive, or cream 3/0 monocord
Tail: Golden pheasant neck wing fibers
Body: Gray, rust orange, olive, or cream dubbing
Hackle: Brown saddle
Interior wing: White calf tail
Head and overwing: Deer body hair
Legs: Medium brown rubber

This highly-effective attractor is one of my all-time favorite patterns today. The actual inventor is unknown, and no one has stepped forward to claim credit for its development. The name is believed to be a combination of the Tarantula (a Guy Turck creation) and the Madam X, from which the Tarantula itself was built upon. It combines features of both of these patterns. From the Tarantula it incorporates pheasant wing fibers for the tail and a dubbed body. From the Madam X, it incorporates the deer-hair head tied rounded bullet-head style.

I first noticed what I believe to be the original version of the Tara X in the Jackson Hole area around 1997-1998. The fly pictured here is a version I tie. I have replaced the original Amherst pheasant-neck wing fibers with wing fibers from a golden pheasant and added brown hackle wrapped around the dubbed body.

While officially an attractor, many area fly-fishers use it as a strict stonefly pattern. An orange dubbed body, or a body dubbed with a squirrel-muskrat fur blend, creates an excellent salmonfly imitation during the June and July hatches on the South Fork. The standing deer hair and calf tail wing gives the fly a fluttering appearance. I will sometimes substitute bear hair for the calf tail to give the wing a more translucent effect. I use an olive body with green legs in a #10 to match little green stoneflies (Chloroperlidae). A variety of Tara Xs are available at different fly shops in the Snake River area. The largest selection can be found at Will Dornan's Snake River Angler in Moose, Wyoming, and the Victor Emporium in Victor, Idaho.

Foam Double Humpy

Fly type: Attractor
Created by Boots Allen, circa 1998

Hook: Dai-Riki 700 or equivalent, size 4 to 8
Thread: Yellow, orange, red, or gray 3/0 flat wax nylon
Tail: Deer body hair
Underbody: Yellow, orange, red, or gray open-cell foam or 1mm closed-cell foam in similar colors. Furry Foam can also be used as a substitute
Shellback: 2mm closed-cell foam in various colors
Wings: White calf tail
Hackle: Grizzly

This pattern combines the best qualities of the Double Humpy and Chernobyl Ant. It builds upon the success of the Super Double Humpy, created by Crescent H Ranch guide Greg Goodyear. Two-millimeter foam is used for the shellback. The Foam Double Humpy is the most common type on the market and the open-cell variety tends to wrap more evenly than closed-cell foam. Recently, however, a few manufacturers have started producing ultra-thin closed-cell foam—1 millimeter and even 1/2-millimeter thick. This material wraps as evenly as open-cell foam and tends to have a smoother finish. It can produce a ribbing effect when wrapped in a certain fashion, which often enhances a fly's imitative quality. This foam is currently being used as the underbody material for the latest Foam Double Humpies. Ultra-thin closed-cell foam is certain to revolutionize tying in much the same way that traditional foam did almost two decades ago.

The Foam Double Humpy is a classic attractor, effective at mimicking a variety of large aquatic insects and terrestrials. It takes full advantage of the large-flies-produce-large-trout theory proposed by the likes of Scott Sanchez, Paul Bruun, Joe Allen, and Ken Burkholder. Simple changes in hook size and body color can allow the angler to better imitate specific hatches if needed. Generally this is not required. The attractive ability of the Foam Double Humpy is often successful whenever and wherever it is fished on the Snake River.

Willy's Red Ant

Fly type: Attractor/Terrestrial
Created by Will Dornan, late 1990s

Hook: Dai-Riki 700 or equivalent, size 4 to 10
Thread: Black 3/0 monocord
Underbody: Red, gold, or tan yarn material
Body: Black open-cell foam
Legs: Medium black rubber
Wing: White Antron

Jackson Hole native Will Dornan is known for designing a wide variety of patterns range from damselflies to caddis nymphs. This modification of the Chernobyl Ant is his most popular creation. Will trimmed the foam for this fly in a fashion that it would more realistically reflect the silhouette of a natural grasshopper or stonefly. The head is a bit more tapered than most other large foam flies. This was the winning pattern at the 2001 One-Fly Competition. Although also offered with gold and tan yarn, red has been the most in-demand color by far. The true impact of color in the fly design scheme is a big topic of debate. While Dave Whitlock would suggest that it plays second fiddle to size and silhouette, anglers like Bing Lempke and Guy Turck suggest that it might be the most important feature for a fly. I tend to at least place it in the same realm of priority as size, silhouette and movement. This was something hammered home to me while growing up under the roof of a professional fly-rodder.

Willy's Red Ant has enjoyed success on the Upper Snake, the South Fork, and tributaries like the Grays and Gros Ventre rivers. The open-cell foam gives it a lot of buoyancy in heavy currents and its visibility is enhanced in these conditions by the distinctive white Antron wing. This pattern is one of my favorites to use with a dropper or trailing emerger.

Plan B

Fly type: Attractor
Creator: Brenda Swinney, circa 1999

Hook: Dai-Riki 300 or equivalent, size 8 to 10
Thread: Tan or yellow 3/0 flat wax nylon
Tail: Yellow Antron of poly yarn
Belly: Gold or yellow ice chenille
Hackle: Brown rooster hackle or grizzly hackle
Body: Tan 2mm closed-cell foam
Legs: Peach or brown rubber legs spackled lightly with black ink
Indicator: Orange 2mm closed-cell foam
Eyes: Black ink on tan foam

The Plan B was created by South Fork guide Brenda Swinney, and is a minimalist version of the Chernobyl Ant. The main differences between this fly and its predecessor are: a thinner body, shorter length, and lighter all-around body color. This toned-down style allows the pattern to ride low in the surface film, yet still ride high enough for easy visibility. The Plan B developed an immediate following after Swinney introduced it in 1999. Anglers fish it as both a golden stonefly and grasshopper imitation. On a #10 hook, it's often fished as a little yellow stonefly. Currently, the Plan B is found in fly shops from Idaho Falls, Idaho, to Moose, Wyoming. Although several color variations are now available, the original version, similar to what is shown here, remains the most popular.

Crystal Creek Stone Nymph

Fly type: Stonefly Nymph
Created by Boots Allen, circa 1999

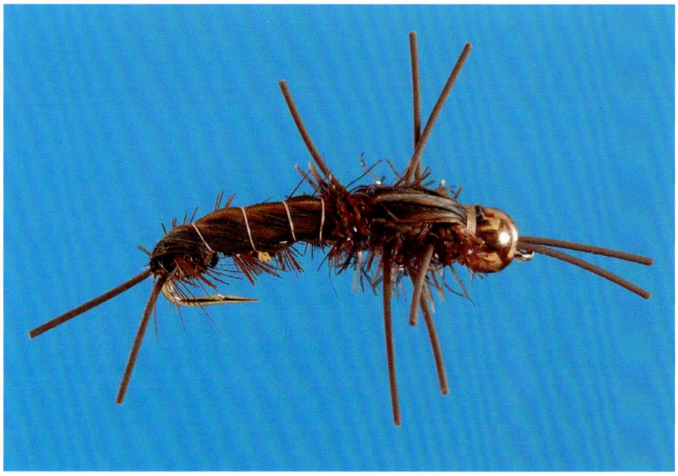

Hook: Dai-Riki 285 Nymph Hook or equivalent, size 2 to 8
Thread: Yellow or black 3/0 flat wax nylon or monochord
Tail: Medium brown or black rubber
Abdomen: Gold or black Ice chenille
Hackle: Brown or red trimmed close
Shellback and wingcase: Woodduck flank feathers (for gold) or Indian hen saddle feathers (for black)
Ribbing: Copper wire
Legs: Medium brown or black rubber
Thorax: Gold or brown Flash Chenille
Head: Large brass bead in front with small tungsten bead following behind
Antennae: Medium brown rubber

The abundance of stoneflies in the Yellowstone region and their importance to trout led me to focus much of my tying attention on these aquatic insects over the past several years. This fly builds upon other successful stonefly nymph patterns in use on the Snake River. Crystal Creek, a small tributary of the Gros Ventre with an unusually strong population of stoneflies, serves as the inspiration for the name of this pattern. The use of Ice Chenille and Flash Chenille does more than just give attractive flash to the fly. It also adds bulk, making it appear full-bodied like a natural. I leave the Flash Chenille longer in the thorax. In the current, the individual fibers move in a way that closely imitates gills on a natural. Wrapping the abdomen with copper wire gives a ribbed appearance and binds the overbody shellback for more durability.

I fish these nymphs close to the stream bottom where stonefly nymphs dwell and feed. The double beadhead is usually enough to get it down. If not, I add a lead-free split shot. Gold and brown are by far the most productive colors. I fish these aggressively while guiding on the South Fork of the Snake River during the salmonfly and golden stone hatches. Dead-drifting Crystal Creek Nymphs along banks just as an emergence was beginning on the Hoback River in late June of 2002 resulted in three cutthroat in as many casts for Justin Hayes, a former guide at the Lodge at Palisades Creek.

Club Sandwich

Fly type: Terrestrial
Created by Ken Burkholder, circa 1999

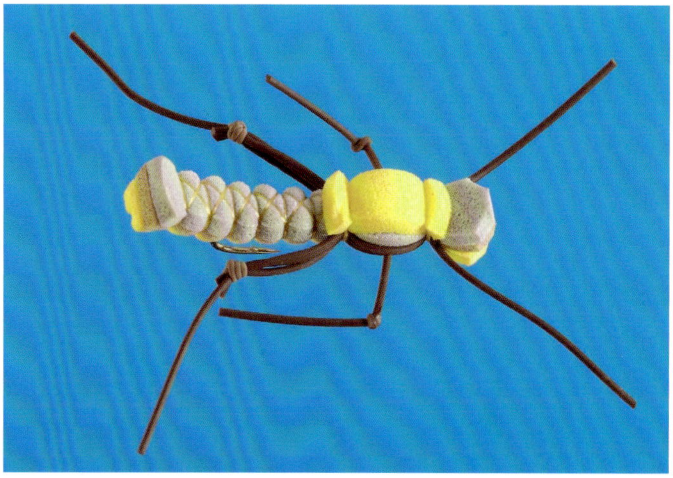

Hook: Mustad 9671 or equivalent, size 6 to 10
Thread: 3/0 brown or yellow monocord, or color to match underbody foam
Body: Laminated sheets of tan, peach, yellow, and gray 2mm closed-cell craft foam cut to shape
Legs: Two strands of knotted medium brown rubber for back legs; one strand of medium brown rubber for front legs
Indicator: 2mm closed-cell craft foam

The Club Sandwich is a major modification to the highly popular Chernobyl Ant. Ken Burkholder, a premier guide and tier on Idaho's South Fork, used pink-flesh foam on his original pattern to capture the color of many grasshoppers found on the Snake River. To match the size of western hoppers, he used #6 and 8 hooks and extended the foam body almost a half-inch past the bend. The result was a truly lifelike pattern that rivals the size of any other surface fly. The Club Sandwich has had unparalleled success throughout the region.

During my time as a guide on the Snake River, I have yet to see a pattern garner such a strong cult following. Stories from its first year reach almost mythical proportions. During the summer of 1999, the Snake River Angler in Moose, Wyoming, sold out of the Club Sandwich several times after being restocked only days before. At the Jackson Hole One-Fly Tournament the same year, Carter Andrews used a Club Sandwich specially tied by Ken to win the competition's professional division. There are even stories of an angler offering to pay a guide $10.00 for one of his Club Sandwiches.

Although technically a terrestrial, several South Fork anglers vary the foam color and tie on deer or bear hair for a wing to imitate salmonflies during early summer hatches. Tied as a #6, it is the perfect size for these gargantuan insects.

Day-2 Midge Emerger

Fly type: Midge
Creator: Boots Allen, circa 1999

Hook: TMC 100 or equivalent, size 16 to 22
Body: Black 6/0 or 8/0 tying thread, depending on size
Ribbing: Copper wire or fine silver tinsel
Wingcase: White 1mm closed-cell foam split down the center
Wing: White or dun colored CDC puff or calf tail

There are several versions of successful midge emergers found throughout North America. This one builds on highly-productive patterns like the suspender midges that Schollmeyer and Leeson's covered with much detail in *Tying Emergers* (2004, Frank Amato Publications). It is by far my favorite midge emerger in a drainage not necessarily known for small patterns that imitate chironomids. The idea behind the Day-2 Midge Emerger was to design a pattern that could be suspended in a more realistic manner than more commonly used emergers, which typically began to sink after a few casts. The split-foam wraps around the previously tied CDC wing. This gives the appearance of midge wings emerging from a splitting wing case. CDC is known for its resistance to water absorption. Together, these two materials create a highly buoyant head.

The Day-2 Midge Emerger was named for its effectiveness on the second day of a three-day early April fishing excursion on Upper Snake River I took with local guide Gary Willmott in the late 1990s. It performs phenomenally well on those first six miles of river below Jackson Lake Dam down to the confluence with the Buffalo Fork. But I prefer to use it on area lakes, particularly those in the Gros Ventre drainage when chironomids make up a higher than normal percentage of total biomass. Emma Matilda and Two Ocean lakes are other waters where this pattern performs well. But most surprisingly, it works well on those parts of the Snake River with classic freestone characteristics. For example, it produces on bluebird days in March and April when air temperatures are warm enough to produce a hatch. In these situations, I fish it in slow-moving currents and pools close to banks.

Tomahawk

Fly type: Wet Attractor
Created by Hunter Ford, circa 2000

Hook: Dai-Riki 710 or equivalent, size 2 to 8
Thread: Black 3/0
Tail: Deer body hair
Body: Medium brown or rust orange chenille
Legs: Large white rubber
Wing: Deer body hair and yellow Flashabou Accent
Head: Spun and trimmed deer body hair

Hunter Ford, a well-known guide for West Bank Anglers in Jackson Hole, Wyoming, created this pattern as an "emergent" stonefly nymph. The original version was constructed of purple and black dubbing for the body and black rubber legs. Hunter later used light colored materials to enhance subsurface visibility. The recipe and sample given above is for this latter pattern, which remains the most popular version today. (The name Tomahawk is also used for a PMD nymph popular on Montana streams.)

While the Tomahawk was first created to imitate a premature emergent stonefly, Ford suggests that it's actually far more versatile, and can imitate stonefly nymphs as well as various baitfish. This is why I list it as a wet attractor. I recall days over the past few seasons when the Tomhawk salvaged otherwise slow days on the Upper Snake River. When nothing was hitting on the surface, and traditional streamers and nymphs were not producing, the

Tomahawk enticed several hard strikes from large cutthroat. During actual stonefly hatches, it's effective when allowed to dead-drift along banks. Short, choppy strips with the line, or a jigging motion with the rod tip, gives the fly motion that appears to attract curious trout. The Tomahawk has proven its worth on stonefly-heavy streams like the South Fork and the Hoback River.

RW's Chamois Caddis

Fly type: Caddis Pupa/Larva
Created by Rob Waters, circa 2001

Hook: Mustad 9672 or equivalent, size 6 to 10
Thread: Black or cream 6/0 monocord
Body: Doubled strip of cream-colored chamois
Legs: Grizzly hackle fibers or pheasant-tail fibers
Thorax: Peacock herl
Head: Gold or brass bead for larva; peacock herl for pupa; or combination

Robert Waters designed this pattern to imitate an October caddis pupa (*Dicosmoecus*), a caddis that becomes active on the Snake River in mid-September. It's similar to Joe Ayre's Chamois Caddis. I like this one better because the chamois is wrapped in a way to produce a more realistic ribbed appearance. It's also easy to color with a prism marker to create the appearance of dark wings and legs just below the head of a natural. A bead head is sufficient weight to sink the Chamois Caddis to the depth where fall caddis larvae dwell. Substitute peacock herl for the bead head to create a pupa making its way to the surface to emerge.

I have relied on R.W.'s Chamois Caddis as a go-to caddis nymph over the past few years. Generally I fish it solo without a dropper or with a double rig, both of which are difficult to do with a large and heavy #6 to 10 nymph, though #8 and 10 are the most imitative and successful versions. R.W.'s Chamois Caddis has produced in conditions when most other patterns fail. On one guide trip on the Upper Snake between Deadman's Bar and Moose Landing in early July, the river was chalky with silt from a heavy rainstorm the night before. During that excursion, only four trout were caught. All were between 16 1/2 and 20 inches, and all were caught on R.W.'s Chamois Caddis.

Lightning Bug

Fly type: Mayfly Nymph
Creator unknown; popularized by Will Dornan

Hook: TMC 2487 or equivalent, size 16 to 22
Thread: Black 8/0
Tail: Pheasant-tail fibers or grizzly hackle fibers
Abdomen: Silver tinsel or Flashabou Accent
Ribbing (optional): Brass wire
Wingcase: Silver tinsel
Thorax: Peacock herl
Legs: Pheasant-tail fibers
Head: Glass bead or silver bead-head

The Lightning Bug is a relatively new creation, having been designed in the 1990s. Still, there are several versions of this nymph as well as several claims of origination. Most agree it was developed either by Madison River tiers in Montana, or by Pacific Coast tiers in Oregon. Regardless, the Lightning Bug has earned a quick, well-respected spot in the hearts of Snake River fly-fishermen, who have added their own unique touches to the pattern.

The material requirements above are for a version that both Will Dornan and I myself tie. We have used it with success throughout the Snake River drainage. The South Fork remains the stream where I have had my best luck with the Lightning Bug. In #14 to 16, I will use it as a dropper off a large surface pattern like a Club Sandwich, Turck's Tarantula, or Tara X. The depth you should fish this or any nymph is dependent on the depth of water you are targeting, time of day, and prevalence of specific hatches. This is covered in greater detail in the South Fork section of this journal.

BMOC

Fly type: Attractor
Created by Brandon Powers, circa 2002

Hook: Dai-Riki 730 or equivalent, size 8 to 10
Thread: Red or orange 6/0 Gudebrod
Belly: Peach foam
Back: Tan foam
Wing: White EP Silky Fibers
Legs: Olive or brown Flexifloss

Brandon Powers, a guide and fly designer for the Jack Dennis Outdoor Shop, has designed some of the Snake River area's most effective patterns in recent years, including his Fluttering Stone and 747 Ant. The BMOC (Short for Big Man On Campus) is one of his most popular designs. It was the top-scoring patterns in the 2003 Jackson Hole One-Fly Competition, continuing the winning tradition of large foam-bodied flies in the tournament. A number of other patterns designed by Powers have had success in this proving-ground competition.

The version above is for the Peachy BMOC, so named for the peach foam used for the belly of the fly. This foam can be substituted for a number of other colors depending on conditions. However, the light hue of peach foam seems to be an attractive color for Snake River trout. Several other successful patterns, including the mayfly-imitating Pink Parachute and Donna Allen's Pink Ant, are testaments to the effectiveness of this color scheme. Flexifloss gives the legs a much more animated quality when on the water. The large, white, silky fibers used for the wing give the fly a fluttering effect when on the water. Like most foam-bodied ant patterns, deliberate movement of the BMOC often draws more strikes from large trout than a simple dead-drift.

Un-Bearable Ant

Fly type: Attractor
Created by Larry Larson, circa 2003

Hook: Dai-Riki 700 or equivalent, size 6 to 10
Thread: Orange, rust orange, olive, or black 3/0
Underbody: Orange, green, or black Furry Foam
Hackle: Brown
Overbody: Brown 2mm closed cell-foam
Legs: Medium brown rubber
Rear indicator: Yellow 2mm closed-cell foam
Wing: Siberian brown bear hair
Forward indicator: Orange 2mm closed-cell foam

This pattern builds upon other foam-bodied flies that Larry Larson ties regularly. The Un-Bearable Ant confronts the low-profile vs. high-rider debate that rages in fly-tying circles. Should a dry fly be designed to ride high on the surface, or to lay low in the surface film? Theories are plentiful and evidence backs up both arguments equally. Many feel that the discussion should not center on dry flies in general, but rather on specific patterns and what they are imitating. The Un-Bearable Ant is specifically designed to lay lower than most other foam ant patterns. Furry Foam, the material used for the underbody, is less water resistant than other foam. This allows the fly to lay on the surface film and present a lower profile than its counterparts.

Like a number of dry flies recently developed on the South Fork, the Un-Bearable Ant has a bear hair wing meant to imitate the translucent affect of a fluttering wing when viewed from below the surface. Bear-hair is hard to come by and there are strong environmental arguments against its usage. Tiers who can't, or refuse to use bear hair, can substitute moose-mane hair or calf tail intermixed with Flashabou or Krystal Flash. These materials do not provide as good a fluttering effect, but they are recognized as classic wing material throughout the fly-tying world.

747 Ant

Fly type: Attractor/Terrestrial
Created by Brandon Powers, circa 2003

Hook: Dai-Riki 730 or equivalent, size 8 to 10
Thread: Black 6/0 Gudebrod
Body: Black open-cell foam
Wing: Clear plastic
Parachute post: White EP Silky Fibers
Hackle: Brown
Legs: Olive Flexifloss

The 747 Ant is one of the latest Chernobyl-style patterns developed by Jack Dennis Outdoor Shop tier Brandon Powers. As with some of his other creations, Brandon uses Flexifloss for legs to produce more animated movement on the water. The version shown here is one that I tie and it deviates slightly from the original. Powers ties his with two parachutes, one at each point of segmentation. Powers also ties the clear plastic wing on at the point of the rear segmentation, whereas I tie mine on at the front with the solo parachute post. Many uninitiated anglers, on seeing the 747 for the first time, are unsure of what to make of it. But if seeing isn't believing, using it certainly is. One day of fishing with the 747 Ant and many fly-fishers are hooked, making it a permanent piece of their overall selection for the Snake River.

Although it's one of the newest patterns on the scene, I've had the chance to fish the 747 throughout the Snake River drainage. It's difficult to pick where I have had the most success. I remember some incredible days fishing this fly in fall 2004 in the Snake River Canyon in Wyoming. Deliberate movement of the fly while fishing below Three-Oar Deal on the whitewater section enticed a strike by a cutthroat that I estimated at close to 20 inches. My inexperienced client unfortunately applied too much pressure as the trout darted for the current, breaking it off and losing the last of our 747s. Needless to say, the angler declared his intention at the end of the day to march into Jack's shop and purchase a dozen of the flies directly from its creator.

Rollans' Stonefly

Fly type: Stonefly Adult
Created by Mark Rollans, circa 2003

Hook: Dai-Riki 700 or equivalent, size 4 to 8
Thread: Orange, tan, or brown 3/0 flat wax nylon
Tail: Gold, silver, pearl, or blended Flashabou accent
Underbody: Black, brown, or root beer Flash Chenille
Hackle: Brown
Legs: Brown Flexifloss
Head: Peacock herl
Overbody: Brown 2mm closed-cell foam over tan or root beer 2mm closed-cell foam
Interior wing: Flashabou accent to match tail
Exterior wing: Calf tail
Indicator: Yellow closed-cell foam

Mark Rollans, Teton Valley resident and a Snake River guide for World Cast Anglers, developed this pattern in his attempt to find a high-riding imitation of giant black stoneflies and salmonflies. Being centrally located in the Victor-Driggs Idaho area, Mark has easy access to the Upper Snake, the South Fork, and even the Henry's Fork and chases stonefly hatches on each, not to mention those that occur on the Hoback River and the nearby Teton River. He designed this fly with similar intentions as Will Dornan when the latter created the Red Ant: a foam fly trimmed in a manner that more accurately represented the silhouette of a natural insect. Allan Wolfe captured the amateur division title in the 2004 One-Fly Competition fishing a Rollan's Stone. There are now a couple of variations of Mark's pattern beginning to make their way up and down the Snake as other tiers design creative substitutes.

The buoyancy of this fly makes it an excellent surface pattern when fishing droppers. I have even used a #4 as a top-water bug to fish lightly weighted Kaufmann's Black Stone Nymphs along shallows and skinny water areas next to banks during emergences on the South Fork. Both work equally well when I employ this strategy.

Purple Haze

Fly type: Mayfly Dun
Creator unknown

Hook: Mustad 94840 or equivalent, size 14 to 20
Tail: Grizzly hackle fibers
Body: Purple 6/0 UNI-Thread or floss
Wing: White calf tail or poly yarn (tied either parachute style or upright and divided)
Hackle: Grizzly

This Pacific Coast transplant is one of the easiest flies a person can tie or fish. Thread-body patterns have a history that pre-date fly-fishing in the western United States. It's a design incorporated into many nymphs as well as some wet attractors, not just top-water bugs. One of the key advantages of a thread-body fly is its slender abdomen and thorax. This is important when trying to imitate small mayflies like blue-winged olives and Tricos. And this is the beauty of the Purple Haze. It's most often fished as a mahogany dun, and some will substitute the white calf tail or yarn with gray Antron or yarn to better simulate the natural color of the wing. A big plus with this pattern is that the body is exceptionally tight. With constant applications of floatant, the body becomes almost impervious to moisture. The result is a minute mayfly dun imitation that keeps producing all day long.

Fat Albert

Created by Brent Taylor
Popularized by Bart Taylor, circa 2002

Hook:Standard dry fly, size 6 to 12
Thread: Flat wax 3/0 in red, gold, or brown
Underbody: Light tan or gray 2mm closed-cell foam
Overbody: Dark tan 2mm closed-cell foam
Wing: White calf tail or Antron
Indicator: Red closed-cell foam
Legs: Medium light tan rubber or Zebra Legs

This large foam attractor gained popularity after veteran guide Bart Taylor of Jack Dennis' Outdoor Shop raved about its effectiveness during the variable water year of 2002. Most are at a loss to explain exactly what it might be imitating. While a stonefly or hopper is an obvious choice, Snake River angler Jason Sutton believes that it is mimicking a simple spider, one of the most overlooked types of trout food on the Snake River. As someone who has spent well over 1000 days on the river during my lifetime, this makes a lot of sense. Although it is rare, I have seen spiders scurrying across the river or their dead bodies floating on the surface.

I have had success with the Fat Albert on several sections of the Snake River, particularly on the middle sections between Moose and South Park and in the Canyon between Pritchard Landing and West Table. It's now making waves on the South Fork where it's bringing up large cutthroat even during the slower weeks in August and early October. Like so many other attractor patterns in use on the Snake River, it's the red-bellied version of this fly that tends to be the most popular and productive.

Part IV: Snake River Legends

Photo Courtesy of Tom Carmichael

Bob Carmichael cooking a trout dinner on the banks of the Snake River, 1953.

Compared to many classic trout streams of the American West, fly-fishing on the Snake River does not have a long history. Even the relatively close waters of the Henry's Fork and the Madison have a heritage that predates the Snake by at least some 30 years. Underdevelopment and the lack of reliable transportation into Jackson Hole, Grand Valley, and Swan Valley didn't facilitate the exchange of information and knowledge that occurred on more well-traveled streams. This rendered the waters of the Snake River a secret known only to a few outside fishermen for many decades. Despite its recent development, the Snake has produced an impressive number of tiers and anglers who have left their mark on fly-fishing. Some have become internationally acclaimed, while others are more regionally known. Regardless, their impact on the Snake River is indisputable. Below are just a few of the tiers, anglers, writers, educators, and conservationists who have made these waters what it is today.

Bob Carmichael

From his first years of guiding in the early 1930s until his passing in 1959, Bob Carmichael was the wise old guru of fly-fishing and tying in Jackson Hole, Wyoming. Accounts of his skill, knowledge, and stern but honest demeanor grace the pages of classic fishing literature, including works by the likes of J. Edson Leonard and Ernest Schweibert. Possibly no other figure did more to advance the sport on the Snake River during its early era. The list of renowned members of the fly-fishing and river-running community that Carmichael directly influenced is long and distinguished. He employed reputable guides such as Clayton Kennedy and Vern Bressler, the latter of whom went on to establish himself as a successful outfitter. Dick Beerkle, step-father of pioneering scenic guide Dick Barker, guided for Carmichael in the 1940s. And Jack Dennis counts Bob Carmichael as one of his mentors.

For years, Carmichael was the official fishing guide of Grand Teton National Park. In 1941, he purchased the general store in Moose, Wyoming, on the banks of the Snake River. From this location, Bob began offering the first high-quality fly-fishing gear in Jackson Hole. This included silkworm gut leaders and handmade bamboo rods, but his greatest contribution came in the form of hand-tied flies. Carmichael collaborated with Roy Donnelly and Don Martinez to create some of the most significant patterns to have originated in the Yellowstone area. The Variant series of dry flies, the Indispensable, and a streamer-style Mormon Girl were patterns developed by this holy trinity of tiers that eventually gained worldwide popularity. Together they helped develop tying styles that became trademarks of their craft, principally the use of upright hackle tip wings and sparse, oversized wraps of hackle for mayfly imitations.

Carmichael's love for Jackson Hole and its native cutthroat trout crossed over into a deep, emotional respect that is well-documented in fly-fishing literature. In *Trout*, Ernie Schweibert recounts a story of being verbally accosted by Bob after the author stated his preference for the fighting ability of brown trout over cutthroat. "When you know enough about this country to have an opinion about fishing," Carmichael huffed, "you will know that there are cutthroats and there are cutthroats! These fish ain't no pantywaists. These are Jackson Hole cutthroats!" Carmichael was one of the first to realize the true greatness of a trout species that can thrive in such a difficult environment. He is recognized as one of the area's first champions of conservation efforts for the river and its trout. As a tribute, the Jackson Hole One-Fly Contest memorialized Carmichael by naming one of its top-guide awards after this truly inspiring figure.

Boots Allen

Leonard "Boots" Allen drifted over Togwotee Pass into Jackson Hole in 1927. The teenager from Indiana had finished high school and was heading west to visit family, but one look at the Tetons and the Snake River changed his plans forever. For the next 60 years, he would be a much heralded fixture of the sporting community in western Wyoming. Working on Jackson Lake Dam and for the Bureau of Reclamation in the 1920s and 1930s kept him close to the region's trout rich waters, which he fished almost every day. He began guiding well-to-do anglers visiting from the East during this time. By the early 1940s Boots was considered one of Jackson Hole's most reputable guides.

In 1945, Allen opened Fort Jackson River Trips and Guide Service in the town of Jackson and began guiding visiting anglers throughout western Wyoming, including the Snake, Green, and Gros Ventre rivers. He was among the first in the Yellowstone region to use rubber rafts for

Boots Allen at the oars, 1949.

guided fishing trips. Allen also helped pioneer area lake fishing and the use of multiple chrome cowbell pop gear on Jackson, Leigh, Lewis, and Heart lakes in Grand Teton National and Yellowstone National Parks. His 41-pound lake trout caught on Jackson Lake in the 1940s was a state record until Doris Budge eclipsed it some 40 years later. His success on the water drew the attention of several high-profile clients, including the likes of Bing Crosby and Roy Rogers.

Boots was considered a colorful character with an unparalleled knowledge of fly-fishing strategies and tactics in Jackson Hole. He was an expert in the use of locally available materials for tying effective dry flies. But it was Allen's popularization of a specific pattern—the Humpy—that would forever secure his place in western fly-fishing lore. With his sons, Joe and Dick, he would crank out over 15,000 flies to sell from his headquarters at Fort Jackson every season. In *A Trout's Best Friend*, Bud Lilly tells of Allen selling Humpies out of his shop by the nail-keg-load in the 1950s and 1960s at 35 cents for one or three for a dollar. According to Jack Dennis, as late as the 1970s, one out of every two flies sold in Jackson Hole was a Humpy pattern!

After selling his outfitting service to his sons in the early 1970s, Allen opened a popular little tackle shop from his home on North Millward Street. His love for fishing kept him away from the business most days, and with no employees he sold tackle on the honor system, with customers leaving money in a bin for the items they purchased while Boots was out. Allen ran the shop in this manner until his death in 1993. His funeral was attended by scores of local and regional fly-fishing personalities, a fitting tribute to a pioneering guide and tier.

Marcella Oswald

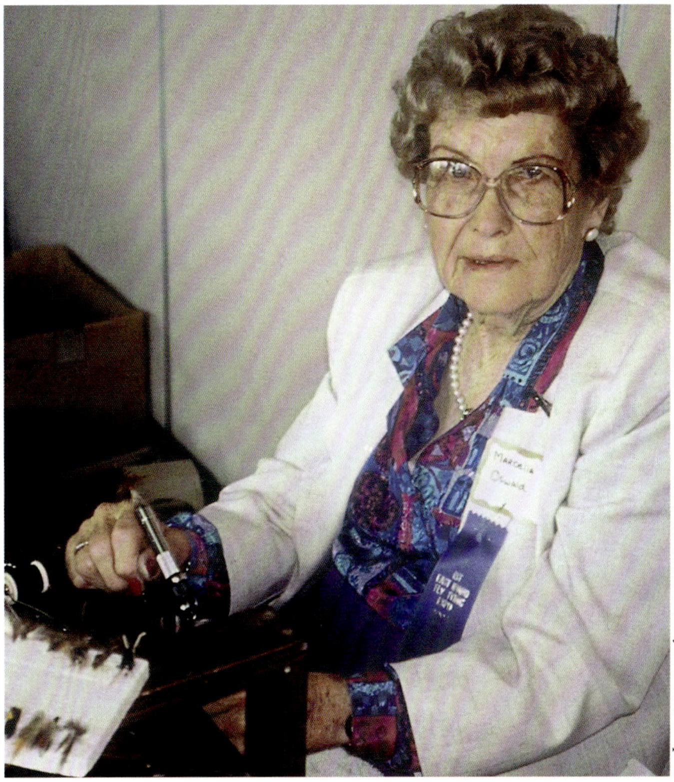
Photo Courtesy of Bruce Staples

Marcella Oswald at the East Idaho Fly-Tying Expo.

I like to think of Marcella Oswald as the Grand Duchess of fly-fishing on the Snake River. Self-taught, she spent evenings learning to tie in the 1940s. In the mid-1940s, Marcella ran a popular sporting goods store on First Street in Idaho Falls, Idaho, with her husband, Harvey. From this location, both helped introduce legions of local and visiting anglers to the sport. They sold quality fishing gear and flies of their own creation that became locally and regionally popular. In fact, tying was Marcella's true calling. For decades she introduced the art to local residents through tying seminars she taught at the Idaho Falls City Recreation Center.

In the 1950s, as fly-fishing was becoming increasingly popular in the area, the Oswalds were inundated with requests for a pattern that could imitate the salmonfly (*Pteronarcys californica*), the large three-inch-plus stonefly that emerges from the South Fork in June and July. Her response was Marcella's Trout Fly, a named derived from the local terminology for the insect it imitated. This fly was built primarily on Pat Barnes' Sofa Pillow and Bird's Stonefly. However, Marcella's creation added heavier wraps of hackle and, more importantly, deer and elk hair for the wing. The Trout Fly was readily accepted and went on to become one of the most popular flies ever used on the South Fork. As recently as the 2004 season, almost half a century after its conception, I witnessed two separate parties of anglers fishing a version of Marcella's Trout Fly with great success!

The store on First Street closed in the early 1980s after Harvey passed away. However, Marcella has continued to supply private clients with her flies and participates in regional fly-tying expos. In 2004, the Snake River Cutthroats, an East Idaho chapter of Trout Unlimited and the Federation of Fly Fishers, honored Oswald with their annual Heritage Award. Her impact on South Fork fly-fishing is unsurpassed to this day.

Vern Bressler

Vern Bressler began guiding under the tutelage of Bob Carmichael before starting his own outfit in the 1960s. Working out of Crescent H Ranch, Bressler offered a stunning variety of fly-fishing excursions, including pioneering backcountry expeditions to the lakes and streams of the Snake River and Gros Ventre ranges. Vern's lasting tribute to the Snake River region was a system of spring creeks he fostered on Crescent H Ranch for over two decades. Along with the stretch of Fish Creek that flowed through the Ranch, Bressler developed these waters into the best

Photo Courtesy of Joe Bressler

Vern Bressler, circa 1960.

privately maintained streams in the region. They were stocked strictly with native cutthroats and nurtured in such an effective manner that successive wild populations have been sustained to this day.

Vern's outfit was a family affair. His wife Ramona was actively involved in the management of the outfit. She was also a noted tier, giving personal touches to already proven patterns, making them even more effective. Her Black Humpy received a loyal following among some of the Snake River's finest anglers. Vern's son Joe became a renowned outfitter who operated extensively in Snake River Canyon, on the South Fork, the Teton River, and the Green and New Fork Rivers. In a 1995 poll, he was voted the number-one guide in Jackson Hole.

Since his passing, Vern Bressler's spirit continues to lives on in a number of ways. Today, the award for top fly-fishing professional in the One-Fly Contest is named in honor of Bressler. And to truly show his enduring impact on the protection of native trout, the Vern Bressler Memorial Scholarship is awarded each year to support the research done by students at the University of Wyoming in the areas of fisheries biology and management.

Jack Dennis

He is recognized everywhere as a true legend of fly-fishing in North America, but the Snake River is proud to call him one of its own sons. It is doubtful that any other name is more synonymous with the Snake River and its cutthroat than Jack Dennis. He has been an ever-present figure on the stream from his earliest days of guiding. Before the age of 20, Jack was a successful outfitter with a well-established tackle shop on Broadway in the town of Jackson, Wyoming. In the early 1970s, he gained national attention through appearances on Curt Gowdy's ABC series *American Sportsman.* Jack's business—the Jack Dennis Outdoor Shop—has continued to grow since, and his staff has guided an unending list of state dignitaries, captains of industry, sports stars, and Hollywood actors. In 2001, *Outside Magazine* picked Jack's shop as the number one fly shop in the U.S.

Like so many legends of the Snake River, it was skill at the tying vise that earned Jack his greatest acclaim. Unlike Carmichael, Allen, and Oswald—who can generally be identified with one or two specific patterns—Dennis is linked directly to several. He has been instrumental in popularizing various styles of Humpies and Irresistables. More recent patterns—primarily his Kiwi Muddler and Amy's Ant—have gained global popularity. But it was the publication of *Jack Dennis' Western Trout Fly Tying Manual* (Vol. I and II), and *Tying with Jackson Dennis and Friends* that produced worldwide celebrity status for the emerging star of Rocky Mountain fly-fishing. The books were groundbreaking in their instructional ability and remain the standard in the industry. All told, over 400,000 copies have been sold. It is not uncommon for tiers from all over the world to credit Dennis for their introduction to the art.

Jack Dennis' impact on the sport of fly-fishing continues with his involvement in several films, videos, and television programs, and an intense lecturing schedule for clubs and organizations around the world. A daily radio show, the *Jack Dennis Fly-fishing Journal,* broadcasting out of Jackson, Wyoming, dispenses information to the angling public on a wealth of topics—flies, lines, strategies, and tactics. But like his mentor Bob Carmichael, Dennis' greatest influence has been in his devotion to the protection of the Snake River and its native cutthroat. In 1986, he helped to initiate the Jackson Hole International One-Fly Competition, a team tournament that raises funds to save cutthroat and protect riparian habitat. He has also been a consistent watchdog for the proper management of stream flows out of Palisades and Jackson Lake dams, so critical to the survival of Snake River and Yellowstone cutthroat. Books, films, TV, and lectures aside, Jack's concern for the Snake River ecosystem and its native trout will be his lasting legacy.

Photo Courtesy of Jack Dennis

Jack Dennis with Curt Gowdy in the early 1970s.

Bob Bean

Bob Bean was known all along the South Fork and its tributaries as an expert angler and tier. But it was his down-to-Earth style, approachability, and eagerness to teach his craft that he will be remembered for the most. Bean fished throughout New York, New England, and Utah before moving permanently to East Idaho in the early 1960s. His skills were already well developed by this time, but now in an angling paradise, they took on a whole new character that touched many.

Photo Courtesy of Mike Bean

Bean made his home in the Blackfoot area of East Idaho. There, he taught fly-fishing, fly-tying, and rod building courses to hundreds of students in high school lifetime sports courses and through the City of Blackfoot Community Education Program. He also provided private group classes at the B&B Bait Shop. Participants in Bob's courses recall intimate settings with no more than ten students per class to maximize individual attention. These courses were the perfect outlet for Bean's personal fly creations, many of which were groundbreaking in their time. Bob's Hopper, first developed in the mid-1960s, was one of the region's first flies to incorporate foam for enhanced floatation. His Doll Hair Thunder Creek Minnow incorporated alternative, but readily available material, for one of the South Fork's most successful big trout streamers. And above all was Bean's Meat Getter, a dry fly that doubles as an adult caddis and a mayfly emerger. Offered commercially, these patterns gained a fast and dedicated following throughout the Snake River drainage. Bob happily met demand by employing his two sons, Tom and Mike, at the tying vise with him. Mike is currently the head guide at the Lodge of Palisades Creek.

Bean was instrumental in introducing the Snake River angling community to the successful fishing found on the lower South Fork and the mainstem tributaries below Idaho Falls. These included the Blackfoot River and spring creeks on the Fort Hall Indian Reservation. Before many of the area's most renowned fly-fishermen had even considered testing these waters, Bob had mastered them. Bean past away in 2000 after battling a brain tumor for almost 15 years. In 2001, the Upper Snake River chapter of Trout Unlimited and the Federation of Fly Fishers honored him with its annual Heritage Award. The Snake River itself will be hard pressed to find a replacement for such a significant loss.

Joe Allen

The youngest son of pioneering outfitter and tier Leonard "Boots" Allen, Joe Allen was born into a burgeoning fly-fishing industry that was beginning to emerge in western Wyoming after World War II. With his brother Dick Allen, Joe guided throughout the Snake River drainage, on the upper Green River, and on lakes and streams in Yellowstone National Park and the Teton Wilderness for almost 50 years. Every season, he would log over 100 days with clients, either in a raft or on horseback through the backcountry. In 1980, Joe left Fort Jackson River Trips and Guide Service, the family tackle shop and guiding business started in 1945, to form his own outfit—Joe Allen's Guide Service. Like his father, he became a favorite guide for Hollywood actors, sports stars, and renowned businessmen.

Allen was a regular fixture on the Snake River before health problems began to sideline him in the 1990s. During his lifetime of guiding, he was a witness to many of the positive and negative changes that occurred on area streams: the construction of levee systems on the Snake River; the change from rubber rafts to fiberglass drift boats as the dominant form of river navigation for fishing trips; and the introduction of slot limits and tackle restrictions to protect trout populations. Joe trained many area guides and future outfitters and was a popular character among the growing number of anglers in Jackson Hole. He was considered one of the best sources of information on fly-fishing strategies and tactics in the Snake River drainage. Noted outdoor photographer Tom Montgomery once commented on Allen's uncanny ability to identify cutthroat holding water, saying, "Joe could pick up trout in runs that you would swear couldn't hold a marlin."

Joe Allen, 1962.

But as popular as Allen was for his fishing knowledge, it was his fly-tying abilities for which he would become most renowned. Joe was a mass producer of hand-tied patterns and at the height of his tying career would produce over 1000 dozen flies during each off-season. His tying room was famed for its piles of deer hair, cabinets full of grizzly and red rooster hackle, and the dozens of pheasant skins that hung from his tying table. In the early 1980s, Allen created the Double Humpy, a quintessential attractor pattern that has become a staple in fly boxes of visiting and resident anglers throughout the greater Yellowstone area. For over two decades, the pattern and its creator were featured in dozens of fly-fishing publications, often with descriptions of Joe's specific material requirements and his unique tactics for fishing the fly.

Joe Allen died of a heart attack in 2003. Ironically, he was on Flat Creek, a stream on which he began guiding walk-in trips at the age of thirteen and one that held his earliest of fishing memories. For an angler so intimately tied to the Snake River and its fly-fishing heritage, it is doubtful that a more fitting place could be found for one to pass.

Joe Bressler

Some Snake River legends are known for their fly tying abilities. Others are more famous for their pioneering work as outfitters. Still others become popular champions of conservation efforts. Joe Bressler is known for his simple ability to find and catch fish on any kind of water. One would be hard pressed to find a better guide or angler anywhere in the American West. Joe had the luck of being born into a family of anglers—his father Vern was a popular outfitter most known for his operation of Crescent H Ranch and the development of some of the best spring creeks in the northern Rockies. The younger Bressler became an outfitter in his own right at an early age, with permits and overnight camps on the South Fork, the Teton River, and the Upper Green River. His guide service—Bressler Outfitters—was one of the Yellowstone region's most active and sought-after fishing operations. Joe made a dramatic impact on the fly-fishing industry when he helped start the Western Rivers Professional Guide School, one of the first of its kind in fly-fishing.

As the twenty-first century dawned, Bressler's already solidly established reputation reached new heights. In an area full of world famous anglers, a community poll named Joe the number one guide in Jackson Hole. In 1995 he won the Jackson Hole One-Fly Competition's Top Gun Award as the high-scoring professional angler with one of the highest point totals ever accumulated by a participant. He became the only repeat winner of the award in 2002. To top all of this off, Bressler was presented with the Competition's Carmichael-Cohen Award in 2004, given to the guide who best exemplifies their profession while making extraordinary contributions to the angling community as a whole. Outdoor writer Paul Bruun called Bressler a natural choice for such an honor, citing his skill with people and his accomplishments as an angler.

Photo Courtesy of Joe Bressler

Though now retired from the outfitting and guiding business, Joe continues to reside in the Jackson Hole area, where he fishes his favorite waters almost everyday of the season. It is a well-earned rest for a man who helped put the Snake River on the elite stage of world fly-fishing destinations.

Paul Bruun

In the winter of 1969, Paul Bruun was introduced to veteran Snake River outfitter and tier Boots Allen. Both were fishing in the vicinity of Baja's East Cape in Mexico. Boots was impressed by the young, adventurous outdoorsman, and invited him up to his home in Jackson Hole, Wyoming, to do some fishing and hunting. Bruun jumped at the chance, and the following September had made his first-ever journey into the land of the Snake River. Like so many before and since who have fallen in love with the Yellowstone region, Paul never left. He became a guide and, later, an outfitter running fishing trips in Bridger-Teton National Forest. In the early 1980s, Bruun and partner Paul Headrick founded South Fork Skiff, a company that produces the lightest and most maneuverable fishing boats in use on western waters.

Early in his career, Paul Bruun became an outdoor writer. With his strong knowledge of all things fishing and an even stronger desire to learn more, he has dispensed a wealth of information to the angling world about the trout paradise that is Snake River Country. Paul has penned columns for almost every fly-fishing and outdoor publication in the United States. Most of these were stories centered directly on fishing opportunities in the northern Rockies. For years, he wrote columns for *Fly Fisherman* on angling in Yellowstone National Park, on the Snake River, and on the Upper Green River. In 1985, Bruun was featured on the television program *Fishing the West*, where he introduced viewers to the fantastic fly-fishing opportunities available on the Snake River. But it's through his continuing weekly outdoor columns for the *Jackson Hole News* that Bruun is

Paul Bruun on the South Fork.

making his greatest impact. This median has allowed the self-employed guide and outfitter to relay his overwhelming knowledge to the general angling public. It would be enough if the reach of his stories was limited to the Yellowstone region, but the skill of his writings has lead to these stories being printed in outdoor journals throughout the country.

Bruun's expertise is not limited solely to his own personal experiences. It is also derived from his extensive networks with some of the greatest in the trade, networks developed because of Paul's complete approachability, good nature, and constant desire to learn more. My personal fishing adventures away from my home waters have taken me from Texas to New Mexico to Oregon. At almost every location, when fellow anglers learn where I am from, I will get the one inevitable question: "Do you know that fella they call Bruun?" This is then followed by either a humorous story of how they discovered a specific tactic or pattern because of Bruun's uncommon communicative skills. Angler's everywhere have Paul Bruun to thank for introducing them to Pete Moyer's lake-fishing tactics, Joe Allen's Double Humpy, Jimmy Jones' J.J. Special, Guy Turck's Tarantula, and John Kiefling's intense cutthroat conservation strategies for the Snake River. Lucky for all of us, *Herr* Bruun is still at it, and more stories and valuable information are yet to come.

Bruce Staples

An accomplished tier and angler, Bruce Staples will be forever known as the historian emeritus of the Snake River. He was introduced to the sport and to fly-tying by some of the area greats—including Stan Yamamura and Pat and Sig Barnes. Later he became acquainted with Charlie Brooks, Rene Harrop, Mike Lawson, Bing Lempke, Ralph Moon, Marcella Oswald, and the Gabettas family. From these individuals Staples gained a deep appreciation for the rich fly-fishing heritage of the region. In the 1980s, he began his tenure as a writer, penning dozens of articles for angling and tying magazines, writing books dealing specifically with fly-fishing in the Snake River area. All of Bruce's writings are steeped in the history, tradition, and heritage of the sport in the Great Yellowstone area. Prime examples of this are his books *Snake River Country* (1991) and *Trout Country Flies* (2002), both of which are as much historical references as they are guides to fishing and tying.

Along with Yamamura, Bruce was instrumental in the establishment of the Snake River Cutthroats, an East Idaho chapter of Trout Unlimited and the Federation of Fly Fishers dedicated to the preservation of the Snake River and cutthroat habitat. He served as the organization's president in the late 1970s. He has been an important part of the organization's conservation efforts, including the regulation of dewatering below Palisades Reservoir and the restoration of cutthroat habitat in South Fork tributaries. In 1977 and 1978, Staples testified against increased phosphate mining in Caribou County because of the negative effects on the Blackfoot River drainage and increased logging in Caribou National Forest.

More than anything else, Bruce Staples is a wonderful teacher of the art of fly-tying. He has chaired numerous fly-tying programs, most notably those for the FFF International Conclaves in 1988,1992, 1998, and 2004 and the immensely popular Eastern Idaho Fly Tying and Fly-fishing Expo. Through his courses and seminars, Bruce passes down the skills and the spirit of the many legends he has befriended over the past four decades. The fly-tying community has tried its best to reward Staples for all his hard work. In 1990, he was awarded the Federation of Fly Fisher's

WRMC Tier of the Year Award. More appropriately, Bruce became the 32nd recipient of the Federation's Buz Buszek Memorial Award for fly-tying excellence in 2001.

Stan Yamamura

Satoshi "Stan" Yamamura appeared on the Snake River fly-fishing scene in the mid-1950s. He was introduced to the sport and to tying early on, and took to it immediately. He had an incredible knack for tying, so much so that by 1960 he was tying commercially. Stan's Flies grew out of his early endeavors. Working out of his home in Idaho Falls, he hired regional tiers to meet the demand of shops and private clients throughout Montana, Idaho, and Wyoming. Throughout the 1960s and 1970s, Stan's operation was one of the most successful wholesale suppliers of flies and tying materials in the northern Rockies.

Stan's speed behind the tying vise was almost mythical. In his 2002 book *Trout Country Flies* (Frank Amato Publications, Inc.), Bruce Staples relates a story of Yamamura accepting a challenge at a FFF Conclave tying demonstration in Jackson in 1968 to construct a Woolly Worm in under two minutes. He completed it in 17 seconds! Stan also was also the creator of his own effective patterns, which he sold out of Stan's Flies. Stan's Willowfly was a popular adult caddis imitation in the 1960s and 1970s. His most popular to date is Stan's Hopper. This pattern achieved greater buoyancy that other hopper imitations due to Stan's use of hollow deer hair as overbody material. Many who still use a version of this fly today will also fish it as a stonefly imitation.

Along with Bruce Staples and Dr. Jim McCue, Stan was a founding member of the Snake River Cutthroats. He was instrumental in initiating the organization's fly-tying program. Unfortunately, Stan died in 1988. For those of us who remain, his legacy lives on in several books that pay homage to his skills, and through the stories of the many anglers and tiers who were witness to his accomplishments.

Photo Courtesy of Bruce Staples

Stan Yamamura instructing one of his many students.

Jay Buchner

A native of Iowa, Jay Buchner moved to Jackson Hole, Wyoming, in the late 1960s. Since then, he has turned his love for fishing and tying into a legitimate career, and has taken his place among the Snake River's list of most influential anglers. In the early 1970s, he began to develop his reputation as one of the region's best tiers with creative patterns such as the Jay-Dave's Hopper, the Chartreuse Humpy, and Jay's Dun Caddis. This trend has continued with more recent patterns, the most well-known of which is his Humpback Emerger. To meet the demand of these and other popular patterns, Jay, along with his wife Kathy, started a successful mail-order business. The Buchners also started High Country Flies, an angling and tying establishment in Jackson Hole that remains one of the best fly shops in all the northern Rockies.

Jay Buchner providing entomology instruction at an annual guide school.

Jay's talents as a tier are matched by his thorough knowledge of entomology. Every year, he conducts popular classes geared toward fishermen at the Teton Science School in Kelly, Wyoming. Buchner is a frequent lecturer on the subject at fly-fishing and guide schools across the West and dispenses his knowledge on fishing and tying to clubs throughout the country.

The Buchners have been at the forefront of conservation efforts on the Snake River and its tributaries. They helped establish the Jackson Hole Chapter of Trout Unlimited where Kathy has been the organization's president for several years. Both were instrumental in bringing the World Fly-fishing Championships to Jackson Hole in 1997. Jay has competed for the United States several times since

1998, lending his superb tying and entomological skills to the team, and bringing back even greater knowledge of the sport, which he dispenses generously to the angling community back on the Snake River and throughout the rest of the country.

Howard Cole

Howard Cole's contributions to fly-fishing and the Snake River are long and distinguished. He is best known for the creative flies he has designed over more than 30 years in Snake River country. In a region known as the home of oversized patterns like the Club Sandwich, Double Humpy, and Double Bunny, Howard has bucked the trend by focusing on highly imitative patterns that are more in line with the smaller trout fare on the Snake River. Two of his most popular—the Sally Emerger and his Ucon series—imitate mayfly, caddis, and small Perlidae emergers on hooks between #12 and 18. He has also created highly popular and effective PMD emerger imitations and a blue-winged olive cripple that ranks with the Quigley Cripple as one of the best challenged-mayfly patterns on the market.

With partner Jimmy Jones, Cole became the proprietor of High Country Flies in the 1980s. Since that time, the two have used this popular shop as not only an outlet for flies, gear, and guiding, but also to distribute information on fishing tactics, cutting-edge equipment, and stream protection to the general angling public. Many fly-fishermen in the Jackson Hole area first learned of the threat of whirling disease and New Zealand mud snails from informational seminars conducted at High Country Flies. When anglers prepare to venture onto the National Elk Refuge and fish Flat Creek, they will find whirling disease sanitation tanks at each entry gate, courtesy of High Country Flies.

Howard Cole inspects his fly selection at High Country Flies.

Howard has continued his zest for teaching by introducing anglers to new facets of the sport. He is considered one of the most knowledgeable Spey casters in the Yellowstone region, and conducts Spey-casting seminars on the Snake each year. But his true impression on the sport is being made in fly-tying. Besides the several patterns he has developed, Cole has demonstrated his tying skills at several expos and fly-fishing shows for over three decades, and he continues to do so today. As Carmichael, Donnelly, and Martinez were to the Snake River 70 years, tiers like Cole are to the Snake today.

Guy Turck

Compared to most on this list, Guy Joseph Turck is a relative new-comer to fly-fishing and the Snake River scene. He did not begin guiding until the late 1980s, but in less than 15 years, he has made an unquestionable impact. As a commercial tier, Guy has created some of the area's most important patterns of recent time. The most popular by far is his Turck's Tarantula, an attractor found in probably every fly shop in the West. In 1990, Montana's colorful George Anderson won the One-Fly Competition with a Tarantula given to him personally by Guy. Turck's other creations include the Power Ant, one of the most effective terrestrials on the market today.

Photo Courtesy of Guy Turck

Guy's enthusiasm for tying and guiding is matched only by his dedication to the protection of his office: the Snake River. Through his website turckstarantula.com, he posts timely discussions of important issues facing the river and the surrounding ecosystem. He has been a consistent critic of the Bureau of Reclamation management practices for the Snake River, specifically the timing of water releases from Jackson Lake Dam and Palisades Reservoir. In 2002, Guy Turck was a leading opponent of the Canyon Club development in Snake River Canyon, which threatened eagle nesting zones, trout habitat, and future river usage by the public. This battle, like many others, continues. So too will Guy's rantings and ravings.

Scott Sanchez

Scott Sanchez has developed such a strong reputation in fly-tying that he might be considered one of the absolute best in the field today. At the very least, he is the most knowledgeable. Growing up in the Rocky Mountains, Scott began tying at an early age. By the time he was 14, he was already instructing tying classes. In the early 1980s, he started working at Jack Dennis' Outdoor Shop. From there, Sanchez started down a path that would be difficult for anyone in the sport to match. The list of patterns he has developed reads like the Christmas wishlist of a hard-core western trout angler. His Double Bunny is debatably the most productive big-trout streamer in use today. It was so successful in the Jackson Hole One-Fly Competition, winning the contest from 1992 to 1994, that hook size restrictions were implemented, rendering this giant obsolete. Sanchez is also credited with the development of the Parachute Crystal Midge, the Foamwing Caddis, the Foam Frog, the Spandex Stone Nymph, the Convertible, and the list goes on and on and on…

Scott Sanchez working his magic at his inline rotary vices.

Quite possibly Sanchez's greatest ability, and contribution to the sport, is his clear and concise understanding of tying materials and how they work. With the possible exception of Bob Bean, no one has incorporated so many innovative types of materials into his flies—everything from foam and elastic materials, to underwing matter from hackle saddles and partridge feathers. Scott is one of the few who can clearly explain why antelope or caribou hair should be used in place of another kind for flaring a fly's body, or why deer hair from the flank gives greater buoyancy than hair from the back.

Scott generously shares his skill with the angling community through private and public seminars. He has demonstrated his craft at dozens of tying expos and fishing shows across the country. Sanchez tying articles have appeared in several national publications and he has been a featured tier in many books and videos. He has an uncanny ability to easily explain and demonstrate what appears to be the most complicated tying step. He is easy to spot at a tying show—glasses, thick mustache, big grin, and dozens of people crowding around his table to watch him work his magic.

Carter Andrews

The name Carter Andrews is synonymous with Bahamas bonefishing and tournament fishing all over the world. The Snake River, however, is proud to call him one of its own. Andrews began his guiding career in 1990 working for Jack Dennis before moving on to the Lodge at Palisades Creek where he was the head guide from 1997 to 1999. His success on the Snake River, be it as a guide, competitor, or just a plain ole fisherman, is unmatched. He has guided individual winners in the One-Fly Competition twice and tied the winning fly for competitors three times. In 1994, this time as a competitor, Carter amassed a record 1209 points over the two days to win the individual category. His record still stands today. He finished second in the casting competition in the 2001 ESPN Great Outdoor Games before capturing the title in 2002.

Carter Andrews has been a strong promoter of fly-fishing and the Snake River. When the 1997 World Fly Fishing Championships were held on the Snake River, Carter co-hosted a series of television programs with Jack Dennis on the contest. In 1999 Andrews represented Team USA at the World Fly Fishing Championships in Argentina. Later that same year he would win the professional division in the One-Fly competition. Today Carter splits his time between his Crooked Island guiding operation in the Bahamas, and the Snake River in Jackson Hole, where he guides for Westbank Anglers.

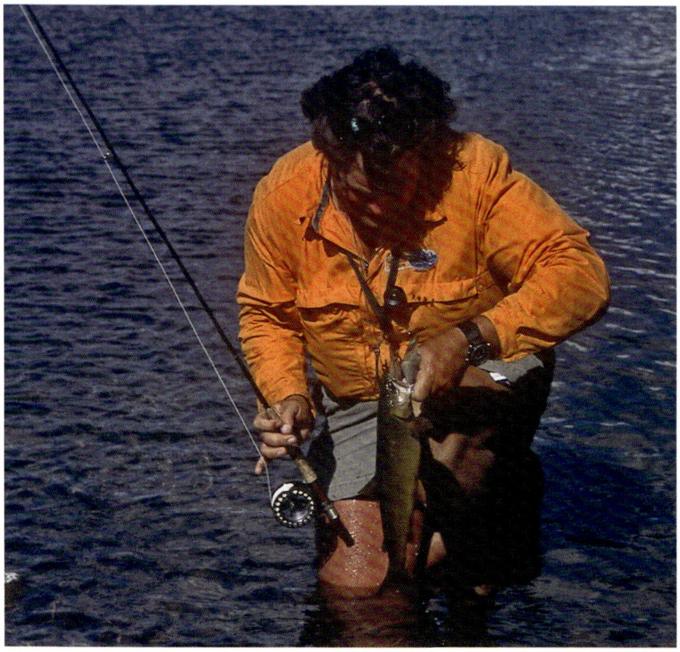

Carter Andrews on a "secret" spring creek.

Index

Names Index

Flies and Patterns Index

References

Allen, Joseph Boots. "The Evolution of the Humpy," *Fly Tyer.* Vol. 8, No. 1, Spring 2002.

Allen, Joseph Boots. "Synthetic Materials for Humpy Patterns," *Flyfishing & Tying Journal.* Vol. 26, No. 1, Spring 2003.

Alt, David, and Donald Hyndman. *Roadside Geology of Idaho.* Montana Press Publishing Company. Missoula, MT, 1989.

Anders, M.H., J. Saltzman and S.R. Hemming. "Neogene ash correlations in eastern Idaho and Wyoming: Implications for Yellowstone Hotspot-related volcanism and tectonic activity." In Bonnichen, W., McCurry, M and White, C., *Tectonic and Magmatic Evolution of the Snake River Plain Volcanic Province.* Idaho Division of Mines and Geology, 2001.

Anthony, Paul V. *The Snake River Levee System Report.* Jackson Hole Conservation Alliance. September, 1998.

Barnes, Antrim "Pat". "Goofus Bug Evolution," *American Angler.* Spring, 1990.

Beers, Cody and Chris Madson, Lance Beeny, David Rippe. "Going Native." *Wyoming Wildlife.* Vol. LXV, No. 5, May 2001.

Behnke, Robert J. *Trout and Salmon of North America.* The Free Press. New York, 2002.

Betts, Robert B. *Along the Ramparts of the Tetons: The Saga of Jackson Hole, Wyoming.* Colorado Associated University Press. Boulder, CO, 1978.

Bruun, Paul. "The Double Humpy," *Fly Fisherman.* Vol. 19, No. 3, May, 1988.

Bruun, Paul. "What Makes J.J. Special," *Jackson Hole Magazine.* Summer, 1996.

Bruun, Paul. "Trout Tackle Turck's Tarantula," *Jackson Hole Magazine.* Summer, 2000.

Bureau of Reclamation, Pinedale Field Office, Wyoming State Office. *Record of Decision: Snake River Resource Management Plan.* U.S. Department of the Interior. April, 2004.

Cantwell, Neil. "Boots Allen's Jackson Hole," *Rocky Mountain Game and Fish.* Vol. 2000, No. 7, July 2000.

Conley, Cort. *Idaho for the Curious: A Guide.* Backeddy Books. Cambridge, Idaho, 1982.

Dennis, Jack. *Jack Dennis' Western Trout Fly Tying Manual.* Snake River Books. Jackson, WY, 1974.

Derig, Betty. *Roadside History of Idaho.* Mountain Press Publishing Company. Missoula, MT, 1996.

Good, John M. and Kenneth L. Pierce. *Interpreting the Landscape: Recent and Ongoing Geology of Grand Teton and Yellowstone National Parks.* Grant Teton Natural History Association. Moose, WY, 1996.

Harward, Lanny. *Snake River Secrets: Floating Guide to the Upper Snake River and its Trout-rich Tributaries.* Frank Amato Publications. Portland, 1996.

Huntington, Rebecca. "Park, State Rethink Lake Trout Stocking: Conservationist Calls Stocking Program "Illegal", *Jackson Hole News & Guide.* March 4, 2003.

Huser, Verne. *Wyoming's Snake River: A River Guide's Chronicle of People and Place, Plants and Animals.* The University of Utah Press. Salt Lake City, 2001.

Jannotta, Sepp. "Angler Catches Great, Terrible Luck at One-Fly," *Jackson Hole News and Guide.* September 15, 2004.

Jobin, D. A. and M. L. Schroeder. *Geology of the Conant Valley Quadrangle Bonneville County, Idaho.* United States Geological Survey. Mineral Investigations Field Studies Map, Map MF-277. 1964.

Kiefling, John W. *Fisheries Technical Bulletin No. 3: Studies of the Ecology of the Snake River Cutthroat Trout.* Wyoming Game and Fish Department. Cheyenne, Wyoming, 1978.

Knopp, Malcolm, and Robert Cormier. *Mayflies: An Angler's Study of Trout Water Ephemeroptera*. Greycliff Publishing Company. Helena, Montana, 1997.

LaFontaine, Gary. *Caddisflies*. The Lyons Press. Guilford, Connecticut, 1981.

Lageson, David R., and David C. Adams, Lisa Morgan, Kenneth L. Pierce and Robert B. Smith. "Neogene-Quaternary Tectonics and Volcanism of Southern Jackson Hole, Wyoming and Southeastern Idaho," in Hughes, S.S. and Thackray, G.D., eds., *Guidebook to the Geology of Eastern Idaho*. Idaho Museum of Natural History. Pocatello, Idaho, 1997.

Leonard, J. Edson. *Flies: Their Origin, Natural History, Tying, Hooks, Patterns and Selections of Dry and Wet Flies, Nymphs, Streamers, Salmon Flies for Fresh and Salt Water in North America and the British Isles, Including A Dictionary of 2200 Patterns*. A.S. Barnes and Company, Inc. New York, 1950.

Lilly, Bud, with Paul Schullery. *A Trout's Best Friend*. Pruett Publishing. Boulder, CO., 1988.

Moller, Sarra, and Rob Van Kirk. Hydrologic Alteration and its Effect on Trout Recruitment in the South Fork Snake River. Project Completion Report for Idaho Department of Fish and Game. Boise, ID, 2003.

Montgomery, M.R. *Many Rivers to Cross: Of Good Running Water, Native Trout, and the Remains of Wilderness*. Simon and Schuster, Inc. New York, 1995.

Piety, L.A., Sullivan, J.T., and Anders, M.H. "Segmentation and Earthquake Potential of the Grand Valley Fault, Idaho and Wyoming," *Geological Society of America Memoir 179*. 1992.

Sanchez, Scott. "Invasion of the Chernobyl Ant," *Flyfishing & Tying Journal*, vol. 24 no. 1, Spring 2001.

Schollmeyer, Jim, and Ted Leeson. *Tying Emergers*. Frank Amato Publications. Portland, 2004.

Schwiebert, Ernest. *Trout, 2nd Edition*. E.P. Dutton. New York, 1984.

Stanford, Jim. "River Users Blast Corp," *Jackson Hole News*. September 25, 2002.

Stanford, Jim. "Bureau Sets Gradual Cut for Snake," *Jackson Hole News and Guide*. September 22, 2004.

Staples, Bruce. *Snake River Country Flies and Water*. Frank Amato Publications. Portland, 1992.

Staples, Bruce. *Trout Country Flies From Greater Yellowstone Area Masters*. Frank Amato Publications. Portland, 2003.

Staples, Bruce. *River Journal: Yellowstone Park*. Frank Amato Publications. Portland, 1996.

Turck, Guy. "Cutthroat Fly Fishing," *Mountain Country*. 2003.

Varley, John D. and Paul Schullery. *Yellowstone Fishes: Ecology, History, and Angling in the Park*. Stackpole Books. Mechanicsburg, PA, 1998.

Other Available Fishing Books from Frank Amato Publications...

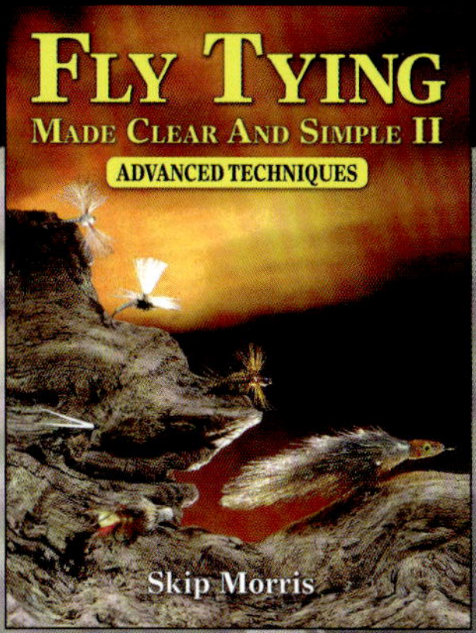

Fly Tying Made Clear and Simple II: Advanced Techniques
by Skip Morris

SPIRAL SB: $24.95
ISBN-13: 978-1-57188-453-4
UPC: 0-81127-00289-4

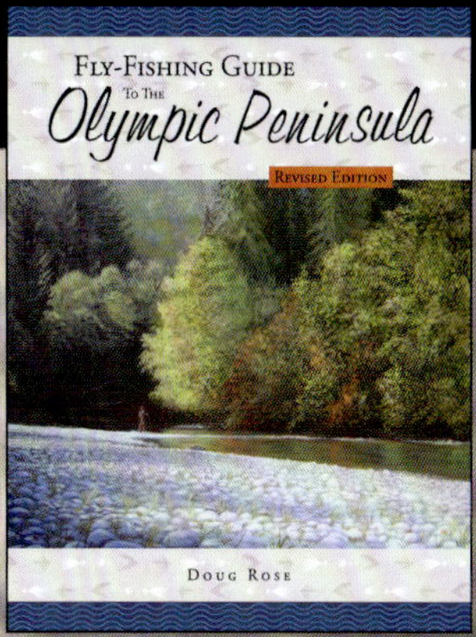

Fly-Fishing Guide to the Olympic Peninsula
by Doug Rose

SB: $29.95
ISBN-13: 978-1-57188-419-0
UPC: 0-81127-00253-5

Fly-Fishing for Alaska's Grayling: Sailfish of the North
by Cecilia "Pudge" Kleinkauf

SB: $19.95
ISBN-13: 978-1-57188-457-2
UPC: 0-81127-00296-2

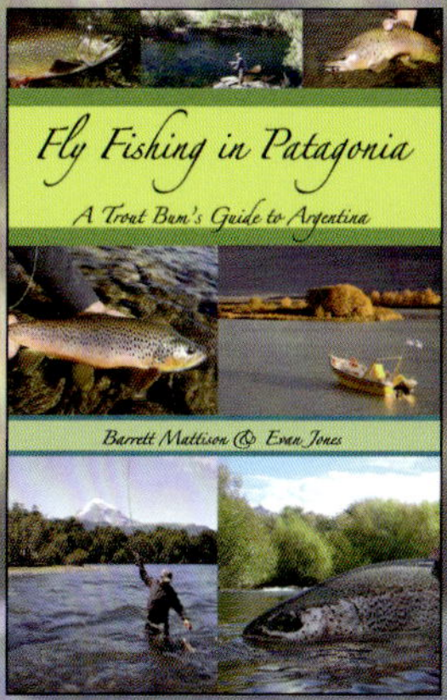

Fly-Fishing in Patagonia
by Barrett Mattison & Evan Jones

SB: $29.95
ISBN-13: 978-1-57188-437-4
UPC: 0-81127-00272-6

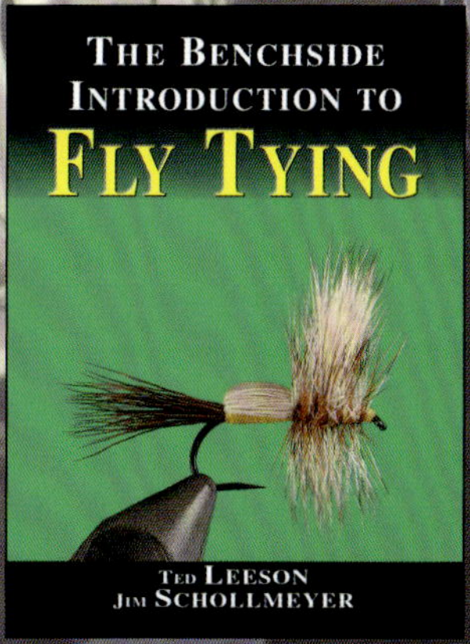

The Benchside Introduction to Fly Tying
by Ted Leeson & Jim Schollmeyer

SPIRAL HB: $45.00
ISBN-13: 978-1-57188-369-8
UPC: 0-81127-00203-0

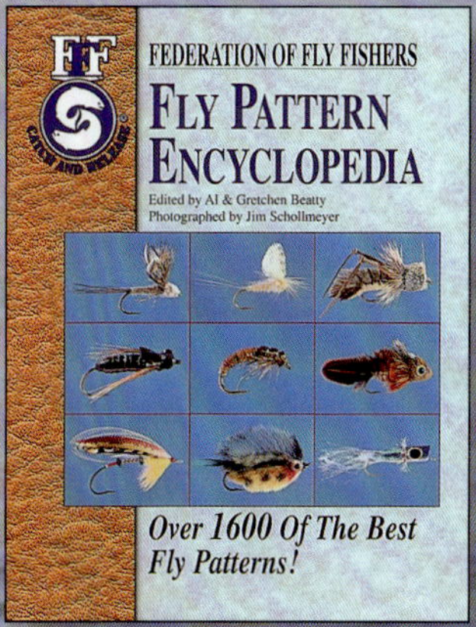

Federation of Fly Fishers Fly Pattern Encyclopedia
Edited by Al & Gretchen Beatty

SB: $39.95
ISBN-13: 978-1-57188-208-0
UPC: 0-66066-00422-2

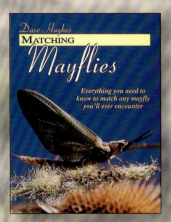

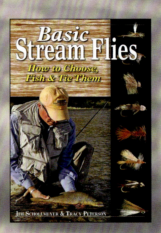

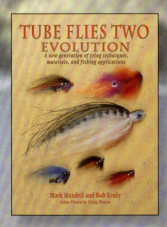

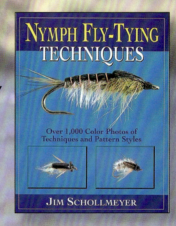

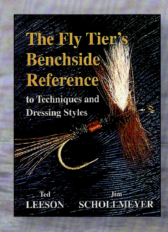